HEROIC HUMILITY

HEROIC HUMILITY

What the Science of Humility Can Say to People Raised on Self-Focus

EVERETT L. WORTHINGTON JR.
SCOTT T. ALLISON

AMERICAN PSYCHOLOGICAL ASSOCIATION
Washington, DC

Published by
American Psychological Association
750 First Street, NE
Washington, DC 20002
www.apa.org

APA Order Department
P.O. Box 92984
Washington, DC 20090-2984
Phone: (800) 374-2721; Direct: (202) 336-5510
Fax: (202) 336-5502; TDD/TTY: (202) 336-6123
Online: http://www.apa.org/pubs/books
E-mail: order@apa.org

In the U.K., Europe, Africa, and the Middle East, copies may be ordered from
Eurospan Group
c/o Turpin Distribution
Pegasus Drive
Stratton Business Park
Biggleswade Bedfordshire
SG18 8TQ United Kingdom
Phone: +44 (0) 1767 604972
Fax: +44 (0) 1767 601640
Online: https://www.eurospanbookstore.com/apa
E-mail: eurospan@turpin-distribution.com

Typeset in Goudy by Circle Graphics, Inc., Columbia, MD

Printer: Sheridan Books, Chelsea, MI
Cover Designer: Beth Schlenoff, Bethesda, MD

Library of Congress Cataloging-in-Publication Data

Names: Worthington, Everett L., Jr., 1946- author.
Title: Heroic humility : what the science of humility can say to people
raised on self-focus / Everett L. Worthington Jr. and Scott T. Allison.
Description: First Edition. | Washington : American Psychological
Association, 2018. | Includes bibliographical references and index.
Identifiers: LCCN 2017041928 | ISBN 9781433828140 | ISBN 1433828146
Subjects: LCSH: Humility. | Courage. | Heroes.
Classification: LCC BJ1533.H93 W665 2018 | DDC 179/.9--dc23 LC record available at https://lccn.loc.gov/2017041928

British Library Cataloguing-in-Publication Data
A CIP record is available from the British Library.

Printed in the United States of America
First Edition

http://dx.doi.org/10.1037/0000079-000

10 9 8 7 6 5 4 3 2 1

To the most heroically humble person I have ever known,
my wife of 46 years, Kirby.
—Everett L. Worthington Jr.

To the woman who demonstrates heroic humility to me every day
and in every way, my wife, Connie.
—Scott T. Allison

To become truly great, one has to stand with people, not above them.
—Charles de Montesquieu

Do nothing out of selfish ambition or vain conceit, but in humility consider others better than yourselves. Each of you should look not only to your own interests, but also to the interests of others.
—Philippians 2:3–4

Desire nothing for yourself, which you do not desire for others.
—Benedictus de Spinoza

CONTENTS

FOREWORD

DAVID G. MYERS

It is widely believed that most folks suffer from low self-esteem, a problem that comedian Groucho Marx had in mind when jesting, "I wouldn't want to belong to any club that would accept me as a member." Psychologist Carl Rogers presumed this low self-image problem (which the Girl Scouts [2002] called a "critical nationwide problem") when objecting to theologian Reinhold Niebuhr's idea that original sin is excessive pretension and pride. No, said Rogers (1958), people's problems arise because "they despise themselves, regard themselves as worthless and unlovable" (p. 17).

As *Heroic Humility* documents with a compelling sweep of evidence, most of us actually have a resoundingly positive self-image. Consider four examples of this scientific retelling of ancient wisdom about the pervasiveness and perils of pride:

- *Self-serving bias*. In most any subjective, socially desirable domain, most people see themselves as better than average—as, for example, more ethical than most people and less prejudiced, healthier, and better able to get along with others. "How do I love me? Let me count the ways."

- *Self-enhancing attributions*. In experiments more numerous than a centipede's legs, people have willingly accepted credit for their successes and good deeds, while shirking responsibility for their failures and misbehavior. The phenomenon has been observed with athletes (explaining victory or defeat), drivers (after accidents), and married couples (among whom conflict often springs from perceiving oneself as contributing more and benefiting less than is fair). We perceive life through a self-enhancing filter.
- *Self-justification*. If an undesirable action cannot be undone, then we often justify it. Every time we act, we strengthen the idea underlying what we've done (especially when we feel some responsibility). If people are induced to deliver electric shocks to another person, they will tend later to disparage their victim: "If I did it, it must be good."
- *Cognitive conceit*. In study after study, people have displayed overconfidence in their beliefs. When answering factual questions—"Is absinthe a liquor or a precious stone?"—we tend to be more confident than correct. And once something happens—the election is over, the game is done, the war is lost—we exhibit hindsight bias. We think we "knew it [the outcome] all along." As the psalmist wondered 3,000 years ago, "Who can detect their errors?"

So pervasive is self-serving pride—the antithesis of humility—that people even see themselves as more humble (with less self-serving bias) than others. They are, in their own eyes, above average at not perceiving themselves as better than average. Others self-aggrandize, people recognize, "but my self-views are accurate." Indeed, even narcissists may see themselves as having superior humility (mindless of C. S. Lewis's aphorism: "If a man thinks he is not conceited, he is very conceited indeed").

Cross-cultural research on individualism reveals that self-serving pride abounds in modern Western cultures such as the United States. As Jean Twenge (2014) has documented, this is the time and place of *Generation Me*. What matters is less the collective "we" (as in Asian cultures) than my individual self. New studies using the Narcissistic Personality Inventory (Emmons, 1984) assess the human tendency toward self-importance, self-focus, and self-promotion with items such as these:

1. I know that I am good because everybody keeps telling me so.
2. I really like to be the center of attention.

As narcissism research has shown—and *Heroic Humility* shows even more convincingly—pride does often go before a fall. Narcissists make good first impressions. But over time, their arrogance, bragging, and aggressiveness get old. In one study of small teams, people's initially positive impressions of narcissists turned negative by the end of seven sessions (Paulhus, 1998).

Now for the good news: The big lesson of this splendid volume is that narcissism's opposite, humility, contributes to human flourishing. Show Everett Worthington and Scott Allison a context where humility reigns—with accurate self-awareness plus modest self-presentation plus a focus on others—and they will show you civil political discourse, happier marriages, more effective leadership, and better mental health.

No wonder humility has been a foundational virtue espoused by the world's five great religions, explain Worthington and Allison. They treat humility as a secular topic, thus keeping the content focused on the psychological, yet they do not neglect the importance of humility in religious and spiritual traditions. My own religious tradition, Christian monotheism, assumes the following at its core:

1. There is a God.
2. It's not me (and it's also not you).

Taken together, these axioms imply our surest conviction: Some of my beliefs (and yours) err. We are finite and fallible. We have dignity but not deity. Ergo, we should hold our untested beliefs tentatively. We should assess others' ideas with skeptical but open minds. And when appropriate, we should use observation and experimentation to winnow truth from error.

This ideal of faith-supported humility and skepticism helped give rise to science. And the ideal is embodied in the aspirations of a "reformed and ever-reforming" religious perspective that encourages us to have open minds and hearts. As St. Paul wrote, "Test everything; hold fast to what is good." Embracing this perspective, one could be a committed person of faith *and* score high on the new Intellectual Humility Scale developed by Mark Leary and his colleagues (2017; agreeing with items such as "I reconsider my opinions when presented with new evidence" and "I accept that my beliefs and attitudes may be wrong").

If that is one version of the multifaith proclamation of humility, the reality—and the reason why the virtue needs continual teaching (and why we need this book)—is that people instead tend, as Benjamin Franklin observed, to "think themselves in possession of all truth, and that wherever others differ from them it is so far error."

Indeed, as Nicholas Epley (2014) has found (and reports in *Mindwise*), most people believe that even God agrees with whatever they believe. And when Epley persuaded people to change their minds about something, they then assumed that God believed their new view. (Epley's research brings to mind J. B. Phillips's classic 1961 book of religious counsel: *Your God is Too Small.*)

People don't just project their beliefs onto God (making themselves into little gods), but they also project them into their religious texts—a phenomenon that enables partisans on both sides of culture war issues (e.g., same-sex marriage) to read them as supporting whatever belief they bring to the text. As a British evangelical white paper on faith and science notes, people of faith often "are not really listening to the Bible, but simply hearing [their] own voices echoing off the pages" (Lucas et al., 2016).

Thus, humility is one of the great religious virtues. Yet the ever-present temptation of religious people is to fashion God in our own image. Oliver Cromwell's 1650 letter to the Church of Scotland reminded it of this temptation and of the church's own "reformed and ever-reforming" ideal: "I beseech you, in the bowels of Christ, think it possible you may be mistaken."

Whether fed by faith or simply rooted in an unassuming and accurate self-appraisal, such humility matters. As Worthington and Allison attest, humility "is key to self- and societal transformation" (p. xiv, this volume). In an era marked by ingroup partiality, clashing worldviews, and extreme political polarization, what the world needs, now more than ever, is heroic humility.

PREFACE

This book is about a particular type of excellence or virtue that we think is crucial for the 21st century. It is critical because in Western culture, we have been immersed in individualism and orientation toward the self, and now culture shifts have brought about increasing discord, angry political diatribes, and even violence. Arguably, this public discord is due (at least in part) to self-absorption and xenophobia. Politicians seem to be locked in mortal combat. Relationships seem to be about individuals wanting their way. Divorces and cohabitation breakups are common. Many religious people are intolerant and fearful of those of different religions. Refugees and immigrants are often not welcome. Disgruntlement with police and new or renewed racial and ethnic tensions abound. There is civil unrest over gay marriage. Instead of civil discourse, leaders seem so keenly aware of their own constituencies that every utterance is made for their own supporters, so opposing sides not surprisingly grow continually further apart.

Youths want life to matter. They sincerely want to help the needy. Sometimes, though, our observation is that some youths only seem to want to help at times and in ways that are convenient to them. Of course, any altruism is usually a good thing, but today, it seems, even altruistic motives can often be tinged with self-interest.

In the private sphere, if there is a private sphere in today's world of social media, things are just as self-interested. In 2014, Google noted that its customers alone—not counting other consumers—take about 93 million "selfies" daily (Brandt, 2014; Van Tongeren & Myers, 2017). Van Tongeren and Myers (2017) reported that Twitter declared 2014 the "year of the selfie." People might, from those data, conclude that humility is the virtue that time forgot. If billions of selfies are shared each year and in the era of blood-sport politics, it is legitimate to ask whether humility matters today.

We believe humility does matter. It is key to self- and societal transformation. Thus, this book is about humility, a commonly recognized virtue. We believe that understanding and building more humility will move individuals and society toward some relief from the tensions that beset our culture. Humility demands that we see ourselves accurately, present ourselves modestly, and orient ourselves toward helping others. Humility serves as a corrective to self-focus and ingroup orientation.

Self-absorbed people think of themselves as more, and occasionally less, important than they actually are. They think they can act with either brash in-your-face egoism or aw-shucks-toe-dragging false humility. They think they can be self-interested and live considering only their own ingroup, and somehow that will promote peace, harmony, and worldwide flourishing. As we shall see, research on narcissism, Machiavellianism, and psychopathy (i.e., the dark triad) and fragile self-esteem suggest that a me-first life orientation does not spread content widely throughout one's social network. Perhaps it is time to look to some new direction. That might be recapturing the classic virtue of humility and then practicing it with heroism even to self-sacrifice.

But humility is not easy to develop or practice in an individualistic culture. It requires courage and moments of extraordinary heroism superimposed over a life of heroic self-sacrifice for the good of others. To help others, leadership is necessary. We thus combine humility, heroism, and leadership in this book.

We hope you will be enriched, enlightened, and encouraged in your study of humility as you read these pages.

HEROIC HUMILITY

INTRODUCTION

Heroic humility is inspirational humility—humility that leads us to want to emulate it. To begin our journey of understanding it, let's consider how heroism, humility, and leadership might intersect. Scott and his colleagues developed a five-factor theory of leadership (Allison & Goethals, 2011, 2013; Goethals & Allison, 2012). The theory focuses on the leader's (a) persona, (b) vision, (c) ethics, (d) actions, and (e) influence. But not all leaders are heroic leaders. Heroic leaders are exceptional. Allison and Goethals (2011) surveyed people and factor analyzed the responses. They identified what they called the Great Eight traits that describe heroes: *caring, charismatic, inspiring, reliable, resilient, selfless, smart,* and *strong.* Where the Great Eight traits of heroes overlap with the five factors of leadership, there is the heroic leader. The intersection centers on helping other people achieve their potential. Heroic leaders have courage and seek to help others, sometimes at great costs to themselves.

http://dx.doi.org/10.1037/0000079-001
Heroic Humility: What the Science of Humility Can Say to People Raised on Self-Focus, by E. L. Worthington Jr. and S. T. Allison

Not all heroic leaders are humble. Genghis Khan was a heroic leader, but he was not humble. Some of the great presidents of the United States were heroic leaders, such as Teddy Roosevelt. Although admired, they were not humble heroic leaders, such as George Washington or Abraham Lincoln. That addition of humility to the heroic leader zeroes in on some very exceptional people—those who are not just pursuing leadership positions for the sake of power and personal aggrandizement, or even self-sacrificially but for the betterment of only their own political group or country. Rather, heroically humble leaders are willing to serve others, lead others, and endure costs for others, even for those who might not be in a narrowly focused ingroup.

Humility has three qualities. Humble people are those who (a) have an accurate sense of self, know their limitations, and are teachable; (b) present themselves modestly in ways that do not put others off by arrogance or by false, insincere modesty or displaying weakness; and (c) are especially oriented to advancing others—not through groveling weakness but through power under control, power used to build others up rather than squash them down. This definition is based on numerous research studies that have accumulated since 2008 from the labs of Worthington, Don Davis, Joshua Hook, Daryl Van Tongeren, and our colleagues. Although the definition derives originally from Worthington (2007) and from D. E. Davis, Worthington, and Hook (2010), it has been elaborated on by adding to it the idea of teachability (see Owens & Hekman, 2012), the concept of modest self-presentation (see D. E. Davis, McElroy, Rice, et al., 2016), and a distinct ramping up of focus on being other-oriented (see Worthington, Goldstein, et al., in press). At this point, no single instrument can assess all aspects of the definition. A set of targeted instruments is required.

It is within the grasp of most of us to rise to moments of humility. In fact, we often see interviews with heroes who say such things as, "I didn't do anything special. I just did what anyone would do." (They may only have run through a hail of bullets into a fire or through an earthquake to save orphans.) Those are indeed humble heroes, and we are usually astounded by their sincerity in such self-effacing statements about their hero status. Yet, as admirable as such humble heroes are, in this book we are more concerned with a different type of humility. We are concerned with people who are truly humble—self-aware, modest, and other-oriented—but who take that to levels and depths that most of us struggle merely to understand. These are not just humble heroes; they are exemplars of heroic humility. Usually, they are leading organizations and social movements, like Nelson Mandela or Mother Teresa did. But sometimes they are just everyday people whom we cannot help but admire. They seem to be uncaring about their own advancement and promote others—sometimes even others they don't know but simply think are worthy of advancement. And as one of those exemplars of heroic humility, they become leaders. In Table 1, we compare aspects of heroes, leadership, and humility to get a sense of what those heroically humble people might be like.

Heroically humble leaders are the noble champions of society that most people are inspired by and aspire to be. They are not weak but are strong at their core. They can employ their assorted virtues to successfully achieve the goals of a group and the people within it. They are virtuous and have worked hard to build positive character, glimpsing the goal to which they personally aspire; practicing virtue until it has become a habit of the heart; meeting tests, trials, temptations, and suffering while maintaining integrity; and experiencing a deep satisfaction (even if they are not exactly happy) because they feel that they are doing the right things.

Most people look up to, and perhaps even learn from and are inspired by, heroic (especially heroically humble) leaders. Although not everyone aspires

TABLE 1
Comparison of Aspects of Leadership, Heroism, and Humility

Five-factor leadership model	Great eight traits of heroes	Definition of humility
Persona: shows high energy, tolerates stress, acts emotionally mature and confident, engenders trust **Vision**: appeals to the values, hopes, and ideals of the followers; embodies society's most noble ideals **Ethics**: uses power wisely consistent with the morals and ethics of society; integrity; honesty **Actions**: acts to benefit the group; works hard to benefit the group; creates (ideas, opportunities, environment for accomplishing goals), communicates, collaborates **Influence**: communicates their vision to others; models energy and loyalty; builds trust and unity; honors commitments; provides feedback; delegates effectively; coaches others to improve; motivates; inspires	**Caring**: compassionate, empathic, kind **Charismatic**: dedicated, eloquent, passionate **Inspiring**: admirable, amazing, great, inspirational **Reliable**: loyal, true **Resilient**: accomplished, determined, persevering **Selfless**: altruistic, honest, humble, moral **Smart**: intelligent, wise **Strong**: courageous, dominating, gallant, leader	**Accurate self-appraisal** including awareness of limitations **Modest** self-presentation **Other-orientedness** that uses one's power under control to lift others up and not squash them down

to be a leader, many people want to build heroic virtues, such as humility, that are uplifting to others and built to last. Not all leaders are humble. Some might touch on humility at times, but few reach the level of heroic humility. Instead, today we are more likely to equate business leadership with just the opposite—hubris, arrogance, and pride.

THE NEED FOR A BOOK ON HEROIC HUMILITY

Humility is a key ingredient for people of today. Yet, finding recent resources about it is difficult.

Generations Have Neglected It

Humility has, until recently, been virtually unaddressed in the popular and scientific literature, though religious resources are more numerous. Many people have been reared on "do your own thing" (the 1960s) high self-esteem (the 1980s and 1990s). Recently, youth have been called "Generation Me" or "iGen," as Jean Twenge (2014) sometimes refers to the generation from their midthirties and younger. Twenge has devoted countless pages to documenting evidence of this increasing self-focus (see Twenge, 2014; Twenge & Campbell, 2009). With the generations of self-focus, humility is increasingly needed. It might be needed to tear apart the welding of political gridlock, to negotiate across cultures and countries, or to prevent breakups and divorces in romantic relationships.

We Have Forgotten Powerful Heroes of Humility

Humility, at first blush, sounds like something only a weakling would do. It sounds like capitulation, like self-imposed humiliation and self-flagellation. It seems anemic. We seem to have forgotten the heroes of humility like Presidents George Washington and Abraham Lincoln, boxer Joe Louis, scientist Marie Curie, activist Harriet Tubman, and rescuer of people in ill-health Mother Teresa. Humility is not a tame virtue. There is power there, but not wild power. Humility involves power under control.

Humility can sometimes be found amid humiliation because humiliation often pushes us to the end of ourselves. Frederick A. Douglass, orator and advocate for freedom from slavery, was raised as a slave. Biographer David J. Bobb (2013) wrote,

> Frederick began to see the power of humility through lessons learned in his early life. Whether by negative examples (his masters and mistresses and slave interests throughout his life) or positive examples (his mother

> and Uncle Lawson), Frederick saw what it took to be humble even in the midst of humiliation. Submission of one sort was thrust on him as a slave, but before he could escape the bonds of slavery, Frederick had to make himself a student. His humility as a learner was preparation for his life as a leader. In humbling himself as a seeker, he gained the pride and dignity that unfitted him for slavery. (p. 188)

Douglass found other exemplars of humility after escaping from slavery. He worked with abolitionist William Lloyd Garrison. After Lincoln released the Emancipation Proclamation, Douglass paid honor to Garrison in a speech at Hillsdale College on January 21, 1863. Even though Douglass had broken with him 12 years earlier, he still recalled how much he owed to Garrison and honored his tireless work. Douglass said of Garrison, "Truth was powerful; a single individual armed with truth was a majority against the world" (Bobb, 2013, p. 181).

Humility Seemed to Be Relegated to Religious People

In the early 20th century, humility was seen as something fit for religion, but to be hidden behind sacred doors and out of secular view. Humility was not a seemly virtue, it was thought, for business or community organizations. During the late 1970s, writers suggested that humility might help organizations. In 1979, Christopher Lasch claimed that the United States had embraced a culture of narcissism. (Oh, how prescient.) He suggested that humility was essential to successful cultural progress. After those early writings, even with the brief popularity of Greenleaf's (1977) servant-leader model, humility lay dormant in both organizations and secular society.

Suddenly the Need for Humility Became Starkly Apparent

In the early 21st century, the need for humility burst through church doors into the halls of corporate power. A series of accusations of fraud and dishonesty occurred. Chief Executive Officer (CEO) of Enron Jeff Skilling and former CEO of Enron Kenneth Lay were accused of fraud in 2001. Bernie Ebbers met a similar fate in 2002. Tyco's CEO Dennis Kozlowski and Chief Financial Officer Mark Swartz were added to the wall of shame. In 2003, HealthSouth's CEO Richard Scrushy (shall we say) slightly exaggerated their assets to the tune of $1.4 billion to appease shareholders, and Freddie Mac's executive management team also exaggerated (by $5 billion) their assets and were caught at it. In 2005, Hank Greenberg (American Insurance Group's CEO) and Lehman Brothers' executives and auditors were caught hiding $50 billion in loans disguised as sales. Not to be outdone, Bernie Madoff used a Ponzi scheme to bilk investors out of $65 billion. The trend continued. In almost all of these cases, analysts agreed that massive pride, hubris, entitlement, and arrogance were root causes (Owens, Johnson, & Mitchell, 2013).

In a decade, these ethical failures, with pride at the base, created questions about business leadership. Were business leaders being trained in profit-at-any-cost self-interest that ignores others—investors, shareholders, individuals in the company, legitimate competitors within the industry, and the general population? Weick (2001) observed that humility was a vital, yet at that point neglected, personality trait for business leaders in the 21st century. Hess and Ludwig (2017) surveyed the recent advances in artificial intelligence and dubbed humility "the new smart" because *smart* humans have to recognize our limits.

Enter a Science of Humility

Fortunately, just as the social, relational, and personal needs for humility became critical, the science of humility exploded. Many studies of humility have burst on the scene in the past 10 years. Several grants have funded subaward grant competitions that, in turn, have funded (or will fund) multiple research labs, principal investigators, collaborators, postdocs, and graduate students. The infrastructure is being constructed right now for a robust science of humility.

One area in the psychological literature could address humility's obverse—narcissism. H. M. Wallace and Baumeister (2002) observed that people with subclinical narcissistic personality traits seek esteem in their own and others' eyes by competitively trying to outperform others and thus win admiration. The level of subclinical narcissism moderates this relationship. People on the high end of the (subclinical) narcissism continuum tend to work harder to reach their goals when they know people are watching, whereas people on the low end tend to work equally hard regardless of whether they believe people are watching. Some of the personal and societal difficulties that we have noted have arisen from 21st-century narcissistic entitlement and to a lesser extent from the millennial mindset. Those might be dealt with by applying basic research to narcissism—especially subclinical narcissism. However, to do so, we believe, would set up a negative framework. It would focus attention on what not to do or how not to be narcissistic. It would not tell what to do. We know that in many areas, the absence of one thing does not necessarily imply its opposite. The absence of diseases does not mean one is healthy. The absence of depression does not mean one is happy. The absence of anxiety does not mean one is peaceful. Similarly, the elimination of narcissism does not mean one is acting humbly in a positive, health-producing, society-benefiting way. Some characteristics need cultivation to promote flourishing. We believe one of those is humility.

Thus, humility might be a virtue that holds promise in an age when vanity in the form of narcissism seems to be an ever-increasing phenomenon (Twenge, 2014). Political humility is needed in an age of embittered, name-calling, belittling gridlocked politics (Worthington, 2017). Relational humility is needed in an age of divorce, couple conflict, organizational power politics, and institutional frauds (D. E. Davis, Placeres, et al., 2017).

INTEREST IN THE SCIENTIFIC STUDY OF HUMILITY

Worthington, Davis, and Hook (2017) searched PsycINFO on July 1, 2016. We adapted their findings in Table 1. In 4-year increments, we summarize next the number of indexed publications that used the word *humility* (see Table 2).

We can see that there is much existing research and theoretical writing on humility. The rate of publication is increasing, and that uptrend started with the initiation of the positive psychology movement (1999–2000). In fact, the rate of increase of publication is a modest exponential curve—an appropriately humble growth rate. Much of the writing prior to 1999 was theoretical. It encouraged developing a virtuous character or recommended humility as a trait for successful psychotherapists. Little research was empirical except for a measure of personality traits (i.e., the HEXACO model on Honesty–Humility). However, since positive psychology (Seligman & Csikszentmihalyi, 2000), with its commitment to the empirical study of the virtues, took hold (probably 2002–2003), the tide has changed. Much research and scientific theorizing has taken place. The doubling time for number of publications has been about 4 years.

We are seeing many signs that a science of humility has taken root. In 2008, I (Ev) was fortunate to receive a grant to study humility in couples making

TABLE 2
PsycINFO Publications Indexing the Word Humility
(1,339 total hits from 1900–2015)

Years	Number of publications indexed in PsycINFO
1900–1995	211
1996–1999	36
2000–2003	77
2004–2007	186
2008–2011	292
2012–2015	537
2016–June 28, 2017 (18 months)	337 (on schedule for 854 in 4-year period)

the transition to parenthood, which gave me a leg up at establishing a program of research on humility. That grant led to a national conference on humility research in Atlanta in 2015 and an edited book on humility (Worthington et al., 2017). In the 2010s, the John Templeton Foundation funded three grants that had provisions for funding more research on humility. Although humility has now been increasingly mentioned in almost 1,700 articles, the direct and principal focus of empirical research articles on humility is less—more like 483 articles in which *humility* is a keyword. This is great news for investigators jumping into its scientific study. There is still much low-hanging fruit.

Research has accumulated in a curve matching the rate of increase in Table 2, but publications are now poised to explode. We estimate that about 30 research teams have been funded on those initiatives. Research teams engage doctoral-level collaborators, use postdocs, train doctoral and master's students, hire paid research assistants, and expose volunteer undergraduate research assistants to the research. The infrastructure of researchers who will study humility in the next decade is growing daily.

Furthermore, the exposure has cut across disciplines. All manner of psychologists—social, personality, health and neuro-, organizational, clinical, and counseling psychologists—have studied humility. Other fields have joined the fun—marriage and family specialists, human development scientists, management scholars, leadership scholars, neuroeconomists, biologists, nurses, physicians, psychiatrists, psychometricians, conflict resolution specialists, and peace workers. We believe that this book will entice people from many disciplines to study humility and could entice a variety of professional applications to diverse other fields.

Although we draw research and illustrations from this variety of disciplines, we have a special affinity for several of the fields because the overlap with and integration into those fields is most obvious. First, we draw heavily from positive psychology, which itself is eclectic. Most positive psychologists would define the field as either the psychological science of character strength and virtue or of happiness and well-being. We find humility to snuggle in most comfortably to a definition that emphasizes character strength and virtue. But as with positive psychology, liberal support is drawn from topics, methods, and styles from personality, social, psychophysiological, clinical, counseling, and other subdisciplines.

Second, we draw on research and theory from social psychology. At the very basic level, we emphasize the power of the situation—with relationships being a key to structuring situations. Thus, we incorporate interdependence theory (Kelley & Thibaut, 1978; Thibaut & Kelley, 1959) and sociometer theory (Leary, Tambor, Terdal, & Downs, 1995), which focus on the ways people shape their personalities (including their senses of self and their self-esteem; see Baumeister, Campbell, Krueger, & Vohs, 2003) and relationships in response to social perception. We clearly acknowledge people's unconscious biases, which Kahneman (2011) helped identify and social psychology expanded by thoroughly investigating self-enhancing biases (Kwan, John, Kenny, Bond, & Robins, 2004). And we examine the difficulty of maintaining and practicing virtuous behavior through referring frequently to topics such as willpower and ego depletion (see Baumeister & Tierney, 2011) and self-control (Finkel & Campbell, 2001).

Third, we often draw on personality psychology as well. We refer to the helpfulness of the person–perception strain of personality (Funder, 1995) in measuring humility, and we examine the personality correlates with humility (for a review, see Leman, Haggard, Meagher, & Rowatt, 2017).

Fourth, we are particularly grateful to counseling, clinical, and organizational psychologies. Together, they help us apply many of the findings from more basic research using positive psychological and social psychological methods.

Accordingly, we hope to address many theoretical, empirical, and practical questions in this book. These are relevant to (a) scientists who study humility and its antecedents and sequelae and (b) psychological scientists who apply the findings to psychotherapy, business, organizations, leadership, political science, and other areas.

FOCUS OF THE BOOK

We seek to analyze the rapidly emerging science of humility. We contextualize it within the current need for heroic humble leadership in society, relationships, and personal lives. We arrive at the fundamental concept of the book—heroic humility. This is a trait by people who practice humility consistently, especially when their ego is placed under strain and the practice of humility is difficult. We are particularly focused on one aspect of heroic humility—its warm orientation toward others, seeking to lift others by using power under control, tempered by promoting good in those others.

What We Seek to Accomplish

David Brooks, *New York Times* syndicated columnist, wrote a brilliant book in 2015, *The Road to Character*. In it, he described Frances Perkins (1880–1965). She was one of two aides to stick with Franklin D. Roosevelt for his entire term as president, and she was a major force in shaping the policies of Roosevelt's New Deal administration. She was the central force in creating Social Security, the Civilian Conservation Corps, the Public Works Administration, and (by way of the Fair Labor Standards Act) the first minimum wage law and overtime law. She was deeply involved in child labor legislation and unemployment insurance. After ending her time in government, she wrote a biography of Roosevelt.

> I began to see what the great teachers of religion meant when they said that humility was the greatest of virtues. . . . If you can't learn it, God will teach it to you by humiliation. Only so can a man be really great, and it was in those accommodations for necessity that Franklin Roosevelt began to approach the stature of humility and inner integrity which made him truly great. (Perkins, 1946/2011, p. 29)

Brooks (2015) described her education at Mount Holyoke College (South Hadley, Massachusetts). We were struck with how much his description captures themes explored in this book:

> A dozen voices from across the institution told students that . . . a well-lived life involves throwing oneself into struggle, that large parts of the most worthy lives are spent upon the rack, testing moral courage and facing opposition and ridicule, and that those who pursue struggle end up being happier than those who pursue pleasure.
>
> Then it told them that the heroes in this struggle are not the self-aggrandizing souls who chase after glory; they are rather the heroes of renunciation, those who accept some arduous calling. . . . It emphasized that performing service is . . . a debt you are repaying for the gift of life.
>
> Then it gave them concrete ways to live this life of steady heroic service. . . . The Mount Holyoke education was dominated by theology and the classics—Jerusalem and Athens. The students were to take from religion an ethic of care and compassion, and from the ancient Greeks and Romans a certain style of heroism—to be courageous and unflinching in the face of the worst the world could throw at you. (pp. 29–30)

Misconceptions We Seek to Combat

We believe that the public perception of humility is sometimes negative. By the end of the book, we hope you will not share those unhelpful perceptions. For example, many people think of humility as follows (misconceptions in italics): (a) *Humility is a Christian topic*. It isn't. It is a human topic. We approach it as a secular topic. Although some studies we review have assessed Christians (and other religious people), most have not. (b) *It is associated with humiliation*. This is a misunderstanding of humility. Our emphasis on heroic humility—humility so deeply embraced that it is of heroic proportions—and on our tripartite definition should easily discredit this. (c) *It means one has to present oneself (and perhaps actually become) a person of low self-esteem, "aw-shucks" modesty, and personal weakness*. That will hamper achievement. Our emphasis on heroic humility should easily discredit this, too. (d) *Humility is thought of as a doorway to being taken advantage of and abused, because it is assumed to be equated with absolute deference to authority*. This is false. We treat it not as a lack of power but as power under control. Professor and writer John Dickson (2011) defined humility (incompletely, we think, but partially true in this regard) as "willingness to hold power in service of others" (p. 24). (e) *Humility is often thought of as something that might be favored by the already powerful but not good for the disempowered and socially marginalized*. We disagree. Gandhi was among the disempowered and socially marginalized, yet he brought the British Empire to heel. Nelson Mandela was imprisoned and abused, yet he, through tender-hearted, tough-minded humility, took down apartheid and united South Africa. (f) *Being more humble is a matter of willpower, self-control, or exerting conscious ego control over unconscious impulses*. We confess that we do hope that many people who read this book will personally conclude that they would like to become more humble more of the time. We believe wholeheartedly that such transformation requires some willpower, self-control, self-regulation (Ng et al., 2012), and grit (Duckworth, 2016) to stick with the transformative process when it threatens to grind to a halt. But grasping at humility by force of willpower is like trying to close your fingers on air. It is elusive. Rather, it is through focusing actively and passionately on others that one finds one has become more humble.

None of these common beliefs is true. Just the opposite of each is actually true. It is for Christians *and* people who are not Christian. It is not being humiliated, which is accepting a position of degraded worth, but it is understanding one's true worth. It is not merely a self-presentational style, but it is an attitude of living that is respectful of self and other. It is not failing to stand up for oneself or others who are needy, but it is using power under control to stand up for those who need power. It is possible to be humble even when having no political or social power and yet emerge with more social power.

Organization of the Book

In the first part of the book, we provide a scientifically informed description of humility. We examine the different types of humility. We also show how humility is measured.

In the second part, we discuss what science has shown to be related to humility, including social correlates; relationships to other virtues and vices; mental health and physical health sequelae; relationships with religion, spirituality, and philosophy; and the promise of connections between humility and a better life for individuals and society.

Then, in the third part, we discuss the need for heroic leadership and humble leaders. In that portion, we argue that heroic humility can be a personally stabilizing, even a world-stabilizing force today.

In the final part, we draw together the insights and integrate them with the scientific findings. We offer direct advice, bolstered by scientific findings, on how people might be more heroically humble, and we describe the results of clinical trials that have studied the efficacy of a workbook to promote humility. In an epilogue, we extract important lessons from the book.

Questions

Several important questions arise from our review. These questions suggest that learning more about humility is vital in this modern world.

Aren't We Just Talking About Learning Humility From Humble Models?

We describe many humble heroes and people exhibiting heroic humility. We draw from well-known leaders, but we also discuss everyday heroes and hope to inspire more. In fact, we pepper the book with exemplars of heroic humility. Cognitive psychology tells us that most learning isn't due to rational, logical teaching. Rather, learning involves intuition and experience, and we can gain much of that intuition and experience by observing models, exemplars, and heroes. But learning humility is not just about copying models as described by social learning theory (Bandura, 1963). Rather, heroic humility is more than demonstrating behaviors or attitudes. We can learn to drive by watching experienced drivers, like our parents, yet from such models we don't usually decide that we want to be the next NASCAR champion. But many people who saw the work of Mother Teresa and Gandhi were inspired to change their lives and also have the humility they were observing. This is the difference between copying models and being inspired by heroic humility.

Will I, a Psychological Scientist, Be Interested in This Book?

Certainly, high-profile researchers like Jean Twenge (2014) and her colleague Keith Campbell (Twenge & Campbell, 2009) have called attention to today's narcissistic trends in "normal" self-expression. This might suggest that research is needed to balance narcissistic pressures. On one hand, more and better research on humility has appeared within the past 15 years. Numerous researchers are studying humility. Even better, young researchers who are looking for a field to devote themselves to can join early in the field's development. Studying humility, providing more information about it, and helping those who wish to become more humble are noble acts. Humility can benefit individuals, couples, families, communities, societies, and the world as a whole. You'll catch that glimpse throughout this book. The supply and demand are coalescing. We hope you agree with our analysis: This is a scientific field on the cusp of explosion.

Will I, a Psychological Scientist, Find the Book and Topic to Be One That Sustains My Interest?

There are several reasons, given next, to believe that people will once again come to embrace humility as a cherished virtue and that this will repay scientific study. People are seeing that some mental health disorders are due to competitiveness, stress, narcissism, and self-focus. Best-selling books by David Brooks (2015) and Jean Twenge's (2014) *Generation Me* suggest that the problems with self-focus and the solutions afforded through humility can make inroads into public consciousness. The need for knowing more about humility is important to life today. This is true for business, professions, politics, religion, relationships, and the person on the street. In fact, Worthington et al. (2017) recently edited a collection of scholarly articles on humility. In their introduction, they pointed out important topics to look for throughout the book. They stated five hypotheses—that humility might be related to virtue, social functioning, health, societal peace, and satisfaction with life—which they thought were vital connections. But they also identified seven other important, but probably not essential, questions. Next, we paraphrase some of those questions regarding religious, political, intellectual, cultural, and relational humility (see Worthington et al., 2017, pp. 8–9).

Religions value humility, and worldwide, most people still are religious (Berger et al., 1999). Virtually all religious and spiritual traditions value humility and provide mechanisms and rituals by which their adherents are encouraged to be more humble. If people exercised more *religious humility*, religious conflict and violence would probably lessen. Religious humility speaks to the conflicts that have recently intensified between radical Muslims and other religions and people in secular societies. This has shown up in such ways as the massacre of over 2,000 people in Nigeria by Boko Haram and by the attacks on a variety of sites in Paris, Turkey, and throughout the world. Muslims of differing theologies need to dialogue to work out a position that decreases violence and prevents worldwide reaction against Islam. In fact, people of all religions need to be in dialogue with each other. Conflicts involve every major religion. Religion is a major motivator of behavior. It is imperative in the modern world to be able to respect others' religions while humbly adhering to one's own religious beliefs and practices.

If people exercised more *political humility*, we might have more civil political campaigns and elections. Political gridlock would be lessened because mutual respect might engage lawmakers more in finding solutions than in pandering to special contingencies. Conflict will likely never be eradicated, but more worldwide political humility might lead to fewer political struggles within nations—and (we can dream) fewer wars. For a civil society that values differences and freedom to talk about those differences, political humility is also necessary. In recent decades, political dialogues have become more polarized. Even within parties, polarization has germinated, sprouted, and grown—like a cancer, some might say. Understanding how humility might mitigate polarization could help promote more thriving and peaceful governments.

If people exercised more *intellectual humility*, they might share more risky ideas, engage in synthetic win–win problem solving, and express less intellectual arrogance. To have civil conversations and discuss ideas that advance knowledge usually requires thinking outside of the box. So, for productive discussions, we need intellectual humility. Ideally, intellectual communities might correct self-interested biases. But we live in a deeply self-justifying world, so we often tend to bolster biases instead of correct them. But, to the extent we can become more intellectually humble, perhaps some of those biases might be put aside. That might help many communities not become so entrenched in the absolute "rightness" of their ideas.

If people exercised more *cultural humility*, we might improve international relations, help international businesses thrive, and have better relations across ethnicities. In today's worldwide culture, we need humility to deal with multinational corporations and in international travel. We spend each day interacting with and exchanging information with people across cultures. (Just today, I [Ev] have arranged a meeting with a lawyer from Colombia, e-mailed a professor from Germany and another from Spain, and worked on a grant with people from both Ghana and South Africa—a typical day.) Within the helping professions, cultural humility is crucial. A helper must understand many people's problems in the context of their culture.

If people exercised more *relational humility*, we might live more peaceably in romantic partnerships, families, workplaces, and communities. Relational humility refers to our ability to place the needs of the relationship over self-interest. Thus, relational humility looks different in different types of relationships. We must be sympathetic to the other person, consider his or her needs, and then—because in humility we are other-oriented—we elevate the other person's agenda for the good of the relationship. We create a context where sacrificing for the relationship becomes self-reinforcing because partners value each other. This can contribute to a sense of trust. In support of a warm other-orientation as an essential component of humility, Thielmann and Hilbig (2015) examined personality traits (using the HEXACO model) within a trust game. Trustworthiness was predicted by unconditional kindness—operationalized by honesty–humility—but not by either positive reciprocity or negative reciprocity. This at least hints at a warmth component of humility. Partners can become more committed when they perceive each other as trustworthy and can enjoy giving to each other. Humility helps relationships thrive.

In short, we believe your interest in humility, and research on it, can be self-sustaining. This is true because its importance and relevance today and in the future will likely increase.

Will the Scientific Study of Humility Enrich Humanity?

Taken together, more knowledge about the varieties of humility and more examples of how people throughout history have acted humbly in very difficult situations can pay off for individuals, families, groups, communities, societies, and the world. The stakes are high. Egos are on display everywhere and conflict with each other. And humility often hides when egos are strained. So, now is the time for us to consolidate the knowledge and experiences we have in a variety of areas regarding humility so that we can formulate agendas that set the next steps to social improvement. In the following chapters, we seek to consolidate scientific knowledge while making an important case that humility is formed and nurtured as people are oriented toward others.

We believe that the field needs consolidation, and we are taking a step in that direction with this book. The new generation of researchers who are actively pursuing research in humility, as well as their postdocs and students, are all pursuing research agendas. We hope to describe some of those agendas in the remaining pages. We try not to "preach" humility as the cure to all ills or human suffering. But we certainly believe that humility has a lot of payoffs, that heroically humble people have things to teach us, and that a nascent science of applying humility can teach us things about self-improvement, character development, organizational living, and leadership.

INTRODUCTION TO AND THEMES OF HEROIC HUMILITY

Throughout the book we keep returning to several major themes.

1. Scientific study of humility has burgeoned. There is consensus about the definition of humility. One major question remains: Is humility merely lack of self-focus, or is it focusing on others (and thereby focusing less on the self)? We take the latter position.
2. The scientific study of humility has progressed because scientists have gotten past the measurement conundrum—that one cannot trust self-reports of humility.
3. Hypotheses can be formulated regarding humility. Many have received empirical support. These include our definition of humility; humility's connection to other virtues; the relationship

of humility to good social relationships; and the benefits of being humble to physical health, mental health, spirituality, society, and one's ultimate life satisfaction.

4. If humility is to experience a cultural resurgence, we must be weaned from the self-focus that Western culture has been nursed on. That will require heroism, leadership, and humility. Developing humble heroic leadership is personally and culturally beneficial.
5. This is possible in our very me-oriented culture. We provide examples in historical, religious, political, and public life that illustrate aspects of humility, show how it looks in practice, and inspire people to move toward development of heroic humility.
6. Many have become heroically humble, some even rising from adversity or from dishonor.
7. We draw researchable life lessons from both the science of humility and from the models of heroic humility that we identified to show how people can develop humility in the midst of a self-focused culture. We discuss the strains and challenges of being humble.
8. Clinical trials have tested the use of a humility-promoting workbook, *PROVE Humility*.
9. There are practical ways that psychological and clinical scientists can help others be more humble and reap humility's benefits.

As we move into the in-depth study of humility, we begin, in Part I, at the most basic level. What is humility? How does it reveal itself? How is it assessed?

WHAT DID WE LEARN IN THIS CHAPTER?

1. Heroic humility is inspirational. It is humility so deeply ingrained in a person and so consistently practiced that we want to emulate it to be a more noble person.
2. Humility has three characteristics: Humble people (a) have an accurate sense of self, know their limitations, and are teachable; (b) present themselves modestly; and (c) are especially oriented to advancing others by using their power under control to build others up and not to squash them down.
3. We need a book on heroic humility because (a) recent generations have neglected humility; (b) we have forgotten many inspirational heroes of humility; (c) it isn't just for religious

people; and (d) arrogance has led to spectacular falls from power in business, and 2016 political campaigning was hardly a paragon of humility on either side.

4. The study of humility—religious, political, intellectual, cultural, and relational humilities—can help people be better and build a better world. It can engage scientists in a new ground floor field, which is on the verge of exploding in activity.
5. We identified nine themes to which we will repeatedly return.

THREE QUESTIONS FOR THOUGHT AND DISCUSSION

1. What are the differences between a humble hero and heroic humility?
2. Where do you stand on the definition of humility? Must people simply be less self-focused to be humble, or do they need to be oriented to help others?
3. Which is the most important reason to study humility scientifically, and why: because deficits in humility show how very much individuals and society need humility or because we might do good things through the study.

I

HUMILITY AND ITS MEASUREMENT

1

WHAT IS HUMILITY?

What does psychological science say humility is, and what does science tell us about humility? Based on the last 10 years of research, here are some conclusions we might arrive at from psychological science.

DEFINITION

In any new science, some of the fundamental battles occur over the best definition for a construct. The field of humility studies is no different.

Weidman, Cheng, and Tracy (2016) noted two limitations in the humility literature. First, they suggested that there is no clear consensus among researchers about what humility is—although we aren't so sure that is the case. Conceptualizations and measures do vary across studies as they summarize. Second, they suggested that most researchers have defined humility as something socially desirable. However, some theological and philosophical traditions

http://dx.doi.org/10.1037/0000079-002
Heroic Humility: What the Science of Humility Can Say to People Raised on Self-Focus, by E. L. Worthington Jr. and S. T. Allison

suggest that humility may have a darker side—a sort of self-downing, poor-sense-of-self type of humility. Weidman et al. conducted a bottom-up analysis of the psychological structure of humility. That is, they wanted to see what "just folks" thought humility is. In five studies ($N = 1{,}479$) that involved (a) cluster analysis and categorization of humility-related words generated by both laypersons and academic experts, (b) exploratory and confirmatory factor analyses of momentary and dispositional humility experiences, and (c) experimental induction of a momentary humility experience, they asked people about humility.

Across these studies, they found that humility took two forms. *Appreciative humility* is elicited by personal success; involves action tendencies that lift and honor others; and is positively associated with authentic pride, guilt, and prestige-based status. In contrast, *self-abasing humility* is elicited by personal failure, involves negative self-evaluations, promotes hiding from others' evaluations, and is associated with dispositions such as shame, low self-esteem, and submissiveness. Self-abasing humility might be part of self-condemnation rather than a different part of humility. As such, it is probably misnamed and is not really humility at all. This may illustrate the dangers of a bottom-up, non–expert-informed approach to trying to define technical terms. At best, such approaches tell not what a concept is but what non-experts might conflate with the concept.

Definitions of humility among researchers abound. In the edited *Handbook of Humility* (Worthington, Davis, & Hook, 2017), each chapter's authors offered a definition. However, in spite of wording differences, we estimated—after reading and analyzing all of the experts' definitions—that there was general consensus, but not full agreement, about what humility is. Here we review some of these definitions and then advance the definition used by our research team (D. E. Davis, Hook, et al., 2011; D. E. Davis, Worthington, & Hook, 2010).

Three Parts Are Necessary

Humility is defined as (a) having accurate self-assessment—not too high, not too low—that involves seeing oneself as a limited agent with a teachable attitude; (b) making a modest—not too high, not too low—(yet consensually true) self-presentation to others; and (c) holding an abiding attitude oriented toward benefiting others (not solely or mainly benefiting oneself) that might be said to exert power under control used to build others up and not squash them down.

Accurate Self-Appraisal

All three aspects are necessary for one to be humble. In our tripartite definition, having an accurate self-appraisal is essential. Being authentic is necessary but not sufficient for humility. A mass murderer might be accurate in appraising the self, have a keen awareness of his or her limitations, and be eager to learn new ways of murder. But clearly the person would not be humble, certainly lacking in our third quality of other-orientedness to lift others up and not squash them down. One could have an accurate view of oneself and be immodest or dictatorial. Humanistic psychology touts authenticity as a laudable characteristic. But being authentic is not the same thing as being humble. Authenticity does not imply that a person is concerned in the slightest about the welfare of others and might be authentically a jerk—completely immodest and self-absorbed. In addition, even a very accurate self-concept as being aware of one's strengths and weaknesses does not imply that the person is open to correction or critique—that the person is teachable and desires input from others. That requires both an accurate understanding of one's limitations and modesty.

Modesty

One could be modest because one had been taught to be modest, not because it arose from an attitude of being teachable and other-oriented. Certainly, though, if people do not appraise a person as modest, the person will not be thought to be humble. In our definition of humility, modesty is an essential part of humility, not something that can be differentiated out.

Other-Orientedness

We believe that humility requires being oriented to elevate others even if, at times, it means not elevating oneself. This third leg of the three-legged stool of humility is the source of some disagreement. Some argue that humility involves simply lack of self-focus. We disagree. One can lack self-focus because one is focused externally or is mindfully contemplating the external world and one's present experience of it. Yet, many externally focused people and many mindful people are not necessarily humble. We believe that an essential component of humility is lacking self-focus *because* one is focusing on others. In addition, one is not focusing on others to use them for one's own ends, but is focusing on others to lift them up and not put them down. One seeks the best for others. At times, one's own benefit comes into conflict with the welfare and benefit of others. If that happens, one must judiciously consider—while being aware of the insidious aspect of cognition that we are self-serving beings and tend to justify acting in our own self-interest—how to optimally care both for the self and other. We believe that our emphasis on the necessity for being focused on elevating others is a distinguishing mark of this book. By the end of the book, we hope you will be convinced that this third plank is an absolute necessity for true humility.

It Takes All Three Parts

Humility comprises all three components. One could be other-oriented and yet be resentful or be desirous of glory from one's philanthropy. One could be modest but not care about others or be completely inaccurate about one's strengths and weaknesses. All three must come together to form the humble character.

So what about Weidman et al.'s (2016) claim about self-abasing humility? We think humility is a lay concept that can be confused by imprecision in its everyday use. This illustrates the difference between what laypeople think a concept is and what experts who attempt to study it scientifically understand it to be. For instance, a lay conception of an atom is a three-dimensional "solar system" with electrons orbiting a small, hard nucleus. But physicists believe that a real atom is a more "smeared out" nucleus with indistinct boundaries and a quantum mechanical probability distribution about where an electron might be. The simple lay definition of an atom has uses—but usually in lay conversation. The expert definition, though, is what scientists use to base science on. We think this is the case also with humility. It has three parts, with only the third part still being controversial. We hope throughout this book to persuade our readers that the warm other-orientation is indeed a crucial part of the definition, not just a quiet ego.

HEROIC HUMILITY IS DIFFERENT FROM HUMBLE HEROISM

Heroic humility is not the same as *humble heroism*. Some heroism might be humble. Other heroism will not be. Immodest heroism might be based on achieving or maintaining self-respect, securing approbation, illustrating self-aggrandizement, and so forth.

Not Humble Heroes

There are some people who seem to rise to the level of doing a heroic act that is (a) not for hidden agendas, (b) modest, and (c) oriented toward building the other or lifting the other person higher even at cost to oneself. Those people show humble heroism.

Some of our most cherished heroes are people who downplay the selfless actions that they took. Consider Wesley Autrey, who was waiting on a New York City subway platform with his two young daughters, ages 4 and 6. Beside them was a 19-year-old film student named Cameron Hollopeter, a complete stranger to the Autreys. Suddenly, Hollopeter had a seizure. Autrey went to assist him, but the writhing young man fell onto the subway tracks.

Autrey saw an oncoming train barreling toward the stricken man. There wasn't enough time to pull Hollopeter to safety. With two young daughters, Autrey could have easily and blamelessly done nothing. But Autrey did the extraordinary: He jumped on top of Hollopeter between the tracks to protect him while five train cars rumbled inches above. Later, Autrey demonstrated extraordinary humility. "I don't feel like I did something spectacular," he said. "I just saw someone who needed help. I did what I felt was right." This was humble heroism.

Not all heroes are humble, of course. We believe that mere hero status is not indicative of humility. Some heroes are downright arrogant. But, for the "typical" hero, we might find a mix of traits. Some of Lilienfeld's research (for a review, see B. A. Murphy, Lilienfeld, & Watts, 2017) on personality traits of heroes shows dominance, impulsivity, even a bit of psychopathology. There are two types of heroes. Some are momentary responders to powerful situations, like Wesley Autrey. Many wartime heroes respond to situational demands with heroic self-sacrifice. The others are lifetime humble people—those who are heroically humble.

We admire Lilienfeld's work. It points to extreme situations when seemingly nonhumble personality traits such as "fearless dominance" can facilitate heroic behavior. For example, in 2004 an Australian man with a criminal history boldly leapt into the water to save 20 people from the Indian Ocean tsunami in Thailand. Lilienfeld's research tells us that at times dire circumstances may require bold, aggressive actions that on the surface may appear to lack humility. On closer inspection, however, these heroic actions are not inconsistent with our tripartite definition of humility as involving other-oriented, rather than self-oriented, focus. The Australian man's boldness was consistent with this aspect of humble heroism during the tsunami, yet that same boldness may have also contributed to his crimes of assault and burglary. He met one of the necessary conditions of humility, but because he did not exhibit modesty or honest self-awareness, he did not meet the sufficient conditions for being a truly humble hero. And because he did not meet the conditions consistently, he is not an example of heroic humility.

Heroic Humility

We are more interested in the heroically humble who pursue humility to heroic lengths of truthful self-appraisal, modesty, and other-orientedness. That hero, like Mother Teresa or Nelson Mandela, has gone through the heroic quest (of Joseph Campbell, 1972) or has built virtue throughout his or her soul. Those heroes are the ones we would say possess "heroic humility." The momentary responder might well be a humble person, but usually it is the situation that draws the heroic behavior and character is incidental.

Likewise, heroes are different from role models and leaders. Kinsella, Ritchie, and Igou (2015b) conducted six studies to make a prototype analysis of the ways people perceive of heroes. Kinsella et al. (2015b) examined laypeople's beliefs about the functions of heroes. They found that heroes serve three psychological functions. They (a) enhance the lives of others, (b) promote morals, and (c) protect individuals from threats. We view this finding as supportive of our conceptualization of humble heroes as ready and willing to assist and mentor others, as described in Joseph Campbell's (1972) monomyth of the hero. It is also consistent with our tripartite view of humble heroism as other-focused rather than self-focused. Interestingly, Kinsella et al.'s third function of "protection" is again reminiscent of Lilienfeld's work on the alleged "psychopathology" of heroism, such that seemingly negative traits associated with dominance may be useful in extreme emergency situations requiring immediate risky action in the service of protecting others from danger. Beyond the main findings, Kinsella et al. did an excellent job of mapping the cognitive perception of laypeople about what heroes are. Their findings are quite consonant with our view of heroic humility. In Study 1, Kinsella et al. had raters sort open-ended descriptions ($n = 189$) of heroes into 26 categories, and in Study 2, participants identified the most central characteristics. People perceived heroes as having humility as a peripheral feature. The central features overlapped with aspects of our definition with (a) accurate self-assessment (see Honest), (b) modest self-portrayal (see Humble = Not arrogant, modest), and (c) other-orientedness (showing power under control to build others up, not put them down). This other-orientation is consonant with heroes being seen as having moral integrity and being willing to protect needy people, as well as being altruistic, self-sacrificial, selfless, and helpful. Heroes also were identified with some central qualities (e.g., being brave, courageous, determined, and honest and having conviction) that do not necessarily map onto humility but round out a picture of heroic humility. Peripheral qualities of heroes included being compassionate, humble, caring, powerful, and able to lead. In Study 3, 33 participants identified the central qualities of heroes faster than they identified peripheral characteristics. In Study 4, 25 participants remembered more central than peripheral characteristics in a surprise recall task. In Study 5, 89 participants identified a hero when given central characteristics more readily than when given peripheral characteristics. In Studies 6 and 7 ($n = 212$ and $n = 307$, respectively), participants perceived role models, leaders, and heroes to have different characteristics.

Finding a balance between selfish and selfless behavior requires creative tension. Even heroes who devote their lives to positive social movements have to eat, find shelter, and meet many basic needs as described in Maslow's hierarchy. So, they are pushed by satisfying basic needs and pulled by other-oriented inspirational needs. A big component of humility is becoming "rightsized," not only with regard to our proper place in the parade of humanity, but also in balancing selfish desires with selfless "generative" behaviors, as Erik Erikson called them.

UNDERSTANDING HUMILITY

One might think that humility requires dealing a death blow to one's ego. However, besides humility involving (a) accurate assessment of self, (b) modest self-presentation, and (c) other-oriented (rather than self-oriented) focus, humility is best observed when the ego is placed under strain (i.e., when conflict challenges one's agenda, recognition for accomplishment). Thus, having an ego is necessary to developing one's humility. Without the pull of egoism toward self-focus, we would not know whether we were developing humility. We can see this easily in thinking of courage. Without situations evoking fear, one would not know whether brave acts were merely foolhardy or courageous responses. Without situations that pull for ego, we cannot know whether we are developing humility.

This last point suggests that humility has several key subdomains. It applies to a broader range of situations than other virtues, such as forgiveness, which refers to how one handles the aftermath of an offense, or gratitude, which involves how one handles receiving a benefit from someone. In contrast, one can imagine that arrogant behaviors can occur across many contexts, and the behavior that indicates high humility depends on social norms in that situation. For example, a college football player who spikes the ball after a touchdown will be viewed as arrogant because the behavior might lead to a penalty and hurt the team. But the same behavior may be viewed as benign for a professional football player because this behavior is accepted as normal.

Researchers have theorized that there are several types of humility, which involve different situations that strain egotism. So a theoretical review and consolidation would contribute to the literature. In Chapter 2, we describe them.

WHAT DID WE LEARN IN THIS CHAPTER?

1. All three parts of the tripartite definition of humility are needed for an unambiguous definition.
2. Within heroic humility, there were similarities and differences with heroism and with leaders, yet people who have developed heroic humility are often characterized by humility and also by heroism and leadership.

3. Having a solid ego is necessary if we are to know whether we are developing higher levels of heroic humility because we must battle against things that place our ego under strain if we are to strengthen our heroic humility muscles.
4. There are different types of humility because there are different arenas in which our egos might be strained and in which we can develop a sense of heroic humility.

THREE QUESTIONS FOR THOUGHT AND DISCUSSION

1. In this chapter, we contend that all three elements of humility must be present or people don't really have humility. Explain why you agree or disagree with this contention.
2. We argue that having an ego and feeling a pull toward self-aggrandizement is a good thing because it shows us we are developing humility when we overcome egoistic urges. Do you buy that argument? Or is that like saying that murder is good because it makes people appreciate life?
3. We argue that finding a balance between selfish and selfless behavior yields humility. This view is like Aristotle's view of virtue as a Golden Mean between two errors. But is this the case with humility? Might humility be something that more of it is simply better? Why or why not?

2

TYPES OF HUMILITY

"Humility is the blossom of which death to self is the perfect fruit," wrote Andrew Murray (2012, p. 40), a turn-of-the-20th-century Christian writer. But this gives a misleading picture of humility as some once-and-for-all-time achievement. After all, we only die once.

Perhaps we might work with this metaphor to give it usefulness consistent with the science of humility. There are many blossoms on a fruit tree. Each of those has a chance of leading to a piece of fruit. Not every blossom leads to a mature piece of fruit. Furthermore, there are many trees in an orchard, and some are star performers, bringing in bushels of fruit. Some are duds. Most are somewhere in the middle, representing a nicely shaped normal distribution. In this example, the blossoms are opportunities for humble acts, and some of those acts come to fruition. Others are bypassed or do not end in something humble looking. The pieces of fruit are humble

http://dx.doi.org/10.1037/0000079-003
Heroic Humility: What the Science of Humility Can Say to People Raised on Self-Focus, by E. L. Worthington Jr. and S. T. Allison

states arising from the acts we attempt. As we know, no disposition or personality trait is characterized by complete consistency. So, the tree of humble fruits is a disposition of humility. In the humility orchard, some people have only a few experiences of true humility, most are somewhere in the middle, and a few take their practice of humility to heroic proportions. They become the exemplars of heroic humility. Those are the people we are writing about.

But let's unpack these different levels of humility. As we do, we will see why it might be simplistic to think about Murray's metaphor as a once-and-for-all-time experience of becoming humble and experiencing "death to self." I (Ev) often speak publicly about humility, and I frequently distinguish among the various types of humility we discuss in the present chapter. I have written more (and sometimes less) about each type in various sources over the years. For two examples that cover similar material, see Worthington (2017) and Worthington, Goldstein, et al. (in press). In addition, Worthington, Davis, and Hook (2017) described the several levels of humility in the *Handbook of Humility: Theory, Research, and Applications*. By consulting these sources, you can supplement what we have summarized in the present chapter.

Instruments have been developed for the reliable and valid assessment of many types of humility. This is not to be taken for granted. In 2000, clinical–social–personality psychologist June Tangney wrote an essay on humility in which she identified the measurement conundrum. If one reports oneself to be "very humble," is this, ipso facto, evidence that one is not humble and might (in fact) be narcissistic? Or, might an exceptionally humble person even be underreporting his or her humility by saying he or she is *only* "very humble," as D. E. Davis, Worthington, and Hook (2010) observed? In short, can a scientist trust someone's self-report of humility? Tangney concluded that humility "may represent one of those relatively rare personality constructs that is simply unamenable to self-report methods" (p. 78).

By now, research on the measurement of humility has accumulated, somewhat like a Sherlock Holmes mystery unfolds. A classic way to minimize socially desirable responding is to hide the items one is concerned about within a long personality questionnaire. As the story goes, respondents who want to "look good" cannot as easily figure out what the assessor desires. That strategy was pursued for years by the Ashton and Lee (2007) HEXACO model. HEXACO stands for a "Big Six" set of personality dimensions: Honesty–Humility, Extraversion, Excitability or Neuroticism, Agreeableness, Conscientiousness, and Openness to Experience. The Peterson and Seligman (2004) VIA-IS (Values in Action Inventory of Strengths) also uses this strategy. Social psychologists have faced measurement difficulties for decades, and one strategy of choice is to design clever experiments that assess constructs behaviorally. That has been done in many ways. Other scientists have recommended indirect measurements, such as implicit associations tests or physiological and biomarker correlates of either self-reports or experimental manipulations. Some personality researchers (Funder, 1995) have recommended third-party assessments, and that too has been applied to assessing humility (D. E. Davis, Hook, et al., 2011).

What do we conclude from this story of scientific sleuthing? Elaborate strategies for ensuring accurate measurement of humility are not needed. That is, scientists do not need always to provide both self-reports of humility (via psychometrically sound questionnaires) and other reports, behavioral indices, or physiological biomarkers. Also, psychological scientists do not need to hide items to assess humility amid a long personality questionnaire. Rather, on the basis of accumulated research, we can say that if there is no overwhelming special interest at work (i.e., a test taker knowing that hiring depends on humble teamwork), then generally self-reports of humility are as good as other reports or additional measures of humility.

Recently, Hill et al. (2017) conducted a thorough review of the ways to assess humility. They identified about 20 measures of humility. In addition, they reported that the area of assessing humility has been awarded grant funding of over $2 million. We will of necessity review some of the instruments reviewed earlier by Hill et al. Our goal is not to attempt a comprehensive scholarly review of all instruments but to describe the variety of instruments available. Thus, we refer the reader to the chapter by Hill et al. for their review of additional measures and more details than we provide here.

ACT OF HUMILITY

An *act of humility* is a single act in which the person exhibits accurate self-knowledge, not taking too much or too little credit or blame. Perhaps he or she is seen seeking information and not coming across as a know-it-all. The person shows that he or she is teachable. Demonstrating teachability is a manifestation of having an accurate assessment of one's strengths and limitations, so it does not always show up. An act of humility also demonstrates modesty in interacting with others. The humble act does not call attention to itself either in a look-at-me grandiosity or an aw-shucks false modesty. In an act of humility, the sine qua non is that the person lays down his or her self-advancement or self-glorification for the good of others (even though it might also benefit the self as a by-product).

STATE OF HUMILITY

Definition

A *state of humility* is a temporary condition in which one is focused on doing acts of humility. Once a humble act occurs, the person might revert to a state of self-interest, exiting the humble state. For example, peace negotiators have vested interests in pleasing their constituencies, but they also want to arrive at a negotiated settlement. Sometimes both parties might be moved to put aside posturing and make concessions, acting humbly even though they return to a self-interested position when the negotiations are complete.

An Example

When Jimmy Carter brokered the Camp David meetings between Menachem Begin of Israel and Anwar Sadat of Egypt, substantial progress was made by the 13th day, but the negotiations then stalled. Begin announced that he was leaving. Carter (2015) described that as the low point of the meetings. Carter, Sadat, and Begin agreed to announce failure and return to Washington, DC. But, as Carter told it, his secretary came to him with a request from Begin to sign photographs of the three leaders to give to his eight grandchildren:

> Without telling [Begin], she had called Israel and obtained their names, so I inscribed them, with love, to each child. I went to Begin's cabin, and he admitted me with a polite but frigid attitude. I gave him the photographs, he turned away to examine them, and then began to read the names aloud, one by one. He had a choked voice, and tears were running down his cheeks. I was also emotional, and he asked me to have a seat. After a few minutes, we agreed to try once more, and after some intense discussions we were successful. (pp. 156–157)

Carter's personal touch created a state of humility in which these two national leaders were able to reopen talks after an impasse. Both were aware of their limitations and reacted with modesty instead of arrogance, and the personal connection made all the difference in orienting them toward working out an agreement that could bless others.

Research Supporting States of Humility

States of humility and how to promote them are important (Kruse, Chancellor, & Lyubomirsky, 2017; Ruberton, Kruse, & Lyubomirsky, 2017). One might imagine how important a state of humility might be in resolving a business conflict or in discussing contentious issues within couples or families. It is useful and important to identify the personal, interpersonal, and situational constraints opposing states of humility, but it also is important for people to know how to promote humble states. Creating a humble state requires developing personal experiences of softening, such as empathy for the other person or side, gratitude, generosity, and forgiveness for past harms. Also each party's acts are crucial. If one or both sides is personally attacking, selfish, manipulative, and self-focused, it is unlikely (and unwise) for the other side to adopt wholesale humility, generosity, and altruism. On the other hand, often it is with one generous or humble act that a turnaround can occur. The game Prisoner's Dilemma—sometimes played as a one-time choice and at other times played as a series of interactions—is one opportunity that could be used to investigate humility. People compete to accumulate the most benefits (see Axelrod, 1984), so this situation puts the ego under strain and makes it difficult for people to act humbly in a way that is focused on others and their welfare.

A huge body of research has shown that an accommodative strategy—playing generously despite what the opponent does—is not a winning strategy. In fact, even the more justice-oriented, tit-for-tat strategy is not optimal. Instead, a bit of humility helps. When computers play against a program that has occasional defections randomly programmed to occur, then the most winning strategy is called *generous* tit-for-tat. In that scenario, a tit-for-tat would interrupt the cooperative flow with a long series of self-interested (both losing) rounds. But in generous tit-for-tat, a defection is met by a similar self-interested defection. If that continues for a few rounds, the generous tit-for-tat program responds humbly. It tries to kick the interactions out of the continuing negative loop by offering a humble, cooperative, other-oriented response. If the opponent responds cooperatively, then the loop can be shortened, and both players can return to accumulating resources.

Assessing States of Humility

Brief Humility Scale

The Brief Humility Scale (BHS; Kruse, Chancellor, & Lyubomirsky, 2017) was initially published in a book by Ruberton, Kruse, and Lyubomirsky (2017), but in July 2017, it was published by Kruse et al. (2017) with full psychometric workup. It is a six-item scale (with three items reverse scored), and the 7-point response options are as follows: 1 = *strongly disagree*; 4 = *neither agree nor disagree*; 7 = *strongly agree*. The items ask respondents to tell whether they feel better than others, deserve more respect than others, and have both strengths and flaws. Generally, these items assess accurate self-assessment to some degree but do not assess modesty or other-orientation. Ruberton et al. suggested that the BHS can be adapted and used to measure trait humility, but it is most unique for allowing assessment of one's present state of humility. The instructions to respondents are to respond as they feel at the present moment. Ruberton et al. claimed strong evidence for construct validity and estimated reliability. Indeed, Kruse, Chancellor, and Lyubomirsky (2017) used 25 samples and over 2,500 adults to develop the BHS. They presented evidence that the scale had good psychometric characteristics, was sensitive to experimental manipulation, and was not related to socially desirable responding. They used the scale to replicate prior findings and show connections between states of humility and creativity, affect, and personality. They also showed that humility differed from modesty. They suggested advantages of using the BHS to assess states. It can be used as manipulation check, dependent measure, or moderator and in longitudinal research. There is potential for intervening to promote states of humility in business, politics, and other human relationships when relationships might be strained. These measurements could help people recognize when they are acting arrogantly and try to change.

Experiences of Humility Scale

D. E. Davis, McElroy, Choe, et al. (2017) used three studies to create and provide psychometric support for the Experiences of Humility Scale (EHS)—a measure of state humility. In Study 1, they used factor analysis with 200 undergraduates to find four subscales: Other-Orientation, Transcendence, Awareness of Selfishness, and Awareness of Egotism. In Study 2, they studied 106 undergraduates and provided initial evidence supporting construct validity. Participants who wrote about a meaningful event reported lower levels of awareness of egotism and selfishness than did participants who wrote about a neutral experience. In Study 3, 155 undergraduates were used to replicate the factor structure and provide more evidence supporting construct validity. EHS subscales predicted spiritual connection and meaning, and they were modestly related to agreeableness, neuroticism, and also (as we might expect) trait humility.

TRAIT HUMILITY

Trait humility is a summary self- or other-evaluation that one acts humbly in virtually all situations and relationships. Trait humility is built up over a lifetime of humble acts and states. It sums across relationships and cultures. It sums across intellectual, political, and religious issues. It requires accumulating a history of humble acts and states and sustaining a humble stance across time and relationships. Trait humility is the sum of a personality indicating consistent and lasting pursuit of humility and sincerity that the pursuit will continue.

Trait humility is not achieved. In fact, in the face of a successful act of humility or experience of a successful state of humility, very quickly the pursuit of humility must resume. It cannot be maintained. At first, this might seem discouraging, but it is similar to life's breath. Immediately on inhaling, one must exhale. It is not discouraging that we are continually in need of the next breath. It is a fact of existence. Similarly, with humility, if we try to hold onto humility, it is like holding our breath. We cannot take in the next needed breath without exhaling the old. The oxygen has nurtured our blood, and the old air, now carbon dioxide–saturated, must be expelled. A humble act or state nurtures our soul, but the more we hold it in, revel in it, and seek to retain it, the more it pollutes and prevents growth in virtue.

THE TRAIT OF HEROIC HUMILITY

Even people who have developed a trait of humility might also have many other traits. They might, by disposition, be forgiving, compassionate, altruistic, and empathic. Heroic humility is what might be considered a central or cardinal trait. That is one of the defining characteristics of a person.

In his book, *Humilitas*, John Dickson (2011), senior research fellow in the Department of Ancient History at Macquarie University in Australia, described the boxer Joe Louis. Louis is rated as the greatest all-time boxer, even above Muhammad Ali (who is number two). Louis had a reputation as a man of humility and generosity. He literally gave away his entire fortune. He was the son of former slaves and was raised in poverty. So, when he became heavyweight champion of the world, a title he held from 1937 to 1949, he wanted to bless others. He gave money to relatives. He gave money to people even if he didn't know them. He gave the City of Detroit money to pay back the welfare his family had received when he was young. An anecdote illustrates how much Louis was able to be fully aware of his strengths, be modest, and be oriented toward others in showing power under control:

> Three young men hopped on a bus in Detroit in the 1930s and tried to pick a fight with a lone man sitting in the back . . . They insulted him. He didn't respond. They turned up the heat of the insults. He said nothing. Eventually, the stranger stood up. He was bigger than they had estimated from his seated position—much bigger. He reached into his pocket, handed them his business card and walked off the bus . . . As the bus drove on, the young men gathered around the card to read the words: *Joe Louis, Boxer*. (Dickson, 2011, p. 26)

This is humility—power under control.

Heroic Humility Is Virtually Impossible to Sustain

One reason we cannot maintain continual humility seems to be that it simply is not in our nature. This is a lesson often learned through privation and suffering. As you will see throughout the book, many of our heroically humble exemplars experienced horrific suffering. For example, take Aleksandr Solzhenitsyn (1918–2008). He was a novelist, social critic of the Soviet Union, and historian, and he won the Nobel Prize for literature in 1970 and the Templeton Prize in 1983. Aleksandr was raised by his mother and an aunt because his father had died in a hunting accident before Aleksandr was born. The family lived in poverty. He grew up during the aftermath of the Revolution, and when World War II rolled around, he served and won decorations for bravery. It was the barbarous war crimes of Soviets against noncombatant Germans (and undoubtedly Germans against noncombatant Soviet citizens as well) that awakened his social sensitivities and set him to think critically about the Soviet system—and earned him a trip to be interrogated at Lubyanka prison in 1945 and a stint of over 10 years in the wilderness in what is now Kazakhstan. In 1956, he was released.

The beauty of Solzhenitsyn's reflections, though, is the way he brings his critical gaze mirror like. In *The Gulag Archipelago*, a summary of his Siberian work-camp experiences and about the system of the Soviets for dealing with dissent, he reflected,

> There is nothing that so assists the awakening of omniscience within us as insistent thoughts about one's own transgressions, errors, mistakes. After the difficult cycles of such ponderings over many years, whenever I mentioned the heartlessness of our highest-ranking bureaucrats, the cruelty of our executioners, I remember myself . . . And I say, "So were we any better?" (Solzhenitsyn, 1973)

This essentially humble attitude is encapsulated in a quote that is seen in many slightly different forms—including speeches, books, and conversations.

> If only there were evil people somewhere insidiously committing evil deeds, and it were necessary only to separate them from the rest of us and destroy them. But the line dividing good and evil cuts through the heart of every human being. And who is willing to destroy a piece of his own heart. (Solzhenitsyn, 1973)

Most of us cannot sustain heroic humility. We are too fallible. But some people can. That's what we would like to find out in this book: What makes such people so able to be heroically humble so consistently?

In addition, humility, especially life-practiced heroic humility such as Solzhenitsyn's, is likely to be associated with other virtues. We have suggested that this is because trait humility, by definition, includes a warm orientation toward others. As we read Solzhenitsyn's writings, we cannot help but be moved by his humility, but also by his panoply of personal virtues and the satisfaction with life he experienced despite the many privations forced on him. For example, he exudes wisdom. Krause (2016) used a nationwide survey of 1,535 middle-aged and older adults. As we might expect from observing Solzhenitsyn, in Krause's sample, greater wisdom was associated with greater humility. In addition, the relationship between humility and life satisfaction was greater when people were wise than when their wisdom was low.

Assessment of the Disposition of Humility

Humility and Modesty in VIA-IS

The Humility and Modesty subscale in the VIA-IS (Peterson & Seligman, 2004), which is (together) one of 24 strengths of the VIA-IS, consists of 10 items using a 5-point response rating (*very much unlike me–very much like me*). For the VIA-IS, humility is defined as nondefensive willingness to see oneself and one's strengths and weakness accurately. That is one of our three core components of humility. Humility and modesty (our second core component) are grouped together. The VIA-IS treats humility as a private self-assessment and modesty, which is limited to not boasting about oneself—as a social component. Humility and modesty are part of the virtue temperance. Temperance scores have an alpha of about .70, which makes the VIA-IS not a precise choice for assessing temperance. Beyond that, humility is hard to parse out from other aspects of temperance. This has been used frequently within the VIA-IS, but its construct validity as a measure of humility is sparse.

Honesty–Humility

Honesty–Humility (HH; Ashton & Lee, 2005, 2007, 2009) is the most often experimentally used measure of humility. However, cautions are advised. The 10-item HH subscale of the six-factor HEXACO Personality Inventory (HEXACO-PI) is the first and most widely used measure of humility. The HH consists of four components: Sincerity, Fairness, Greed-Avoidance, and Modesty. Sample HH items using 5-point ratings include "I wouldn't use flattery to get a raise or promotion at work, even if I thought it would succeed," and "If I knew that I could never get caught, I would be willing to steal a million dollars" (reversed score). Thus, HH is far removed from our conceptualization of humility. It emphasizes genuineness, cooperation, and fairness, even when exploitation of others will not be punished (Ashton & Lee, 2007). Only the two-item modesty subscale of the HEXACO assesses anything close to our definition of one aspect of humility. Hill et al. (2017) suggested that because the dark triad (narcissism, Machiavellianism, and psychopathy) is negatively correlated with this measure, then HH (including all four subscales) might be assessing something like the goodness of one's character, not humility. They concluded that even though the HH subscale is named Honesty–Humility, and even though it has strong psychometric support for predictive validity, the evidence supporting its construct validity for humility is weak.

The Quiet Ego Scale

The term *quiet ego* describes a self-identity that has transcended the preoccupation of egotism. This is hypothesized to allow a compassionate orientation toward the self and others (Wayment, Bauer, & Sylaska, 2015). Though other positive attributes such as self-compassion, and other-oriented virtues such as gratitude and forgiveness, also characterize a quiet ego, the concept is aligned with humility (Kesebir, 2014) and most closely represents the third component of humility—non–self-focus more than other-orientation. Scores on the Quiet Ego Scale (QES; Wayment, Bauer, & Sylaska, 2015; see also Wayment & Bauer, 2017), a 14-item, 5-point response format (*strongly disagree–strongly agree*), were correlated with other measures of humility. We would assess the estimated reliabilities as adequate and evidence supporting construct validity as good. In general, ego quietness is consistent with a Buddhist conceptualization of humility, which prioritizes the internal. Wayment and Bauer (2017) used the QES to provide additional construct validity. The QES was related to a sense of balanced values. It was also related to goals of compassion and to universalism, benevolence, and self-direction.

CEO Humility

CEO Humility (Ou et al., 2014) seeks to assess humility in corporate leadership. Thus, it is not a dispositional measure of humility but borders on being a relational humility measure. This 19-item measure uses a 6-point response rating. It yields six subscale scores: a cognition-of-a-transcendent-self view, underlying motivations of low self-focus and pursuit of self-transcendence, and behavioral manifestations of self-awareness, openness to feedback, and appreciation of others. Estimated reliabilities of scores are acceptable for research (about .8). Validity data at this point are sparse.

Humility-Arrogance Implicit Association Test

The Humility-Arrogance Implicit Association Test (IAT-HA; Rowatt et al., 2006) provides a different type of method for measuring humility. It was modeled after existing implicit association tests (Asendorpf, Banse, & Mücke, 2002). Participants were shown attributes such as *humble* or *modest* and others such as *arrogant* or *egotistical*. They responded to each word as like self or like either an arrogant or humble exemplar. When the perceived self is like the exemplar, reaction times are short, but when the perceived self is different from the exemplar, reaction times are long, with differences requiring more cognitive processing. The IAT-HA had good alphas. The assessment of humility by non-self-report or by other-report is an excellent ideal. Implicit measures are only one way of doing this. Inconsistencies suggest circumspection in using the IAT-HA at present. In the future, perhaps other IAT assessments can be developed that contrast humility with not-humble-but-also-not-arrogant exemplars, which might expand the range of use of IATs.

Measuring Dispositional Humility in the Future

We anticipate improved self-report measures, development of behavioral assessments of humble behaviors in particular settings (e.g., occupational decision making, couple conflicts, counseling, and other instances when the ego might be under strain and self-protective ego-defending behaviors might be common), and use of brain imaging (fMRI, PET technology, EEGs, and evoked potentials) to assess humility.

TYPES OF HUMILITY: RELATIONAL HUMILITY AND CULTURAL HUMILITY

We suggested previously that trait humility was a summary self- or other-evaluation that one acts humbly in virtually all situations and relationships. We think it is useful to also think in terms of different types of humility. We do not want to recreate the debate over intelligence, which we do not believe has ever conceptually been resolved (even though it seems clear that there is an overall *g* factor [general intelligence]), factors of verbal and performance intelligence (and other ways of slicing the pie), and specific factors making up those broad factors. But it seems clear that people might have humility when talking about religion but not politics (or vice versa), in relationships with a romantic partner but not a supervisor at work (or vice versa), or in empathically understanding a colleague from another culture while believing one's country might be superior to other countries. Thus, from a practical standpoint—but not from hard philosophical commitment—we suggest that several types of humility exist.

What Are Relational Humility and Cultural Humility?

One type of humility is *relational humility*, which refers to humility in the context of one's relationships.

Humility differs with roles. It is important to note that one's roles and relationships may affect the level and expression of humility across different contexts. Thus, humility may look different if a person is a humble student or professor, client or counselor, business leader, middle manager, or worker.

Humility differs with contexts. Also, one may express different levels of humility across different contexts, depending on factors such as one's needs and sense of security within these different settings. Relational humility has been thoroughly investigated by Sandage, Worthington, Davis, and their colleagues, with many empirical articles having been published.

Humility differs with duration. It might be relationship specific and enduring across time, a brief state, or even an act of relational humility.

Humility differs with relational variables. Generally, relational humility will be influenced by relationship qualities such as the amount of care and concern partners have for each other; their identity as a unit (e.g., as a family, couple, member of a workgroup); and the relative power among the unit's participants to influence each other's behavior, feelings, and ideas.

Humility differs with culture—cultural humility. A subtype of relational humility is *cultural humility*. A culturally humble person is open to and sees value in people of different cultures. Most people explicitly or implicitly view themselves as a group as morally superior to others; this is a difficult by-product of morality in groups. Being culturally humble involves not overgeneralizing one's core values and beliefs to other people, who may hold different core values and beliefs. Instead, one treats individuals, families, and groups on their own merit, while at the same time understanding that individuals' personalities and relationships are conditioned by their culture. Cultural humility is particularly important for smooth interpersonal relationships, and it is most relevant when people from different cultures come into contact with each other and attempt to understand each other or when people within a multiethnic country seek to understand people from different ethnic backgrounds. There is a burgeoning body of research in cultural humility (see the book by Hook, Davis, Owen, & DeBlaere, 2017). I identify two types of cultural humility, which like any relational humility can be an act, a state, or a trait.

Empathic Cultural Humility

The person empathically understands the cultural difference of another person, has sought to master knowledge about the other culture, yet treats the person as a valuable individual who has an individual story to tell within the cultural framework. Empathic cultural humility means the person does not presume to know the other person merely because he or she might be well versed in knowledge about the person's culture.

Nonpartisan Cultural Humility

Nonpartisan cultural humility is having humility about the strengths and limitations of one's own culture and being able to recognize, without judgment, the strengths and limitations of other cultures.

Research on Cultural Humility

Mosher, Hook, Farrell, Watkins, and Davis (2017) reviewed 49 articles on cultural humility. Of those, 31 were theoretical and 18 were empirical articles. The theoretical articles represented three themes. Some sought to define and provide a conceptual framework for cultural humility. Others aimed to distinguish *cultural humility* from terms like *cultural competence*. Still others sought to identify the relevance of cultural humility for other fields. The remainder of this section summarizes research reviewed by Mosher et al.

Core qualities of cultural humility were present across definitions: (a) Cultural humility requires lifelong learning. It isn't an achievable end point or even an asymptote that one nears. Interpersonal interactions are unique, so we must be always vigilant and flexible. (b) Cultural humility presupposes cultural self-awareness. Culturally humble people test their cultural assumptions and biases through reflection. (c) They seek to understand other people not through stereotypes but by interaction and active listening (Foronda, Baptiste, Reinholdt, & Ousman, 2016). (d) Respect is essential when interacting. (e) Cultural humility differs from cultural competency. Cultural humility involves lifestyle and attitudes; cultural competency involves knowledge and skill-sets. Cultural humility is relevant to helping disciplines, cross-cultural interactions, and international relations.

Mosher et al. (2017) found that only 11 of 18 empirical studies were solely quantitative. The high number of qualitative studies likely reflects the newness of the field. One scale—the Cultural Humility Scale (CHS; Hook, Davis, Owen, Worthington, & Utsey, 2013)—has been developed to assess cultural humility. Mosher et al. found three groupings of studies. They found that seven studies described cultural humility within the helping professions and how it develops over time. For example, Hilliard (2011) examined eight culturally humble physical therapists. Hilliard found five themes describing cultural humility: (a) open-mindedness, (b) responding to clients' emotions, (c) affirming clients' goals, (d) promoting empowerment, and (e) directing clients to their community's needs and assets. Mosher et al. found that nine studies used training to help people act more culturally humble. All programs had desired improvements. They promoted confidence and self-awareness, elicited clients' beliefs about treatment, and led to better relationships with the clients. Mosher et al. also found two quantitative studies that related cultural humility to counseling outcomes. When clients rated counselors as culturally humble, they had stronger working alliances and more symptom improvements (Hook et al., 2013).

Cultural humility is important in supervision of psychotherapy as well as in psychotherapy itself. Watkins and Hook (2016) considered the role of cultural humility within psychoanalytic supervision of psychotherapy. Culture has become increasingly relevant to the practice of supervision. However, Watkins and Hook argued that psychoanalytic supervision literature has stayed very limited in addressing culture and diversity. They suggested a view of psychoanalytic supervision that is based on teaching supervisees about and modeling cultural humility. A safe space for interaction can be experienced as the supervisor is culturally transparent and accepting. Watkins and Hook argued that creating such a safe space in supervision prepares the way for a psychotherapist to create such a space in psychotherapy.

Owen et al. (2014) explored religious and spiritual cultural humility. Favorable client perceptions of a counselor's cultural humility toward religion predicted better working alliances and outcomes. However, religious commitment of clients moderated that relationship. For clients with higher religious commitment, cultural humility predicted religious and symptom-change outcomes. For clients with lower religious commitment, that prediction did not hold.

Assessing Relational Humility

Self-Reporting Humility in Relationships

As of this point, no self-report measures have been developed to assess oneself in specific relational context. Self-reports are needed of humility specific to marriage, work, friendship, and other relationship. There are other reports of humility in various relationships, as detailed next.

The Relational Humility Scale

The Relational Humility Scale (RHS; D. E. Davis, Hook, et al., 2011; D. E. Davis, Worthington, & Hook, 2010) is a 16-item, other-rated scale that assesses the rater's opinion of the target's humility. The RHS conceptualizes humility as a personality judgment (D. E. Davis, Hook, et al., 2011; Funder, 1995). Relational humility was defined as an observer's judgment that a target person (a) is interpersonally other-oriented rather than self-focused, and accordingly, (b) is marked by a lack of superiority to others, and (c) has an accurate view of self—one that is neither too inflated nor too low. Not surprisingly, this definition is close to the one we use throughout the present book. The RHS has three subscales: Global Humility (which assumes other-orientation), Superiority, and Self-Awareness. Responses use a 5-point rating

(1 = *completely disagree*, 5 = *completely agree*). For the full scale, in various studies, alphas ranged between .90 and .95. Subscale alphas ranged between .79 and .97 (D. E. Davis, Hook, et al., 2011). Evidence of construct validity of interpretations of RHS scores as indicating humility is relatively strong.

The Expressed Humility Scale

Owens, Johnson, and Mitchell (2013) assumed that aspects of humility are observable by others and affect interpersonal interactions. They developed the Expressed Humility Scale (EHS) for organizational leadership. Expressed humility assumes the rated person has demonstrated (a) being willing to view the self accurately, (b) appreciating others' strengths and contributions, and (c) being teachable. Each of the three components is assessed by three items (nine items total) using a 5-point response format (*strongly disagree* to *strongly agree*). Alphas were strong. Evidence for construct validity was good.

Round-Robin Judgments to Assess Relational Humility

D. E. Davis et al. (2013) used a round-robin design to assess relational humility. Round-robin designs allow people to interact and then rate all of the people within a group or organization. D. E. Davis et al. (2013) suggested and tested five propositions about relational humility. First, they defined humility as involving accurate self-perception, other-focus, and modest self-presentation. Second, they proposed that it is easier to accurately detect humility in others than in oneself. Third, humility helps strengthen relationships. Fourth, emotions influence humility judgments. Fifth, humility is most easily assessed when it is challenged. In their first study, they recruited people with an interpersonal harm within the most recent 2 months, and they assessed them weekly for 6 weeks. Humility at any one time predicted forgiveness at the next time. In the second study, 84 college students in small groups completed three tasks requiring cooperation. In each group, participants used round-robin ratings at three measurement occasions to evaluate whether trait humility predicted formation of strong social bonds. In contrast to Meagher, Leman, Bias, Latendresse, and Rowatt (2015), when people rated participants to have high trait humility, that rating was associated with greater group status and acceptance. Meagher et al. concluded that support was provided for the proposition that humility can help repair and form relationships with strong social bonds.

Assessing Cultural Humility

The Cultural Humility Scale

We discussed two types of cultural humility as examples of relational humility. *Empathic cultural humility* is sensitively understanding the cultural differences of a person from the perceiver's culture. *Nonpartisan cultural humility* is being humble about the strengths and limitations of one's own culture. In psychotherapy, empathic cultural humility plays an important role. Hook et al. (2013) developed a scale to measure empathic cultural humility, which they defined as an ability to stay other-oriented (i.e., open to the other) regarding parts of clients' cultural identities that they value most. Hook et al. posited that those who are culturally humble will exude respect for and lack of superiority toward another individuals' cultural background and experience. The CHS (Hook et al., 2013) has clients rate their psychotherapist on a 12-item scale of the psychotherapist's cultural humility. CHS scores had a high alpha for both full scale ($\alpha = 0.86$) and its two subscales. When clients rated psychotherapists higher on the CHS, those ratings were positively correlated with a better working alliance and with improvement in psychotherapy.

Other Reports of Cultural Humility

At this point, there are no other reports of cultural humility of someone such as a counselor or leader who must interact with people from a variety of cultures. There is a need for such reports.

TYPES OF HUMILITY: INTELLECTUAL HUMILITY

Intellectual humility, a subtype of general humility, involves the way people relate to each other when sharing ideas. When people differ intellectually, the ego is strained, which can reveal humility or lack of it. People personally invest in many topics. For example, people might have strong ideas about how to conceptualize current events, how to interpret history, or how to describe a concept within an academic discipline. Intellectual humility allows people to respect others' ideas, beliefs, and values. Many relationships revolve around exchanging ideas. For some, the ideological debate is embedded within the personal relationship and might (or might not) be important. For example, philosophical political differences might form the bulk of the relationship between political rivals, ideological differences between two scholars in a common field, and theological differences among church members. This gives rise to subtypes of intellectual humility imbued with particular emotional significance—political and religious humility.

General Intellectual Humility

Intellectual humility is the ability to treat one's ideas as subject to modification and to negotiate ideas fairly, representing another person's ideas respectfully and honestly rather than framing his or her ideas manipulatively to influence decisions of others. Holding strong convictions strains intellectual humility. It is needed to facilitate discussion of conflicting ideas, concepts, and worldviews. Intellectual humility is arguably foundational to advancement of knowledge, as communities seek to create a forum for sharing and evaluating the merit of different ideas. Intellectual humility has recently been studied by numerous grant-funded research teams, so this area is ripe for a review or meta-analysis.

Intellectual humility is a domain-specific humility. It is unclear how much it overlaps with general humility and how much it is a manifestation of it. Researchers have developed instruments that assess intellectual humility. Some research has shown it to be quite general. For example, Krumrei-Mancuso (2017) found that intellectual humility was associated with higher levels of empathy, gratitude, altruism, benevolence, and universalism and with lower levels of power seeking. This suggests support for the third element in our definition of humility, that humility requires a warm orientation toward others and therefore is associated with other-oriented virtues. This contention is supported because the interconnections among humility and other virtues that involve other-orientation are strong and consistent.

D. E. Davis, Placeres, et al. (2017) suggested the *span hypothesis*—being willing to accept challenges to one's intellectual span and adjust the span if the data or a persuasive argument warrants. They claimed that humility allows people to process information fairly and negotiate ideas with reduced self-interest. Humility allows people to change their minds when new evidence is presented. Humility encourages people to seek new evidence, not just search for supportive evidence. D. E. Davis, Placeres, et al. evaluated the evidential support for the hypothesis as mixed. One challenge for evaluating support for the intellectual even-handedness hypothesis is that values may affect how people understand and practice humility. Imagine a person exchanging ideas about peace and war with a skinhead or with a dedicated Buddhist. We might reasonably expect to be more intellectually open to one than to the other, depending on our values and beliefs.

People often judge others' intellectual humility, and that judgment might affect one's own intellectual humility. Confronted by a braggart, a natural impulse is to show the person up, and if intellectual ideas are the topic of conversation, one can be provoked to less intellectual humility than in most other situations. Judgments of people's intellectual humility depend on the context. Wilson, Ottati, and Price (2017) found that people judged intellectual closed-mindedness as more positive when the closed-mindedness was about either socially normative attitudes (depending on one's socially normative group) than when the closed-mindedness was about beliefs and values one held as personal values. It is easy to see how situation dependent intellectual humility might be.

D. E. Davis, Rice, et al. (2016) differentiated intellectual humility (IH) from general humility (GH). In Study 1, with 1,097 undergraduates, they used confirmatory factor analysis to show that IH and GH were different. IH predicted unique variance in openness to experience relative to GH. In Study 2, they studied 355 undergraduates. IH predicted unique variance in need for cognition, objectivism, and religious ethnocentrism relative to GH. From the research of D. E. Davis, Rice, et al., it seems that intellectual humility is more about openness to experience and ideas superimposed on warmth, nurture, and empathy toward others, which predominates in general humility.

Dunlop et al. (2016) showed that intellectual humility was related to openness to experience and ideas. They studied overclaiming—in which individuals overstate their level of familiarity with items. Overclaiming has been suggested to indicate a positive self-presentation. Dunlop et al. conducted four primary studies using six samples, and they presented a meta-analysis. People overclaim because of egoistic self-enhancement, intentional impression management, and biased memory. Dunlop et al. tested whether overclaiming would best be predicted by a dispositional tendency to be curious and explorative or self-centered (i.e., low Honesty–Humility). All of their findings supported a curiosity—that is, openness to experience—rather than a self-centered explanation.

However, it might not be as simple as that. Deffler, Leary, and Hoyle (2016) examined whether intellectual humility was related to recognition memory. Indeed, higher intellectual humility was associated with higher likelihood of recognizing when one had been exposed to a belief before. The connection held regardless of whether the items were congruent or incongruent with participants' own beliefs. Intellectual humility might, then, involve an ability to put aside personal biases and report correctly on facts, regardless of personal bias. Individual differences in intellectual humility may partly reflect how people process information and judge what they do and do not know.

Before discussing how intellectual humility is assessed, let us note that in Chapter 1, we described the research of Weidman, Cheng, and Tracy (2016), who studied a folk understanding of general humility. Samuelson et al. (2015) did the same with intellectual humility in three separate studies of a "folk" understanding of an intellectually humble person. They arrived at a complex portrait of an intellectually humble person. Self-knowledge, self-orientation, and other-orientation were each important in lay understandings of intellectual humility. As we have found repeatedly, humility of all types requires (a) accurate self-assessment and teachable attitude, (b) modesty, and (c) a warm orientation toward others, but different types of humility superimpose other emphases on top of those qualities.

Assessing Intellectual Humility by Self-Report

The Intellectual Humility Scale

The Intellectual Humility Scale (IHS; Hill et al., 2015) is a 17-item self-report measure of intellectual humility with three subscales: low concern of intellectual status, perspective taking that admits to intellectual shortcomings, and intellectual defensiveness. The alphas for two subscales (i.e., low concern for status, $\alpha = .85$; perspective taking, $\alpha = .88$) are strong, but not for low intellectual defensiveness ($\alpha = .66$). Evidence supports both predictive validity and construct validity of the HIS.

The Comprehensive Intellectual Humility Scale

Krumrei-Mancuso and Rouse (2016) developed a 22-item Comprehensive Intellectual Humility Scale (CIHS). They drew on theoretical descriptions of intellectual humility, pilot studies, reviews of experts, and both exploratory and confirmatory factor analyses. The CIHS sees intellectual humility as being aware of one's intellectual fallibility without undue threat to self. The scale assesses four interrelated aspects of intellectual humility. These are independence of intellect and ego, openness to revising one's opinions, respect for others' opinions, and not being intellectually overconfident. They reported psychometric support for the CIHS. For example, the CIHS's four subscales have alphas between .73 and .89 (full scale alpha is .88).

Assessing Intellectual Humility By Other-Report

The Intellectual Humility Scale–Other. The Intellectual Humility Scale–Other (HIS-o; McElroy et al., 2014) is an other-report of intellectual humility. Intellectual humility was conceptualized as openness to ideas based on the recognition of one's limited knowledge and on the ability to regulate arrogance by reacting nondefensively to views that are different from one's own. There are two subscales, intellectual openness and intellectual arrogance. Construct and predictive validity evidence is reasonably strong but has received some critical attention (Meagher, Leman, Bias, Latendresse, & Rowatt, 2015). Meagher et al. (2015) used round-robin rating to ask people in short- and long-term interactions to rate each other on intellectual humility. They conducted two studies of intellectual humility and intellectual arrogance. Unacquainted participants in brief interactions provided round-robin judgments following a set of collaborative tasks. In round-robin judgments, each partner rates all others. However, in those brief interactions, they could reach no consensus on the group members' humility or arrogance. To the contrary, a round-robin rating design following months of cooperative course work did produce consensus on ratings of both humility and arrogance. Self-reported intellectual humility was positively associated with self-enhancement. However, ratings of intellectual humility by other group members were not related to self-enhancement.

Political Humility

Defining Political Humility

Political humility is yet another subtype of intellectual humility. When people are engaged in politics or the way politics are practiced, they can become quite emotionally invested, and political humility is difficult. That can also be true for those who are politically identified or patriotic. In general, political humility is about negotiating and respecting others' political ideas, and this manifests often in the public square. Worthington (2017) suggested a postmodern reconceptualization of political philosophy. Modern communication frequency, transparency, and availability to one's ingroup have changed politics. Traditionally, elections emphasized distinctions between political opponents. However, after the election, the elected officer could be a statesperson—someone who governs opponents and supporters impartially. With social media, though, candidates' communications are tracked by supporters, and deviations from the party line are punished and extremist politics are reinforced. This was apparent recently. Republican Eric Cantor had risen to the highest level of leadership in his own party in the House of Representatives. Yet, he was defeated by a never-elected-previously Tea Party (conservative Republican) candidate (David Bratt), because Cantor—in compromising—had become considered too accommodating of Democratic ideas.

Worthington (2017) argued for a resurgence in political humility, the ability to have a civil discourse in which people can hold and advocate their own political positions and can be respected by people within their community for doing so. With political humility, people can adhere firmly to core positions and yet value other positions enough to discuss, to sometimes compromise, and to work out viable agreements without caving in.

Assessing Political Humility

Hoyle, Davisson, Diebels, and Leary (2016) developed a nine-item scale that can be applied to multiple domains within intellectual humility. For example, typical items are like this: "My sources of information about ______ might not be the best." The specific domain of interest—political humility, religious humility, stance about the proper definition of humility—is what is placed in the blank. Domain-specific measures might account for more variance than general measures of intellectual humility.

Religious Humility

Defining Religious Humility

Another subtype of intellectual humility is *religious humility*. In today's climate of religious extremism, religious humility might be necessary for preserving world peace. This is a particularly important subtype of humility because it involves not just intellectual commitment to ideas but also what people identify as sacred. It is thus connected to the beliefs, values, and practices that give life meaning. People count many things as sacred. For example, they could be invested in their religious identity (Christian vs. Muslim vs. religious none). Or they could be invested in a particular subtype of a major religion (i.e., Protestant, Baptist, Roman Catholic, Evangelical, etc.; cf. Sunni versus Shiite Muslim vs. Hindu vs. Sikh, etc.). Religious commitments could also be toward particular theological stances (i.e., liberal or conservative), particular congregations, or even particular beliefs (i.e., whether supernatural healings should be expected today). Religious humility thus is challenged by any of a number of strong religious or spiritual commitments. In addition, religious commitments affect how people live. Thus, theological, religious, or spiritual commitments frequently tend to bleed over into political beliefs. Even the position of whether religious commitments should bleed over into the political arena is at once a matter of political philosophy and religious theology.

Assessing Religious Humility

The Intellectual Humility Scale Specific to Religious Beliefs (IH-Religious; Hopkin, Hoyle, &Toner, 2014) is based on the assumption that intellectual humility is domain specific (see Hoyle, Davisson, Diebels, & Leary, 2016). The IH-Religious has four subscales: awareness of fallibility of religious beliefs, discretion in asserting religious beliefs, comfort keeping beliefs private, and respect for others' beliefs. Subscale alphas were between .71 and .89. Hoyle et al. (2016) also developed a nine-item scale that can be applied to multiple domains within intellectual humility. For example, typical items are similar to this: "My sources of information about ______ might not be the best." The specific domain of interest—political humility, religious humility, stance about the proper definition of humility—is what is placed in the blank. Domain-specific measures might account for more variance than general measures of intellectual humility. In Study 1, Hoyle et al.

reported the scale's development. In Study 2, they established measurement invariance and adduced evidence of convergent and discriminant validity. In Study 3, they showed that the measure was not just associated with beliefs about religion, but also applied to intellectual humility across several beliefs.

SPIRITUAL HUMILITY

Spiritual humility is not a form of intellectual humility. It is humility in the face of what one considers sacred (D. E. Davis, Hook, Worthington, Van Tongeren, Gartner, & Jennings, 2010). For many, God—as understood by their religion—is sacred. Or, other religious constructs (e.g., Bible, religious identification) might be considered sacred. Some hold nature or environment to be sacred. Others hold humanity in reverence. For still others, that which seems transcendent or beyond the ordinary is considered sacred. Some marvel at the mystery of the self. Some stand in awe over consciousness, identity, and a personality that can seem beyond comprehension. For many people, spiritual humility might involve more than one of these simultaneously (D. E. Davis, Rice, Hook, et al., 2015). Thus, a secular person could embrace spirituality of nature, humanity, the transcendent, and the self. A thoroughly religious person could embrace humility toward the sacred but also be dedicated to nature spirituality, humanistic spirituality, transcendent spirituality, and self-spirituality.

The Spiritual Humility Scale (SHS; D. E. Davis, Hook, Worthington, Van Tongeren, Gartner, & Jennings, 2010) is a four-item scale to assess humility as it relates to generic spirituality. Respondents report (three items) on the degree to which they accept or feel comfortable with their place in relation to the Sacred and know their place in relation to nature (one item). Response options range from 1 = *completely disagree* to 5 = *completely agree*. Alpha is strong. The SHS can be used as a self- or other-report instrument. Validity data at this point are sparse.

SECULAR HUMILITY

Secular humility disavows religious commitments but not necessarily spiritual commitments. For example, secular humility could acknowledge awe before a splendid cosmos or deep dedication to humanity that seems mysteriously interconnected through a principle of shared brotherhood or sisterhood of humans. Secular humility could also acknowledge things transcendent even though they seem mysterious and unexplainable. No one has yet developed an assessment for secular humility.

WHAT IS REVEALED FROM THIS ANALYSIS OF TYPES OF HUMILITY?

In addition to reviewing the rapidly accelerating work on subdomains of humility, theoretical advancement is needed to map and integrate the various subdomains of humility. So these chapters will literally lay a theoretical foundation for the emerging science of humility.

From the measurement pessimism of Tangney's (2000) article, the field has come a long way. The diversity of assessments of general humility is a reflection of the instability of definitions. Some of the most used instruments have confounded definitions, and so using those instruments requires nuanced interpretation of the findings. As yet, investigators have not frequently offered such nuanced interpretations. Rather, many investigators treat their findings as showing what "humility" is or isn't related to. This introduces a conceptual muddle when it comes to reviewing results of studies on humility.

Most scales agree generally that humility needs to consider accurate assessment of one's strengths and weaknesses. Many treat this as humility, although it is clearly an inadequate definition by itself. People can have accurate assessments of themselves and still be jerks. Fewer might add that one is open to correction or is teachable or has a quiet ego. Even when added to the first leg of the definition, this suggests that humility is primarily about an internal self-understanding and no need to aggrandize oneself or belittle oneself. This seems inadequate because there is no apparent social dimension. It seems that humility requires action so that it is manifested. Virtue theory requires virtues to be tested in the muck and mire of life. Internally focused definitions allow a person to believe he or she is humble and never find out for sure. This is like believing one is courageous but then when put to the test, cowering or running away. Mark Twain once talked of his (brief) career as a soldier and war hero in the American Civil War. "I had in my first engagement three horses shot from under me. The next ones went over my head, the next hit me in the back" (quoted in Safire, 1997, p. 53).

As far as the social aspects, modesty is included in about half of the instruments and other-orientation in about half—not the same half. So, many instruments recognize a social component to humility, but they are not ready to commit to whether it is about modesty or serving others or both.

Reflecting on the types of humility, we find that instruments to measure the varieties of types are still needed. For example, there are several instruments to assess intellectual humility, including one that looks at religious humility. However, none assesses political humility. The topic of cultural humility is assessed in a single instrument, but we pointed out that there were at least two types of cultural humility: empathic and nonpartisan. Thus, there is much room to develop additional measures of cultural humility, which is an increasingly important topic in the global marketplace and global social arena. All major religions advocate humility as a virtue, yet there are no existing measures of Christian humility, Muslim humility, Buddhist humility—or indeed humility from any specific religion's point of view. There is one spiritual humility measure that is global, yet it is more suited to the Abrahamic religions than to Eastern religions.

Most of the measures are user-friendly. Except for the HEXACO and VIA-IS, which assess multiple constructs, including one that involves humility confounded with other constructs, most direct measures of humility are admirably brief—usually from five to fewer than 20 items. This makes the use of psychometrically supported humility measures particularly convenient for social, personality, and health psychologists. However, given the well-known numerical fact that the estimated reliability of scores is proportional to the length of scale, this has resulted in alphas on the order of .75 to .85, which is acceptable for basic research. However, this is unacceptable for clinical research, where a minimum standard of alpha (about .9) is generally accepted. In clinical research, precise assessment is necessary because one is dealing with individuals. Social, personality, and health researchers are more interested, usually, in averages and in differences among groups. Thus, the field is open for development of a clinically usable measure of humility. Establishing its bona fides will require not only good reliability of scores (hence longer scales) but also good evidence supporting construct validity (hopefully assessing both the intrapersonal and interpersonal aspects of humility) and predictive validity (involving relationships with physical health, mental health, relationships, and perhaps spirituality).

We have come a long way. We have a long way to go.

WHAT DID WE LEARN IN THIS CHAPTER?

1. Acts of humility, states of humility, and a trait of humility are different. We can probably expect different antecedents and consequences of each.
2. There are different levels (i.e., acts, state, trait) and different types (i.e., general, intellectual, relational) of humility. Within each type, there are subtypes. So, relational humility differs depending on type of relationship. Intellectual humility includes religious and political humility. Spiritual humility reflects people's stance in regard to what they consider sacred, and secular humility is humility apart from sacred commitments.

3. The variety of definitions and the lack of precise agreement have yielded a plethora of instruments, most of which measure only one or two aspects of humility. To assess humility adequately, people must consider multiple measures and also consider whether to assess for humility generally or a particular type of humility in a particular setting.
4. Psychometrically sound measures need to be created to assess different types of humility. Short, psychometrically strong measures are essential for good research and clinical work.

THREE QUESTIONS FOR THOUGHT AND DISCUSSION

1. Are there really different types of humility, or is humility one and the same, just applied in different areas? Is political humility an oxymoron? How do people embrace intellectual humility when they believe they are correct?
2. The HEXACO-HH and the VIA-IS can both assess humility and have been used in many studies to do so. But there are concerns about the validity of what they are assessing. Other instruments have been used far less often, but their psychometrics are stronger and seem to have more evidence supporting construct validity. This presents an assessor with a dilemma. Discuss the times when one might opt to use the oft-used instruments and times when one might opt for the less-used but more precisely defined instruments.
3. Given that the HEXACO-HH, the VIA-IS, and many specific measures appear to assess radically different things, what good are meta-analyses?

II

WHAT THE SCIENCE SHOWS

3

HUMILITY AND RELATIONSHIPS

Becoming humble is becoming "rightsized," which means knowing one's true place as an equal in human worth to other human beings. This chapter describes the ways in which gaining this humble attitude prepares people for a life of service. We review research suggesting that humility elevates one's compassionate and empathic responses to others and thus elevates morality and selflessness. We lay the groundwork for the notion that part of the social effectiveness of humility resides in being inspired by heroically humble people. People see the excellent interpersonal effects of humility, reflect on their own heroes of humility, and realize that they like to interact with humble people, too. Thus we draw on Scott's work to create a justification and motivation to read the stories in the second part of the book.

This chapter summarizes research on the social hypotheses. Humility is usually associated with prosocial outcomes. The social bonds hypothesis asserts that humility strengthens most social bonds. Various authors have written or

http://dx.doi.org/10.1037/0000079-004
Heroic Humility: What the Science of Humility Can Say to People Raised on Self-Focus, by E. L. Worthington Jr. and S. T. Allison

published research articles that we have drawn from in this chapter (see D. E. Davis, Placeres, et al., 2017; D. E. Davis et al., 2013; McElroy et al., 2014; Van Tongeren, Davis, & Hook, 2014). The social oil hypothesis asserts that humility promotes sacrifice for others. The social buffering hypothesis suggests that it buffers the social wear-and-tear of competition on the relationships. Humility usually promotes better communication in a long-standing social relationship (i.e., friendship, partnership, business relationship, romantic relationship). It often results in partners who are healthier mentally (and perhaps physically). When one partner is more humble, that often affects not only the humble partner's mental health but the spouse's as well. That is the social health transmission hypothesis. Each of these sub-hypotheses has been supported by research.

PROFILE OF A HUMBLE PUBLIC FIGURE—GEORGE H. W. BUSH

We begin the discussion of the all-important social hypotheses with an extended case study. George H. W. Bush, 41st president of the United States, is one of the few recent presidents not to write an autobiography or life memoir—a fact telling in itself. However, because he wanted to make sure that history was as accurate as historians could make it, he edited a collection of his letters, memos, diary entries, and miscellaneous writings that reflected on his life. He wrote in the preface that

> The book is not meant to be an autobiography. It is not a historical documentation of my life. But hopefully it will let you, the reader, have a look at what's on the mind of an 18-year-old kid who goes into the Navy and then at 19 is flying a torpedo bomber off an aircraft carrier in World War II . . . [and] what a President is thinking when he has to send someone else's son or daughter into combat. It's all about heartbeat. (Bush, 1999, p. 22)

Bush was also other-oriented and attentive to close relationships. Two excerpts from letters show this well during his navy years. On December 12, 1943, he wrote a love letter to Barbara:

> I love you, precious, with all my heart and to know that you love me means my life. How often I have thought about the immeasurable joy that will be ours someday. How lucky our children will be to have a mother like you. (Bush, 1999, p. 38)

Then, shortly afterward, on December, 29, 1943, he wrote to his mother:

> I changed my allotment check, so starting either at the end of January or the end of February the check for 143 dollars will come to you every

> month. . . . If it is made out to you and I am lost, the checks will continue to come in until it is definitely established that I am safely in heaven. (Bush, 1999, p. 39)

But Bush was not just concerned with close family relationships. On December 11, 1977, he had completed his stint at the CIA. He was contacted by Michael Randall Hewitt, apparently someone Bush did not know personally, who asked Bush whether he would write to Hewitt's 1-year-old nephew, David Robey, so that, on reaching 21, Robey could read a collection of letters from Bush and other leaders. We might imagine the way presidential hopefuls of today might respond to such a request. Bush penned a personal seven-paragraph letter. He responded humbly and other-oriented. In the note he said,

> Your uncle asked me to send you this note—what a guy he must be to think in these terms. . . . The future holds in store for you great treasures, the greatest of which is freedom. . . . I am optimistic. I see enormous problems at home and abroad but they can be solved by 1997. I wish I were a little guy 1 year old. There is so much to do, so far to travel, so much happiness to give. Good luck, kid. (Bush, 1999, pp. 273–274)

Bush was concerned about people enough to invest his time in them, even when there was no possibility of political advantage. For example, Ruthie, a young political supporter, donated money to his unsuccessful campaign to run for president. On September 18, 1979, he wrote her back.

> Ruthie, . . . it is impossible for me to accept your generous contribution. You see, I cannot accept money from anyone under 18 years of age. I have enclosed a check for $1.79, which is the combined total of your two contributions. I am sending you a George Bush for President T-shirt to let you know how grateful I am that you are one of my best supporters. When I get back to Houston, I hope I can meet you in person. (Bush, 1999, p. 281)

In 1980 (February 10), Bush responded to a letter from Ray Goodman of Boston suggesting that Bush tout himself as a statesman rather than a politician. Bush thanked Goodman and concluded his three-paragraph letter with, "Then again there's the famous definition given by the 19th century Speaker of the House of Representatives, Tip Reed. He said a statesman is a politician who has died" (Bush, 1999, p. 287). Bush had the humility not to take himself too seriously.

He was genuinely modest. In 1989, at the Republican national convention, rumors abounded that Reagan would ask former President Gerald Ford to be his running mate. Reagan opted for Bush instead. "No one was more surprised that I was when I answered the phone in my hotel suite and Ronald Reagan was on the other end of the line" (Bush, 1999, p. 299).

Exhibiting great political humility, he told of receiving one of his first congratulatory phone calls from Senator Walter "Fritz" Mondale, who was to be the vice presidential candidate on the Democratic ticket. He wrote a thank-you note to Mondale on July 19, 1980. "Thank you for your courteous call. It was most thoughtful of you to call all the way from Africa" (Bush, 1999, p. 299). That political humility—having respect for political opponents—was evident throughout his life. On November 8, 1980, after Reagan and Bush had won the election, Bush wrote Mondale. "I'd love to sit down with you. Thank you for your wire, your call, your just plain decency. I've lost—plenty—I know it's no fun" (Bush, 1999, p. 302).

Bush never lost touch with simple relationships. As vice president, he penned a note to Mrs. H. Webster Smith, who in 1973 had permitted the White House to use a beautiful piece of furniture—a bookcase. "It just occurred to me," he wrote, "that having lent this beautiful piece to the government, you might have a personal interest in where it is. I am attaching a picture. I am the one standing next to your beautiful mahogany piece." We love the humility of identifying himself in the picture—as if the just-elected vice president might not be recognizable.

Bush appreciated the talents of others. He wrote to Katharine Hepburn after she won an Oscar for *On Golden Pond.*

> We so enjoyed our meeting—too brief of course; but for Barbara and me, a highlight not soon forgotten. We respect you so—and I guess as a little kid I thought you were the meowest of the cat's meows. . . . But this is about last night's Oscar too. Hooray for you—3 cheers for excellence and style and class and honor and warmth. 3 cheers for your decency—Affectionate regards from yet another Hepburn fan. (Bush, 1999, p. 317)

Bush began his first day as president-elect (November 9, 1988) going to church, showing spiritual humility. After the sermon, he even wrote the speaker, the Right Reverend Maurice M. Benitez, a note: "Your being there today made our special service—extra special. Thanks for that. The awesome nature of what lies ahead is just beginning to sink in" (Bush, 1999, p. 404). Colin Powell recounted an anecdote from that same day. He said,

> I was returning to my West Wing office, and since we were next-door neighbors, the Vice-President and I walked together. "Well, Mr. Vice-Pres—excuse me, Mr. Pres—Mr. President-elect. What should it be now?" I asked. Bush laughed and said he did not know. (Powell & Persico, 1995, p. 388)

How typical of Bush. Most of us, if just elected president, would have rehearsed what people should call us hundreds of times—that day alone—but Bush hadn't thought about it.

He maintained his generosity to former political opponents after he became president. Former President Jimmy Carter, reflecting on his relationships with former presidents, identified his close relationship with Jerry Ford as noteworthy. But he reflected,

> My best and most enjoyable experience with presidents was with George H. W. Bush and his secretary of state, James Baker. Throughout their term in office, they used the resources of our Center as fully as possible, encouraged our involvement in politically sensitive areas, and even sent a plane to bring me directly to the White House for a report after some of my foreign visits. (Carter, 2015, p. 235)

As Bush reached 90, a biography by Jon Meacham (2015) stirred the pot. Bush was a bit critical of George W.'s presidency, chiding his son for bellicosity and swagger. But he reserved more criticism for Dick Cheney and Donald Rumsfeld, referring to each as "iron ass." As columnist Kathleen Parker (2015) told it, "Cheney, who was secretary of defense under the first Bush, has responded that he considers the description a compliment, while Rumsfeld replied that Bush is 'getting up in years.' Then again, perhaps the 83-year-old Rumsfeld was projecting" (p. A11).

THE SOCIAL BONDS HYPOTHESIS

The social bonds hypothesis states that humility strengthens most social bonds. Eleven studies support this hypothesis. Humble people who were dating were rated more favorably by their partners and had more forgiveness and relationship satisfaction (Farrell et al., 2015; Van Tongeren, Davis, & Hook, 2014). In 230 Canadian students, sexual faithfulness was related to high humility.

McElroy et al. (2014) provided initial evidence relating intellectual humility to social bonds. People who held different beliefs about religion, politics, or ideas and shared them respectfully experienced more forgiveness, had more trust, and enjoyed higher relationship quality than did those lower in intellectual humility. Intellectual humility was also related to trust and forgiveness of a religious leader and attitudes toward the Sacred.

Besides couples and churches, other types of social relationships have also been studied. For example, in groups that come together for some ad hoc purpose, D. E. Davis et al. (2013) found humility of group members to be related to status and acceptance in the group. Additionally, in psychotherapy, Hook, Davis, Owen, Worthington, and Utsey (2013) reported that clients who viewed their therapists as more culturally humble tended to report stronger working alliances. When people are humble—especially when partners can readily detect that—this promotes the forming of tight social bonds.

Cultural humility tends to strengthen the bonds between clients and psychotherapists. Owen et al. (2016) surveyed 247 clients who were treated by 50 psychotherapists. Owen et al. compared client ratings of their psychotherapists' cultural humility to client perceptions that the psychotherapist missed opportunities to discuss cultural identity. Clients who rated their psychotherapist as more culturally humble reported better psychotherapy outcomes. Clients who perceived that their psychotherapist missed opportunities to discuss the client's cultural heritage reported worse psychotherapy outcomes. Client ratings of cultural humility of their psychotherapist moderated the relationship between cultural opportunities and psychotherapy outcomes. For clients who reported that their psychotherapist was less culturally humble, missed opportunities and negative outcomes were related. But for clients who reported that their psychotherapist was more culturally humble, missed opportunities were not associated with outcomes.

RELATIONAL HUMILITY

The empirical literature on relational humility has been independently reviewed by Green et al. (2017); Garthe, Reid, Sullivan, and Cork (2017); and D. E. Davis, Placeres, et al. (2017). They each found that due to the core aspects of humility, humility can be difficult to measure. For instance, people have self-serving biases. Furthermore, they have self-interested personality styles that might have been long practiced. Arrogant people might overreport their own levels of humility. Also, if they are socially sensitive to others' expectations, they might report inaccurately on their humility if they think that inaccurate report is valued by the person they are talking to (D. E. Davis, Worthington, & Hook, 2010). In addition, out of modesty, even humble people may underreport their humility.

Given the self-serving bias (see Van Tongeren & Myers, 2017) and the tendency to over- or underreport humility because of social perception of others' expectations (D. E. Davis, Worthington, & Hook, 2010), Worthington (2007) suggested that a measure of relational humility might be warranted. Relational humility is the self-report of a relational partner of the target's humility. D. E. Davis, Worthington, and Hook (2010) provided a precise definition: Relational humility, in romantic relationships, is perceiving and reporting a target romantic partner to be other-oriented, thus showing qualities such as empathy, sympathy, compassion, love, and gratitude toward the reporting partner. It also involves regulating self-oriented emotions such as pride, superiority, and competitive motivations. Additionally, it involves (relatively) objectively perceiving the target partner (D. E. Davis, Worthington, & Hook, 2010). If one believes one's partner is humble, usually the relationship benefits: People experience increased trust, intimacy, and deepness of bonds within that romantic relationship (D. E. Davis, Worthington, & Hook, 2010). In conflictual situations, high stress, or life transitions, D. E. Davis, Hook, et al. (2011) found that relational humility "counteracts the natural tendency of these situations to cause instability in relationships" (p. 227).

That is, we might believe that a spouse would give a more accurate report of our behavior—at least in that relationship—than we might give ourselves. A friend might give a more accurate report of our behavior than we might give ourselves. A supervisee might give a more accurate report of our behavior than we might give ourselves. And a composite of others' reports across a variety of relationships might give a more accurate picture of our trait of humility than we ourselves might give.

Each person who gives the other report has only a partial view of our behavior and does not have access to our motives. But, within a relationship, over time, the person has usually seen how we have met challenges to our ego and thus might report without being unconsciously governed by our own self-serving biases and our own motives to look good. Such reports, of course, have more weaknesses than mere lack of complete knowledge. The other people have their own self-serving biases and social expectations that will unconsciously govern their reports. Yet, we presume that rating us will not be as ego involving for the other person as would rating themselves.

A model of relational humility is emerging. (a) Relational humility is relationship-specific humility, often measured by other-report for a person in each relationship and thought to be especially revelatory when the ego is under strain. (b) Relational humility is a generalization within a relationship for numerous instances of state humility in the presence of the other. (c) Summing relational humility for each relationship over time yields trait humility. (d) Relational humility predicts positive social outcomes, which are summarized by (1) the social bonds hypothesis (i.e., relational humility is related to stronger formation, maintenance, strengthening, and repair of social bonds), (2) the social oil hypothesis (i.e., a relationship characterized by strong social bonds helps partners act humbly and sacrifice for each other), (3) the social buffering hypothesis (i.e., relational humility buffers against negative social outcomes when stress occurs), (4) the social communication hypothesis (i.e., high humility is leads to better communication), (5) the leadership-in-social-groups hypothesis (i.e., effective leadership is related to perceived leader humility), and (6) the social health–transmission hypothesis (i.e., positive relational characteristics contribute to the mental and physical health of partners). Although these five propositions might form the skeleton of the model, what is missing is a theoretical explanation for the model.

INTERDEPENDENCE THEORY AS A FRAMEWORK FOR THE SOCIAL HYPOTHESES

In their review of relational humility, Green et al. (2017), Garthe et al. (2017), and D. E. Davis, Placeres, et al. (2017) arrived at a similar conclusion. Interdependence theory (Kelley & Thibaut, 1978; Thibaut & Kelley, 1959) might provide a parsimonious theoretical framework to aid in understanding the research that has accumulated to date. Interdependence theory focuses on interactions within a couple. It considers outcomes for each partner when several possible combinations of behaviors occur. Sometimes outcomes are *correspondent* and satisfying, which happens when partners have the same preference, such as when partners have the same attitude toward visiting relatives during holidays. Sometimes, though, outcomes are not correspondent, such as when partners disagree over the frequency of sex. Such disagreements are inevitable in stable relationships, though the frequency in some relationships is less than in other relationships. When preferences differ, partners experience a *dilemma*. Interdependence theory holds that the acid test of a relationship occurs when partners must deal with dilemmas that pit divergent outcomes against each other. (Virtue theory identifies such dilemmas as tests that must be met to prove a virtue; Worthington et al., 2014.) Each partner must choose to either attempt to maximize his or her own well-being or make the partner the priority, thus valuing the relationship. Dilemmas can involve conflict, difficult discussions, silent resentments, different goals and desires, and sometimes transgressions against the other person.

Humility is relevant to these dilemmas (Green et al., 2017). Interdependence theory claims that whether people resolve differences (or not) affects health, well-being, satisfaction, commitment, and longevity of the relationship. Disagreements affect each partner as well. These situations are *diagnostic situations* because one partner's transformation of motivation—acting in non-self-interested ways (i.e., giving a humble response)—reveals information to the other partner about the first partner's relationship values, priorities, and goals. In diagnostic situations, partners have two options. They can act consistently with either the *given situation* or with the *effective situation*. The given situation brings forth "gut-level," self-interested acts. The effective situation brings forth concordance. Both the partner and the long-term health of the relationship are valued. In healthy relationships, other-oriented motivations become habits. Partners might not even pay attention to their own desires, having gotten into the habit of valuing the partner and the relationship's well-being (Righetti, Finkenauer, & Finkel, 2013).

Partners who maintain successful, healthy relationships have become motivated to do so by internal and relational exigencies. For example, social norms, dispositions, and relationship-specific motives feed into whether individual motivations are transformed into relationship motivations. But those factors act outside of consciousness. More accessible experiences, such as cognitive beliefs, values, and preferences and momentary thoughts, gut feelings, emotions, moods, and practiced habits, are more often sensed as conscious motives for relationship transformation.

The relationship-specific motives of trust and commitment strongly affect transformation toward a relational orientation. *Trust* emerges when individuals have confidence in their partner's positive orientation toward themselves. Trust develops as a history of choices reveals that the other person will value the partner instead of the self. Trust is acting on a sense that the other person will consistently try to meet one's needs. The other-orientation of humility suggests that trust should permeate relationships in which both partners are humble, and perhaps even the humility of one of the partners might bring about relational trust. *Commitment* is a feeling that one can trust in the long term. Rusbult, Olson, Davis, and Hannon (2001) found that commitment is characterized by adult attachment to the partner that indicates that one intends to persist in the relationship. Commitment leads to positive cognition, motivations, emotions, and acts within the relationship (Rusbult et al., 2001). Benevolent thought, emotion, and behavior all are shaped by high commitment (see Farrell et al., 2015). Trust and commitment feed on each other. Both are strengthened as partners see that each other's motivations have become more relationship-oriented, and to complete a mutual cyclical growth pattern, partners who see the other value the relationship over their own interests respond in kind.

Yovetich and Rusbult (1994) found that time is needed for motives to be transformed and the transformation to be detected and then acted on. Gut-level self-interested acts are evolutionarily supplied but not acted on except in valued relationships. Parent–infant bonds are experienced early. But romantic bonds are usually late to develop after self-interested responses have been long practiced. Self-interest is hard to dislodge. Yet, transformation to relational motivation can become habitual. Dwiwardani et al. (2014) found that humility negatively predicted an avoidant attachment style, which might mean that insecurely attached people did not develop positive relational attachments with primary parents, making it harder for them to develop humility than it is for securely attached adults. Observing a partner acting humbly as an other-oriented prorelationship partner may help the observing partner feel valued—and might eventually erode even insecure attachment habits and promote humility.

HUMILITY IS ASSOCIATED WITH HEALTHY RELATIONAL MAINTENANCE

Maintenance mechanisms are processes that maintain positive relationships (Rusbult et al., 2001). These involve processes such as accommodation, self-sacrifice, forgiveness, and gratitude. Humility has been hypothesized to enhance each of these, and some empirical research supports that hypothesizing.

Accommodation

Accommodation is a prorelationship response to dilemmas. When faced with a partner's transgression or violation of expectation, people usually desire retaliation to restore a sense of justice in the relationship. Retaliation might involve a prorelationship reproach (Schönbach, 1990; Worthington, 2003), and that might bring about a prorelationship account (e.g., a concession, a well-timed and well-delivered excuse; Schönbach, 1990; Worthington, 2003). But it also can lead to poorly delivered reproaches and destructive accounts, such as denials, justifications, and clumsy, ill-timed, responsibility-evading excuses.

Accommodation is responding positively instead of yielding to retaliatory gut feelings. When given a limited time to respond to a hypothetical transgression by their partner, people often responded with retaliation rather than accommodation (Rusbult et al., 2005). Presumably, inhibiting gut feelings and replacing them with prorelationship accommodation takes time and energy. Accommodation takes energy (Worthington, 2003). Because it requires effort and self-regulation, it also can be short-circuited by ego depletion (see Baumeister & Tierney, 2011). Finkel and Campbell (2001) showed that accommodative responses are reduced when people are ego depleted. People who have developed high trait self-regulation tend to be accommodative more often (Baumeister & Tierney, 2011), which is likely because self-regulation has become habitual. Accommodation is also related to higher commitment, which also indicates that it has become habitual (Rusbult, Bissonnette, Arriaga, & Cox, 1998). Baumeister and Exline (2000) suggested that self-control is needed for humility, and when humility becomes more trait-like, people are less likely to become ego depleted in acting humbly. Thus, humble responses are more likely to result in accommodation and other prorelationship acts such as self-sacrifice, forgiveness, and gratitude.

Self-Sacrifice

Conflicts occur in even the closest relationships. When partners have different preferences, some humility seems needed to resolve the dilemma. Humility is using one's power under control to lift the other up and not put the other down. Partners acting with other-oriented humility tend to make small or large sacrifices to deal with dilemmas, and those sacrifices communicate love to one's partner. Higher commitment to the relationship also reliably predicts sacrifice (Agnew & Dove, 2011).

Forgiveness

When an offending partner is humble and when a humble person is offended, humility on both sides of the offense predicts forgiveness (Sheppard & Boon, 2012). This is especially true when relational commitment and trust are present (Farrell et al., 2015). When partners believe they are both other-oriented (i.e., humility), have made attributions that the partner is trustworthy (i.e., trust), and are in the relationship for the long haul (i.e., commitment), accommodation is likely. Partners are motivated to repair the relationship and forgive and reconcile (Worthington, 2003). Thus, humility, commitment, and trust produce more relationship satisfaction and stability.

Humility can lead to forgiveness by victims because humble transgressors are often more empathic of the hurt they have caused, contrite about their transgressions, expressive of regret, apologetic, willing to make restitution, and willing to ask for forgiveness (Jennings et al., 2016). When an offender is usually other-oriented, that inspires more trust, evokes less fear of being exploited by the partner, and conveys that the partner is valued and valuable (Burnette, McCullough, Van Tongeren, & Davis, 2012). Offenders who are high in humility usually have inflicted fewer and less serious transgressions on victims than those low in humility (Green et al., 2017). Likewise, humility can lead to forgiveness because victims, too, are other-oriented. Humble, other-oriented victims can respond vengefully (K. Lee & Ashton, 2012). Humble victims are more empathic of the suffering of the offender, and thus they might be more merciful.

Research has supported other links between humility and forgiveness. For example, D. E. Davis et al. (2012) studied people who were hurt by their romantic partner, following them for 6 weeks. Judgments of greater humility in the offending partner (i.e., relational humility) predicted less unforgiveness over time. Van Tongeren, Davis, and Hook (2014) discovered that distance does not make the heart grow fonder. People in long-distance romances were less forgiving of their partners than were those in face-to-face romances.

However, when the people viewed their romantic partner as humble, the impact was greater in the distance relationships.

Gratitude

Kruse, Chancellor, Ruberton, and Lyubomirsky (2014) found that what they called an upward spiral of humility was produced by an intervention inviting people to express their *gratitude* to partners. Merely writing a grateful letter led to increased state humility, which in turn increased the amount of gratitude experienced. Both gratitude and humility involve both low self-focus and other-orientation. In couples, both gratitude and commitment require orientation to the partner's acts and investments in the relationship. Some attribute this to lack of focus on the self or to a hypoegoic state (Leary, Adams, & Tate, 2006). We prefer to think of it as also involving an orientation to the other.

WHAT IS KNOWN ABOUT THE SOCIAL HYPOTHESES

We described a relational humility model previously and stated that it led to six hypotheses that related relational humility and social outcomes. Let us now examine the evidence bearing on those hypotheses.

The Social Bonds Hypothesis

This hypothesis claims that when people are judged to be humble, that is related to strong social bonds, emotionally laden connections of affinity toward someone that induce the person to act as if the partner's or group's interests are similar to his or her own interests (D. E. Davis et al., 2013; D. E. Davis, Placeres, et al., 2017; McElroy et al., 2014; Van Tongeren, Davis, & Hook, 2014). Social bonds motivate unselfish other-oriented acts. However, feeling a social bond can work unfairly against a person when the partner draws strength from the bond but does not act with reciprocal other-orientation. Thus, social bonds need to be regulated. D. E. Davis et al. (2013) argued that perceptions of humility pull humility from the partner, yielding stronger social bonds. If people see their partner act selfishly, they view him or her as less humble. That can weaken the social bond and thus weaken commitment. However, if people see their partner act unselfishly, they view the partner as more humble. That can strengthen commitment to the relationship.

The social bonds hypothesis is well supported by research in the formation, maintenance, and repair of relationships. Regarding forming relationships,

Van Tongeren, Davis, and Hook (2014) found that humility was negatively related to acting manipulatively during romantic relationships and thus promoted more and longer lasting romantic relationships. People reported more favorable attitudes toward developing relationships with individuals who were viewed as more humble. People also reported greater likelihood of initiating romantic relationships with people they perceived to be humble. Regarding maintaining relationships, humility is related to better relationship quality (Farrell et al., 2015; Peters, Rowatt, & Johnson, 2011). Regarding repairing relationships, humility predicts forgiveness (Carmody & Gordon, 2011) and apology (Dunlop, Lee, Ashton, Butcher, & Dykstra, 2015).

The Social Oil Hypothesis

The social oil hypothesis states that to the extent that a relationship is characterized by strong social bonds, it is easier for partners to act humbly and sacrifice for each other. Eleven studies within eight articles have supported the social oil hypothesis. This has been investigated in the Prisoners' Dilemma game. In that game, two people are placed in a situation in which they both benefit if they cooperate. However, if they defect—taking the rewards and letting the other player suffer—they reap even more benefit. But if they defect and the other player also defects, they suffer losses. Zettler, Hilbig, and Heydasch (2013) found that high humility was related to a higher cooperation index. Furthermore, considering humility added to predictability based solely on the Big Five personality traits. However, high humility was not related to indiscriminant cooperation to the level that highly humble people could be taken advantage of. Other games, like Dictator and Ultimatum, yielded similar results (Hilbig, Zettler, Leist, & Heydasch, 2013). Owens, Wallace, and Waldman (2015) found support for the social oil hypothesis. Subordinate-rated narcissism of health care managers was negatively related to their effectiveness as leaders and to employee job performance. However, humility moderated the connection: The correlations were weaker in leaders of higher humility.

The Social Buffering Hypothesis

High humility buffers the social wear-and-tear resulting from competition in relationships. This too has been supported. High humility has been related to more forgiveness when wrongs occur (Van Tongeren, Davis, & Hook, 2014) and to apology (Dunlop et al., 2015). Sheppard and Boon (2012) found that low humility was related to higher likelihood of seeking revenge after being offended, even after weighing the costs. Both offender and victim benefit by high humility.

The Social Communication Hypothesis

High humility is hypothesized to be related to better communication in a long-standing social relationship (i.e., friendship, partnership, business relationship, romantic relationship). In 257 Roman Catholic couples, Estephan (2007) found that higher humility was related to positive relationship qualities. But Estephan did not measure communication directly. Communication was assumed to be better if relationship quality was better. At this moment, the social communication hypothesis has not been supported.

The Leadership-in-Social-Groups Hypothesis

The leadership-in-social-groups hypothesis states that effective leadership is often related to perceived leader humility. However, in groups in which survival is on the line (e.g., military), perceived leader humility can take a back seat to survival, producing authoritarian leadership. Only two studies have tested this hypothesis. E. De Vries (2012) assessed 113 leaders and 201 subordinates. High scores on the HEXACO-HH scale were related to ethical leadership and negatively related to task-oriented leadership. Owens, Wallace, and Waldman (2015), which we mentioned earlier, found that even narcissistic leaders could overcome some negative effects of their narcissism if they showed humility.

The Social Health–Transmission Hypothesis

The social health–transmission hypothesis states that because of positive relational characteristics (social bonds, social oil, social buffering, social communication), the mental health and physical health of partners in relationship with humble people is likely to be positive. Wiltshire, Bourdage, and Lee (2014) provided indirect evidential support. In studying 268 employees, they found that perceptions of organizational politics were related to four outcome measures—counterproductive work behavior, impression management, job satisfaction, and job stress—through the moderator of humility. That is, for those high in humility, involvement in organizational politics tends to produce positive outcomes (e.g., low counterproductive work, low job stress, high work satisfaction). For those low in humility, however, involvement in organizational politics produced negative work outcomes. The relationship of humility to stress in the social work environment was the most pertinent to the social health–transmission hypothesis. Generally this is not well supported.

SUMMARY

Overall, humility is centered on the social aspects of community. The social hypotheses are among the best supported. Virtues thrive and flourish in community, so we next turn our attention to hypotheses about virtues and vices that humility might be related to.

WHAT DID WE LEARN IN THIS CHAPTER?

1. The social hypotheses—social bonds, social oil, social buffering—are the best supported.
2. Humble people are other-oriented. That orientation toward helping others is probably the reason why humility has such powerful social effects.
3. Perhaps the best theoretical perspective for organizing the social hypotheses is interdependence theory.

THREE QUESTIONS FOR THOUGHT AND DISCUSSION

1. Humility is an individual virtue, and yet one of the strongest sets of hypotheses involves social effects. Why do we see strong social transmission in humility, altruism, and forgiveness, but not necessarily in other virtues like self-control, conscientiousness, etc.?
2. How are interdependence theory and family systems theory alike and different?
3. If humility requires simply non–self-focus or quiet ego (and not an other-orientation), would we still expect such strong support for the social hypotheses?

4

HUMILITY AND OTHER VIRTUES (AND VICES)

Humility is a trait and should be normally distributed across the population. Moderate levels of humility are expected to have modest correlations with virtues or vices, usually on the order of .2 to .3. Because other-oriented attitudes and self-control are the roots of many virtues, high humility will likely be related to most virtues and will be expected to be present when people show exceptional virtue in any demonstrated area.

High humility is expected to be related to altruism, forgiveness, generosity, compassion, and gratitude—all other-oriented virtues. Low levels of humility will likely be related to vices, especially self-focused ones, such as the dark triad, which is composed of narcissism, Machiavellianism, and psychopathy (Muris, Merckelbach, Otgaar, & Meijer, 2017). Let's look at these. But first, a word about methodology. You'll recall from our chapter on types of humility when we discussed measurement that the HEXACO model and its

http://dx.doi.org/10.1037/0000079-005
Heroic Humility: What the Science of Humility Can Say to People Raised on Self-Focus, by E. L. Worthington Jr. and S. T. Allison

Honesty–Humility measure conceptualize humility differently than do many other measures of humility.

A METHODOLOGICAL PREFACE

Some research has investigated the relational correlates of the Honesty–Humility dimension of the HEXACO personality model. The HEXACO model was developed to account for some replication discrepancies in the Big Five model of personality in lexical studies of personality adjectives across different countries (Ashton & Lee, 2007). The defining feature of the HEXACO model is its inclusion of an Honesty–Humility (HH) factor besides the five other factors similar to the Big Five (Emotionality, Extraversion, Agreeableness, Conscientiousness, and Openness). The HEXACO-HH has several facets—Modesty, Sincerity, Greed-Avoidance, and Fairness. Modesty is the only facet correlated with relational humility (D. E. Davis, Hook, et al., 2011)—not sincerity, greed-avoidance, or fairness. Trait humility is positively associated with many of the relationship maintenance mechanisms we talked about in the previous chapter.

Thus, we will make some distinctions when the HEXACO-HH and measures other than the HEXACO-HH are used. Sometimes those distinctions are important because the HEXACO-HH is more heavily weighted toward truthfulness and honesty and their opposites, such as deceit or cheating on a romantic partner, which probably reflect its heavy emphasis on honesty more than humility per se.

HUMILITY AND POSITIVE TRAITS

High humility is, in fact, related to many virtues. Let's begin with a look at some virtues that humility is almost certainly related to. Worthington, Goldstein, et al. (in press) reviewed the literature and found that the interconnections of humility to other virtues have been shown in 15 independent articles reporting 20 studies. Others have reviewed the literature independently (see Green et al., 2017; Leman, Haggard, Meagher, & Rowatt, 2017).

Humility has been related to a host of virtues. Philosophers and theologians from Augustine to Andrew Murray have treated humility as a gateway to virtues. We might hypothesize that among the many virtues, humility is most likely to be related to those that depend on a positive, prosocial orientation to others. These might include altruism, forgiveness, gratitude, generosity, cooperation, and the like.

Altruism

Sir Edmund Hillary (1919–2008) and his Sherpa, Tenzin Norgay, conquered Mount Everest in 1953. But Hillary was also one of the people at the peak of altruism. He felt that the Nepalese people had given him much in his quest to climb Mount Everest. So, he established the Himalayan Trust in 1960, and with the monies in that trust, he had hospitals and schools built and provided the means to accomplish other projects to benefit the Nepalese. He did not use his riches for his selfish comfort and glory. Rather, he acted altruistically.

He was altruistic with his time as well. He served as Honorary President of Mountain Wilderness, an international NGO aimed at protecting the mountains of the world. His humility was the core of his altruism. His humble orientation to others was what made altruism possible. But Hillary showed his humility in other ways as well. For example, he cared about others—even strangers—and did not want to see them embarrassed. John Dickson (2011) related an anecdote that captures this. Hillary was visiting the Himalayas after he had conquered the mountain. A group of tourists spotted him and asked him to pose for a picture. As the photographer set up the shot, he handed Hillary an ice ax and posed him. Just then a climber walked by. Not recognizing Hillary, he stopped and chided Hillary about the way he was holding the ice ax, then patiently explained the proper way to wield it. Hillary listened attentively and thanked the young man for his pointers. Hillary was secure in the knowledge of his strengths and weaknesses. He did not require bluster or making an offense public to be confident in his abilities, and he was modest in front of the group of tourists and the helpful young man.

It is not just anecdotal evidence that supports a humility–altruism connection. Worthington, Goldstein, et al. (in press) identified nine articles reporting 10 studies that related humility and altruism (e.g., Hilbig, Thielmann, Wührl, & Zettler, 2015; Hilbig & Zettler, 2009). Krumrei-Mancuso (2017) found that intellectual humility was associated with altruism in three separate studies (one in Sweden and two in the United States). Bergh and Akrami (2016) found humility and altruism to be correlated on the order of $r = .4$.

Forgiveness

Forgiveness and its link to humility have been vigorously studied. Worthington, Goldstein, et al. (in press) identified eight articles reporting 13 studies that related humility and forgiveness (i.e., D. E. Davis, Hook, et al., 2011). Dispositional humility positively predicted forgiveness in master's level students (Jankowski, Sandage, & Hill, 2013; Sandage, Jankowski,

Bissonette, & Paine, 2017). In addition, trait humility predicted less willingness to engage in calculated revenge (K. Lee & Ashton, 2012). People who are low in Honesty–Humility perceive revenge as less costly and more desirable than do those high in Honesty–Humility (Sheppard & Boon, 2012). In couples making the transition to parenthood, humility has been found repeatedly to predict forgiveness (Nonterah et al., 2016; Ripley et al., 2016). D. E. Davis et al. (2013) used ratings of humility and forgiveness at six weekly intervals after partners experienced a relational hurt from the other person. Humility at any one of the first five assessments predicted forgiveness at the subsequent assessment occasion. Humility predicts forgiveness.

I (Ev) have studied forgiveness since the 1980s—first in psychotherapy and couple therapy and later applying science and clinical science to its study. I have been privileged to have traveled throughout the world and met some of the most forgiving people I can imagine. I frankly am humbled that so many can forgive so much. So, choosing someone to profile was very difficult.

I had the privilege in 2008 to sit beside Immaculée Ilibagiza in a 2-day meeting in Nassau and then to hear her tell her story on one of the nights. Immaculée survived the massacre of 800,000 fellow Tutsis in Rwanda in 1994. As a 22-year-old woman, she hid in a Hutu pastor's bathroom with seven other women—cramped, terrified, starving—for 91 days. Her brother and most of her extended family and friends were murdered during those 100 days of genocide. Yet Immaculée emerged not bitter but forgiving and with a revitalized faith in the goodness of God. After the killing ceased, she had the opportunity to confront Felicien, the man who had killed her brother and mother. A powerful politician, Semana, who had been like an uncle to Immaculée, brought Felicien to meet the woman his murders had harmed:

> Semana pushed Felicien into the office, and he stumbled onto his knees. . . .
>
> "Stand up, you killer!" Semana shouted. "Stand up and explain to this girl why her family is dead. Explain to her why you murdered her mother and butchered her brother. . . ." Semana screamed even louder, but the battered man remained hunched and kneeling, too embarrassed to stand and face me. . . .
>
> I wept at the sight of his suffering. . . . He was now the victim of his victims, destined to live in torment and regret. I was overwhelmed with pity for the man. . . .
>
> Felicien was sobbing. I could feel his shame. He looked up at me for only a moment, but our eyes met. I reached out, touched his hands lightly, and quietly said what I'd come to say.
>
> "I forgive you." . . .
>
> [Semana said] "What was that about, Immaculée? That was the man who murdered your family. I brought him to you to question . . . to spit

on if you wanted to. But you forgave him! How could you do that? Why did you forgive him?"

I answered him with the truth: "Forgiveness is all I have to offer." (Ilibagiza, 2006, pp. 203–204)

For a truly humble person, what else is there to offer?

Gratitude

Worthington, Goldstein, et al. (in press) reviewed articles investigating the relationship between humility and gratitude. They identified three articles reporting six studies that positively related humility and gratitude.

Kruse, Chancellor, Ruberton, and Lyubomirsky (2014) uncovered a positive, reciprocal relationship between state gratitude and their measure of state humility. That is, increases in state humility predicted increases in state gratitude from day to day, and vice versa, even when controlling for base rates of each. Recall our analogy early in the book about acts of humility, states of humility, and traits of humility being like blossoms producing fruit (acts of humility) that yield states (pieces of fruit) and eventually characterize a fruit tree as having a weak, moderate, strong, or truly heroic level of dispositional humility.

Entertainers and celebrities can inspire us with their humility. Fred Rogers, who was the beloved "Mr. Rogers" to countless children, showed remarkable gentleness and humility. Actor LeVar Burton (http://www.ew.com/article/2003/12/26/farewell-levar-burton-pays-tribute-fred-rogers) recalled a time when Rogers was invited to a gathering at the White House, and he asked everybody, including President Clinton, to close their eyes for 60 seconds and think about someone who had helped shape them. People in attendance soon began to weep. "Fred felt it was critical to acknowledge those who have helped us come into being," said Burton. "And Fred's legacy is that he is that person for so many of us." Fred Rogers was a humble person, and it showed up in a spontaneous expression of gratitude that touched those present.

Generosity

Exline and Hill (2012) developed a self-report measure of humility that predicted generosity. Generosity was measured behaviorally. Even after statistically removing the variance accounted for by the Big Five, self-esteem, entitlement, religiosity, social desirability, and dispositional gratitude, self-reported humility still predicted generosity in the form of donations, completion of a mail-in survey, and kindness motives.

Others have studied generosity more recently. Zettler, Lang, Hülsheger, and Hilbig (2016) examined the dictator game. The dictator game allows a target to split $10 with another person, but the division must be agreed to by the other person. Typically, in general populations, a $7 to $3 ratio is encountered in this constant-sum game. The prosocial personality traits of agreeableness and honesty–humility often result in more egalitarian distributions of wealth in the dictator game. Recently agreeableness and HH have predicted more equal ratios than a 7-to-3 split. Zettler et al. (2016) examined 560 participants, who completed a series of economic games in which allocations in the dictator game were compared with those in the generosity game, a non-constant-sum wealth distribution task where proposers with fixed payoffs selected the size of their partner's payoff ("generosity"). They also examined response to the partner's previous move—either a negative or a positive move—and sought to determine whether reciprocity occurred. Generosity and positive reciprocity were popular strategies. Allocations to the partner in the generosity game were more than in the dictator game, especially in following a positive move by the partner. Men were more generous when this was costless. Women were more egalitarian overall. Honesty–humility predicted dictator, but not generosity allocations, so there is support for a connection between honesty–humility and generosity, but not in all cases.

Sir John Templeton earned his fortune investing in Pacific Rim technology companies when "Made in China" or "Made in Japan" signified cheap or poor-quality products. That changed when technology boomed, and Sir John earned a fortune. Yet, Sir John always retained his humility. Humility was one of the main thrusts for the John Templeton Foundation. I (Ev) had the pleasure of meeting and interacting with Sir John on numerous occasions. He was always positive and upbeat—one of the most genuinely positive people I have ever met. And he passed that quality along to his children. I also knew Dr. John M. (Jack) Templeton Jr. and worked closely with him during the time I served as executive director of A Campaign for Forgiveness Research, a nonprofit formed to raise additional money to fund forgiveness research. Jack was the president and chief fundraiser. He also donated a huge amount of money as a complement to the time he donated to promote forgiveness. He had learned well the lesson Sir John taught—that humility was the root of generosity.

Humility and Personality

Humility has been found to be related to a wide variety of personality traits and dispositions. In addition, humility is related to other virtues.

Self-Control

Tong et al. (2016) conducted four experiments that examined the relationship of humility to self-control. Participants were induced to recall humility experiences, and then they were subjected to self-control tasks. Even when personal variables like compliance and achievement motivation and self-esteem were controlled, participants who recalled humility experiences were better able to squeeze a handgrip, persist in a frustrating task, and resist eating chocolates than people who recalled neutral experiences.

George Foreman was born poor and without a stable family. As a youth, he was troubled. In the Job Corps, he was attracted to boxing, and a date was set for his first sparring session. He told all of his friends to come see him. In an interview with Gordon Marino, a philosophy professor, Foreman said,

> I got whupped very badly. It was so embarrassing that I never wanted to box again. . . . That beating taught me humility in this sense. It taught me never to think that I was better than anyone else. It taught me that on any given day, you can be beaten. This always helped me to prepare for my bouts. A few years later, after I knocked out Joe Frazier and won the heavyweight title, I forgot that lesson in humility and again, I had to pay the price by getting beaten and embarrassed by Muhammad Ali in Zaire. (Marino, 2010, p. 44)

But those lessons stuck. Humility was related to self-control. Foreman became a minister after retiring from boxing, but he trained young kids in boxing. Marino said,

> I once pressed him on how he could be a Christian and at the same time teach young kids how to hurt people. Foreman responded, "Because the discipline of boxing gives you practice with your emotions, emotions like fear and anger. In time, the kids learn to control rather than to be controlled by those powerful feelings. People who have control over their emotions are less violent." (Marino, 2010, p. 44)

Sexual Fidelity

People who are low in Honesty–Humility are more likely to engage in one-night stands (but are equally likely to be in long-term relationships) compared with those high in Honesty–Humility (Jonason, Hatfield, & Boler, 2015). These findings show a consistent pattern that trait humility across social situations may promote other-oriented motivational focus as well as relationship commitment in close relationships.

Ego Quietness or Mindfulness

Ego quietness is a lack of self-focus, which can include mindfulness, detachment, or simply a lack of self-focus as a personality characteristic that has more to do with lack of personal awareness than with humility. On the other hand, people like the Dalai Lama certainly possess a quiet ego, and it is highly related to their humility. Thus, in a population, we would expect to find some modest statistically significant correlations between ego quietness or mindfulness and humility, and this has been the case (Schwager, Hülsheger, & Lang, 2016). That inclusive measure of humility correlated positively with the quiet ego scale, which includes perspective taking, detached awareness, inclusive identity, and growth as different facets (Bauer & Wayment, 2008; Wayment, Bauer, & Sylaska, 2015).

Verdorfer (2016) examined two samples—a sample of nonleaders and one of leaders—to examine the degree to which mindfulness related to servant-leader characteristics. In nonleaders, Verdorfer found a positive relationship between dispositional mindfulness and humility as well as a non-self-centered motivation to lead, both representing essential features of a servant attitude. In leaders, in a second study, Verdorfer found that dispositional mindfulness reported by leaders was positively related to their direct reports' ratings of servant-leader behavior, leader humility, and authenticity of leaders.

Example of Self-Regulation and Humility

Some of the greatest political figures in history endeared themselves to the public through their humble nature. George Washington, for example, was known as America's Cincinnatus. Cincinnatus was a Roman general who voluntarily stepped down at the height of power, returned to his life as a farmer, and was called into service later. After rescuing the nation, he once again stepped voluntarily down and returned to civilian life. Washington was granted by the Continental Congress absolute rule over the military. He refused to abuse that power, and he continually appealed to the Congress to supply the needs of the army instead of seize resources in power. That was not an easy decision. The states were not inclined to give up resources to fund the war effort. The states were not united, but they acted like 13 free riders. Washington used sincere requests, even begging, instead of using legitimate military might to seize resources. There is another anecdote that two men went walking in the snow during the winter at Valley Forge. They entered a barn and saw Washington kneeling in prayer for his troops. Quietly they backed out (Lichtman, 2000, Lecture 3, George Washington—American Liberator). Instead of using his power, he used power under control, one of the linchpins of humility.

When he had emerged victorious in the Revolutionary War, he could have continued as a powerful military ruler. But, 8 years after the war started, Washington chose to lay down his sword. In a circular to the states, he did not lay out a grand plan for a powerful nation. Rather, he spent most of his time imploring state leaders to pay their share of salary for his troops. He closed with a prayer, that God would "dispose us all, to do justice, to love mercy, and to demean ourselves with . . . charity, humility, and temper of mind" ("Circular to the States," in Allen, 1988, p. 242). On December 23, 1783, he resigned, becoming what King George of England foretold: "If he does that, he will be the greatest man in the world" (quoted in Wood, 1992, p. 208). He established, in resigning, civilian control over the military, something quite unique in history.

In 1797, after two terms as president, George Washington stepped down once again. That set a long-standing precedent that presidents were not lifetime rulers but servants of the people for a limited time. Washington chose not once but twice to leave the pinnacle of power for the good of something more than his own personal ambition—the good of the new nation he had helped found. He thus earned the recognition he deserved as America's Cincinnatus.

He did not come to this humility naturally—which is good news for the rest of us. Rather, Washington was "prone to excessive pride . . . tempted to vanity, concerned about his appearance, and guarded about his reputation. His humility eventually became a habit, as he combatted these temptations" (Bobb, 2013, p. 52). Early in his career he was driven to greatness, willing to do anything to achieve greatness. Yet, he eventually realized that greatness at any price is not true greatness. He acquired humility methodically by copying and living out in constant practice 110 rules for civility.

> Rather than cloaking his ambition, Washington recognized that the more he served others and the cause of justice, the more his success would matter. The less his ambition was about his own fame, the more he would deserve the honors he received. (Bobb, 2013, p. 57)

Other Connections Between Humility and Personality

Leman et al. (2017) reviewed research on the connections between humility and personality. They found humility to be related to numerous personality virtues. These included cooperation, harmony at work and school, and sociopolitical dominance, and interested readers are referred to Leman et al. for reviews of research on those variables.

Positive Outcomes in Important Aspects of Life

Given the positive qualities that seem to be associated with humility, it would seem likely that humility would result in some positive outcomes in life. We found research associating humility with child rearing, work satisfaction, academic achievement, and self-esteem. For instance, in Israel, using the Values in Action Inventory of Strengths (VIA-IS; Peterson & Seligman, 2004), Shoshani and Aviv (2012) found that both parents' and children's temperance predicted better child emotional and behavioral adjustment. However, the VIA-IS combines Humility–Modesty with forgiveness/mercy, prudence, and self-regulation (Peterson & Seligman, 2004). Thus, it is impossible to determine the contribution of humility alone to those outcomes. In Sweden, temperance predicted work satisfaction among phone workers in a call center (Moradi, Nima, Rapp Ricciardi, Archer, & Garcia, 2014). Similar difficulties as we found with the VIA-IS in the Israeli study occurred in trying to determine why people worked in what might be considered a nonrewarding job as a caller. An implicit measure of humility (relative to arrogance) correlated positively with college students' grades in an academic course when other variables were controlled (Rowatt et al., 2006). In addition, good grades—the dependent variable—might not be a product of virtue either. Some people are brilliant but morally are wrecks. For others, getting grades is demanded by parents. It becomes a strong situation that overpowers personality, much as Milgram's (1974) studies found obedience to overshadow personality. Other research using self-reports has shown that honesty–humility is related to measures of academic performance. A. De Vries, R. De Vries, and Born (2011) supported that connection in two studies. To get at a more laser-like assessment, many researchers have employed non–self-report scales—such as report by knowledgeable third parties—to understand humility (D. E. Davis, Worthington, & Hook, 2010). In their review, Leman et al. (2017) pointed out three examples. In one, Gregg, Hart, Sedikides, and Kumashiro (2008) used a prototype analysis. In the third example, Rowatt et al. (2006) used semantic differentials and a single thermometer item (very arrogant/very humble) to relate humility to self-esteem. In Rowatt et al., scores on the humility semantic differentials were correlated with implicit self-esteem and scores on the Rosenberg (1965) self-esteem scale as well as satisfaction with life, agreeableness, openness, spiritual transcendence, forgiveness, and gratitude, while negatively correlated with unhealthiness and neuroticism.

Dinger et al. (2015) examined the relationship between honesty–humility and achievement goals in 173 high school students. Honesty–humility correlated positively with goals focused on mastery and negatively for goals focused on performance approach and performance avoidance. Even people very high in the need for achievement can benefit by humility. Take the field of military leadership. People can still succeed at a high level in the competitive field of military service while showing great humility. Consider the story of Pat Tillman, the NFL player who turned down a million-dollar contract to serve his country as an Army Ranger. We will tell a bit more of his story in Chapter 10.

HUMILITY AND POSITIVE RELATIONSHIPS

Generally, virtuous behavior is likely related to better relationship functioning. Worthington and his colleagues have studied couples making the transition to parenthood. Such periods of disruption in practiced life patterns and renegotiating new patterns can be times of conflict. One hypothesis, though, is that people who are humble are likely more willing to behave in ways that value their partner and also that reflect virtuous behavior in many areas. Another hypothesis is that transitions place the ego under strain and can therefore reduce humility within the couple relationship.

When partners view each other as humble, this tends to increase commitment and relationship quality. Nonterah et al. (2016) expected that greater stress over the transition to parenthood would reduce relational humility. Participants were 69 heterosexual married couples that were followed from 3 months prior to childbirth until 21 months after childbirth. Individuals who are more stressed perceive their partners as less humble across the transition into parenthood. Ripley et al. (2016) used the same sample. They found that higher levels of relational humility predicted lower levels of stress initially and over time. With its orientation toward benefiting others and generally desirable interactional style, relational humility promoted more positive social support, which in turn reduced perceived stress over time.

VICES

Low humility has been found to be related to a variety of vices. Whereas this involves some subclinical antisocial behavior, it also involves three related characteristics that together form the *dark triad*.

Developmental Subclinical Antisocial Behavior

In adolescents and young adults, evidence is accumulating that honesty–humility is related to more antisocial behavior. Allgaier, Zettler, Wagner, Püttmann, and Trautwein (2015) assessed 307 on honesty–humility. At a second time, the adolescents responded to vignettes describing realistic school situations, and their responses were coded regarding the degree of anti-social and prosocial behavior. Adolescents higher on honesty–humility later reported lower levels of antisocial behavior and higher levels of prosocial behavior. In addition, for adolescents low in honesty–humility, situational characteristics had more influence in determining antisocial or prosocial behavior. Similarly, Gylfason, Halldorsson, and Kristinsson (2016) assessed 143 undergraduates in a cheap talk game. Dishonesty was predicted by people high in extraversion and low in honesty–humility (see also Zettler, Hilbig, Moshagen, & de Vries, 2015). Fiddick et al. (2016) found honesty–humility to be related to maintenance of social contract behaviors. Worth and Book (2015) surveyed 219 university students. Aggression during videogame play was associated with honesty–humility.

The Dark Triad

The dark triad describes three related attributes that often bother people who interact with possessors of them. These attributes are (1) *narcissism* (i.e., entitlement, grandiosity, and a desire for social admiration), (2) *Machiavellianism* (i.e., manipulativeness and self-serving interactions with others), and (3) *psychopathy* (i.e., reckless impulsivity and callousness toward others). These are not just characteristics of disagreeable people. Ashton and Lee (2007) suggested that disagreeable people focus on not being taken advantage of, but people low in honesty–humility are more attuned to how to take advantage of others. So, narcissism, Machiavellianism, and psychopathy seem to be linked by pursuing one's own agenda for one's own benefit, regardless of the cost to others. We might call this combination of negative traits an extreme lack of other-orientation—or worse, an other-orientation that is more concerned with exploiting than with valuing others. Two studies found that people low in honesty–humility were focused on taking advantage of others (K. Lee & Ashton, 2005; K. Lee et al., 2013).

Leman et al. (2017) reviewed the research on the dark triad through 2014 (with two citations in 2015), and we urge readers to consult their excellent review for summaries of numerous studies. In 2017, Muris et al. published a meta-analytic and critical review of the research on the dark triad. They found the HH subscale of the HEXACO model to be associated with all three elements within the dark triad. They drew several conclusions about the dark triad. Dark triad traits were substantially intercorrelated. Men exhibited them more than women. They were negatively related to agreeableness and honesty–humility. They also were generally associated with several negative psychosocial outcomes.

Narcissism

Let's briefly examine each of the elements of the dark triad independently. Low humility has been shown to relate to high scores on all three personality dispositions that make up the so-called dark triad. Low humility has been related to high levels of grandiose narcissism (Owens, Wallace, & Waldman, 2015), vulnerable narcissism (Sandage, Jankowski, Bissonette, & Paine, 2017), self-absorption, entitlement (Sandage et al., 2017), and emotional reactivity (i.e., neuroticism; Maltby, Wood, Day, & Pinto, 2012). On the other end of the spectrum, high humility has been related to low levels of narcissism (Muris, Merckelbach, Otgaar, & Meijer, 2017). Owens, Wallace, and Waldman (2015) surveyed 876 employees. They found that even narcissistic leaders can have positive effects on followers when the leaders show humility. Effective leaders are more likely to be people who can learn to harmonize some of their negative personal qualities with more positive, and often humble, leadership qualities.

Muris, Merckelbach, Otgaar, and Meijer (2017) found that what might be considered normal narcissism is also related to low Honesty–Humility scores. Baiocco et al. (2017) found that low Honesty–Humility scores were related to number of selfies (own self, partner and self, and self within a group) posted. Sandage, Jankowski, Bissonette, and Paine (2017) examined vulnerable narcissism. Whereas grandiose narcissism has often been investigated, *vulnerable narcissism* involves an entitled self but tends to respond to wounds to the ego with shame, self-condemnation, and guilt. Higher levels of vulnerable narcissism have been found to be related to lower forgiveness and humility. Sandage et al. examined 162 seminary graduate students in training for mental health careers. Vulnerable narcissism, a kind of privileged entitlement that is related to more manipulative one-down narcissism than is grandiose narcissism, was related to low forgiveness of others, low humility, and high levels of depression. Differentiation of self, the degree to which a person can maturely act autonomously while not forsaking the give-and-take value of relationships, mediated between vulnerable narcissism and all outcomes. More mature differentiation-of-self lessened the connections of vulnerable narcissism to lower forgiveness and humility and higher depression.

Machiavellianism

People high in Machiavellianism are pragmatic, self-serving, and willing to and capable of manipulating others to get their way. In several studies, high HH was related to low Machiavellianism (Leman et al., 2017). Muris, Merckelbach, Otgaar, and Meijer (2017) found Machiavellianism to be related to honesty–humility overall ($r = -.40$) and to three of the four subscales on the HEXACO-HH scale: sincerity ($r = -.29$), fairness ($r = -.34$), and modesty ($r = -.23$), but not greed avoidance. Recent research continues to support the association between honesty–humility and manipulation. Austin and Vahle (2016) surveyed 380 participants and found that low HEXACO-HH scores predicted attempts to manage or manipulate others' emotions. Much of the research supporting the connection between manipulation and honesty–humility has used the HEXACO-HH. That scale is heavily influenced by items assessing honesty. Thus, it is not clear the degree to which *humility* per se is related to manipulation of and dishonesty with others.

Psychopathy

Psychopathy consists of antisociality, low empathy, flat affect, high impulsivity, and willingness to take advantage of others for personal gain (Hare, 1991). HH has often been negatively correlated with psychopathy (for a review, see Leman et al., 2017). Muris et al. (2017) found Machiavellianism to be related to honesty–humility overall ($r = -.28$) and to two of the four subscales on the HEXACO-HH scale: sincerity ($r = -.37$) and fairness ($r = -.34$), but not modesty or greed avoidance.

Other Vices

Humility has consistently been shown to be related to the dark triad, as summarized by Leman et al. (2017). But what about other vices? Schwager, Hülsheger, and Lang (2016) investigated mindfulness and its relationship to counterproductive academic behavior (i.e., cheating). They tested, in 281 graduate students, the moderating role of conscientiousness and honesty–humility between mindfulness and counterproductive academic behavior. Students completed self-reports of all measures. Self-ratings of counteproductive academic behavior were made 3 months later. Mindfulness, conscientiousness, and honesty–humility all were negatively related to counterproductive academic behavior. Both conscientiousness and honesty–humility moderated the relationship. Low mindfulness–high counterproductive behavior links were stronger for students low on conscientiousness and low in honesty–humility.

VIRTUES, VICES, AND THE CROOKED-TIMBER TRADITION

New York Times columnist David Brooks (2015) wrote a brilliant account of a life of virtue, *The Road to Character*. He began by reflecting on what he called the "resume virtues" versus the "eulogy virtues." The resume virtues are those related to achieving autonomously. "Oh the Places You'll Go!" wrote Dr. Seuss, and it became the fifth best-selling book ever. And it is still selling hundreds of thousands of copies every graduation season. The eulogy virtues, though, are the ones you hope people will say about you at your funeral. They are fueled by humility. After tracing the philosophical transformation of modern worldviews, Brooks closed the book by providing a 15-point Humility Code. He saw this as the way to get back to a time of moral realism—recognition that Kant was right and nothing straight can be made from crooked timber. And humans are crooked timber. Moral realism accepts personal limitations, struggles against them, and spends a lifetime at the struggle. "The purpose of the struggle . . . is not to 'win,' because that is not possible; it is to get better at waging it" (Brooks, 2015, p. 263).

Here is a digest of Brooks's (2015) Humility Code: (1) Live for a great purpose, not for happiness. If you work for the purpose, the happiness will come. (2) The long road to character begins with understanding our crooked-timber nature. (3) While flawed, we are splendidly endowed. Seek to know your strengths as well as flaws. (4) In the struggle against your bent nature,

> Humility is the greatest virtue. Humility is having an accurate assessment of your own nature and your own place in the cosmos. Humility is the awareness that you are an underdog in the struggle against your own weakness. Humility is an awareness that your individual talents alone are inadequate to the tasks that have been assigned you. Humility reminds you that you are not the center of the universe, but you serve a larger order. (Brooks, 2015, pp. 262–263)

(5) Pride is the central vice. (6) Once the necessities of life are satisfied, the main life struggle is to get better at waging the war for virtue and against vice. (7) Character is built by confronting your inner desires that pull toward pride. (8) In the long term, seek virtues of lasting value. (9) No one can achieve self-mastery alone. Everyone needs redemptive assistance from God, family, friends, ancestors, rules, traditions, institutions, and exemplars. (10) Progress, when it happens, is U-shaped. It involves repeated patterns of advance, failure and struggle, and redemption. (11) Defeating weakness requires quieting the ego so you can struggle against weakness by self-effacement. (12) Wisdom starts when we truly admit we don't know enough to succeed. (13) No good life is possible unless it is organized around a vocation. "A vocation is not found by looking within and finding your passion. It is found by looking without and asking what life is asking of us" (Brooks, 2015, p. 266). (14) The best leaders lead along the grain of the crooked timber of humanity—realizing that they and those they lead are fallible. (15) The person who struggles successfully against weakness and sin will not become rich and famous but will be mature.

SUMMARY

People who are humble are those you want to be friends with. They are altruistic, forgiving, agreeable, good parents, good workers, achievers, and self-controlled, and they have quiet egos that do not need to be continually stoked. They are people you want to hang out with. In fact, we admit, we would really like to be like those people because then people would want to hang out with us. We could look to have our choice among many fulfilling romantic partners because they would be attracted to us. We could also do significant things with our lives—have great relationships, achieve in our jobs and life work, and live at peace with ourselves and the world.

On the other hand, people truly low in humility are not rewarding people to interact with. If one has to do so, care is prudent.

But being humble and developing virtues is not easy. In fact, it's downright difficult. And commitment to a life of virtue requires a radical shift in worldview. Brooks would have us balance a life of striving for virtues and recognizing the pull of vice by embracing a crooked-timber view of life. For Brooks, humility is about seeking redemption more than imposing our will on life. From the stories and research in this chapter, we see that seeking humility is a road to virtue that leads through vices, against which we struggle alone and, we fervently hope, with others' aid.

WHAT DID WE LEARN IN THIS CHAPTER?

1. The virtues most often predicted by humility are those involving a positive orientation toward others, like gratitude, generosity, compassion, altruism, and forgiveness.
2. The lack of other orientation is a key to predicting narcissism, antisocial behavior, and manipulation.
3. David Brooks (2015) wrote about virtue in *The Road to Character*. Resume virtues are accomplishments. Eulogy virtues are character traits. Brooks finds a satisfying life in focusing on the eulogy virtues.

THREE QUESTIONS FOR THOUGHT AND DISCUSSION

1. Philosophers like Augustine and Thomas Aquinas see all virtues as unified. Humility is often seen as a gateway to the other virtues. Why might humility hold a special place among the virtues?
2. Can you identify barriers in your life to developing a humbler and more virtuous life? If so, what can you do to lower, knock down, leap over, or run around those barriers?
3. Recall a specific time or times in your life when you felt you were particularly altruistic, grateful, forgiving, or loving? In those times, did you also feel humble?

5

HUMILITY, MENTAL HEALTH, AND PHYSICAL HEALTH

In this chapter, we review research demonstrating effects of humility on mental health and physical health and well-being. We draw heavily on two recent reviews of research. One by Worthington, Goldstein, et al. (in press) surveys the field of humility and summarizes the findings to this point in a set of hypotheses. The other, by Toussaint and Webb (2017), is a careful look at humility and mental and physical health. But here we also updated those studies by including newer research.

WHAT WE LEARN FROM THE TWO RECENT REVIEWS

In these two reviews, we gained a basic understanding about how relationships, mental health, and physical health interrelate. Humility is related to personality characteristics within the Big Five as well as to situational characteristics, such as stress.

http://dx.doi.org/10.1037/0000079-006
Heroic Humility: What the Science of Humility Can Say to People Raised on Self-Focus, by E. L. Worthington Jr. and S. T. Allison

Relationships, Mental Health, and Physical Health

The *mental health hypothesis* suggests that to the extent that one is humble, one will experience better mental health (Worthington, Goldstein, et al., in press). Humble people are likely to experience fewer disruptive negative interpersonal stress-related experiences. The *physical health hypothesis* states that to the extent one is humble, one will have better physical health. Humble people tend to be more agreeable and conscientious (Ashton, Lee, & de Vries, 2014). Agreeableness is likely related to calmer responses to stressors, thus stress-related disorders are likely to be infrequent. Conscientiousness is related to better health care behavior, which should result in better physical health (Visser & Pozzebon, 2013). In addition, high humility is related to better mental health, and this has physical sequelae.

Finally, high humility is related to better relationships, as we saw in Chapter 3, and that should result in better and more health-promoting social support, which affects mental and physical health (Contrada & Baum, 2011). The effects of humility on physical and mental health are more often indirect than direct. Thus, humility will affect people's stress—perhaps most directly through their relationships—which might in turn affect mental health. Humility will also affect physical health through affecting people's stress, mental health, and relationships—again, generally indirect relations.

Toussaint and Webb (2017) reviewed the existing studies in the area and posited a theoretical model relating humility and both mental and physical health. They provided a schematic diagram of the interconnections (see Figure 5.1). Path A shows a direct link between humility and health and well-being. We expect that humility should be related to mental and physical health for a variety of reasons. Humility is thought to make people generally satisfied with their lives, which might not lead to happiness because being other-oriented is costly. But Worthington, Goldstein, et al. (in press) put forth the ultimate satisfaction hypothesis—that ultimately humble people will be satisfied with their lives.

Other-Focus as a Bridge Between Humility and Health

We can see this connection between humility and mental health in Viktor E. Frankl's (1959) book, *Man's Search for Meaning*. Frankl was in a death camp under the Nazis, and one of his big lessons was that a sense of meaning could foster endurance. Later, he showed that a sense of meaning was also related to flourishing in times when deprivation was not an issue.

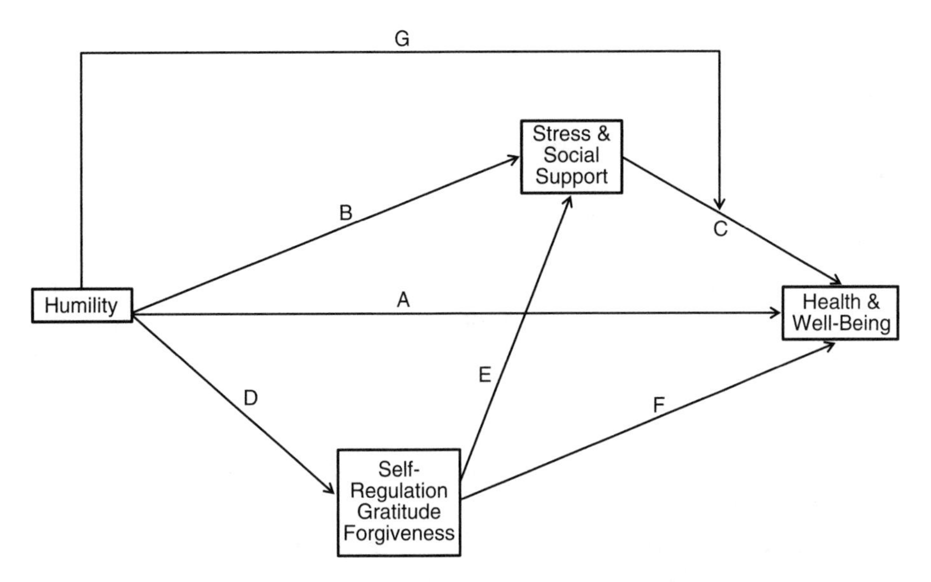

Figure 5.1. Theoretical model relating humility and both mental and physical health. From *Handbook of Humility: Theory, Research, and Application* (p. 180), by E. L. Worthington Jr., D. E. Davis, and J. N. Hook (Eds.), 2017, New York, NY: Routledge. Copyright 2017 by Taylor and Francis. Reprinted with permission.

Other-Focus When Health Is Threatened

Frankl's essential humility is evidenced throughout his entire account of his 3 years of experiences in Auschwitz. We see what he admired:

> We who lived in concentration camps can remember the men who walked through huts comforting others, giving away their last piece of bread. They may have been few in number, but they offer sufficient proof that everything can be taken from a man but one thing: the last of the human freedoms—to choose one's attitude in any given set of circumstances, to choose one's own way. (Frankl, 1959, p. 104)

But why did these humble men Frankl so admired do the other-oriented, self-sacrificial acts they did? Were they driven to self-sacrifice morally or religiously? Frankl (1959) answered clearly:

> Man is never driven to moral behavior; in each instance he decides to behave morally. . . . [H]e does so for the sake of a cause to which he commits himself, or for a person whom he loves, or for the sake of his God. If he did it for the sake of having a good conscience, he would become a Pharisee and cease to be a truly moral person. (p. 158)

Frankl was not talking about actualizing oneself in Maslow's sense of having dealt sufficiently with all of the deficiency needs and finally seeking actualization through acting humbly. He was talking of people stripped of everything, completely deficient in having their basic physiological, safety, love and belongingness, and esteem needs met. Yet, their existential essence is found by these few in humility—accurate knowledge of their self (they literally are nothing in the eyes of the world and know it), modesty (how else can they present themselves?), and other-orientation using the only power they retain under their control (the power to choose their reactions) to lift others up and not put them down. Humility is the core of their humanity. For them, *humus*, the Earth, is what they are rooted in—humanity and humility blend together in their connection to the Earth.

Identity and Health

The first link (Path A) in Toussaint and Webb's (2017) model is humility to health and well-being. Chancellor and Lyubomirsky (2013) reviewed ways that humility might facilitate better health. Humility might lead to more stable, self-accepting identity and thus less rumination about the self, more control of negative affect, and openness to experience that taps into Fredrickson's (2013) broaden-and-build hypothesis. As we see from Figure 5.1, humility can directly decrease stress and increase social support (D. E. Davis et al., 2013; see Figure 5.1, Path B), which leads to health (see Figure 5.1, Path C).

Relational Mediators Between Humility and Health

There are important mediators to the relationship between humility and stress and social support (see Figure 5.1, Path D and Path E)—such as forgiveness, gratitude, and self-regulation (and others). Each virtue strengthens the connections between humility and both lower stress and higher support. Also, forgiveness, gratitude, and self-regulation may have direct connections to health (see Figure 5.1, Path F).

Humility might also buffer the effects of stress on health (see Figure 5.1, Path G). In aging, religious adults, evidence supports this hypothesis (Krause, 2014). Toussaint and Webb (2017) suggested that humility might moderate stress–health relationships. Humble people accurately assess their own role in conflicts (and can act to avoid or lessen conflict), act more modestly (and thus less provocatively), and are other-oriented and thus more concerned for others. Therefore, highly humble people experience less stress and more support, which might lessen physical problems and depression. Moreover, humble people might perceive interpersonal stress as less severe, have better coping responses, or avoid stressful circumstances (Orth & Luciano, 2015).

Ruberton et al. (2016) investigated the relationship between physician humility, physician–patient communication, and patients' perceptions of their health during a planned medical visit. Primary care physicians ($n = 100$) and patients ($n = 297$) had physician–patient interactions that were rated for the physician's humility and the effectiveness of the physician–patient communication. Physicians and patients reported their satisfaction with the interaction. Patients self-reported their overall health. As physician-rated humility fluctuated, self-reported patient health mirrored it. Different levels of humility across physicians predicted effective physician–patient communication. This was true regardless of whether the physician was frustrated with the patient or whether the patient was dissatisfied with the visit. Ruberton et al. suggested that humble, not paternalistic and arrogant, physicians are most effective at working with their patients and might have an effect on the health of patients. They advocated training physicians in humble behavior to promote better physician–patient interactions.

In summary, Toussaint and Webb's (2017) model integrates research and theory about humility and health. It suggests numerous research hypotheses that could be tested to support each path in the model. But what about the empirical evidence supporting the model?

Toussaint and Webb (2017) reviewed the research on humility and mental and physical health organized according to their model. They imposed strict criteria for inclusion of empirical research in their review. A study had to assess humility, not just a suspected correlate like self-esteem or narcissism. And it had to assess actual mental or physical health. They found only 14 studies that met their criteria. As a result, they made several observations at the outset of their review. First, that the evidence base is small. Second, most studies investigate college students. Third, no widely accepted measure of humility was used. Fourth, 12 studies are cross-sectional and correlational. Causal statements are premature because only one experimental study and one prospective population-based study have been done. Fifth, only self-report measures of health were used. No objective health indices and no biomarkers were used.

What Then Can We Expect?

Given Toussaint and Webb's (2017) methodological observations, we can see that we are on thin ice in drawing conclusions about the relationships between humility and mental health or physical health (only three studies!). Toussaint and Webb were mindful of the limited data base, and they suggested that their conclusions are more suggestions for a starting place for future research. Given the limited base of literature we are dealing with, let's turn our attention to what is there by looking at the two reviews.

HUMILITY AND MENTAL HEALTH

Humility has been found to be related to positive mental health. Substantial support was present early in the investigations of humility, and support has continued to build supporting that relationship.

The Mental Health Hypothesis

Worthington, Goldstein, et al. (in press) reviewed the literature on humility. They proposed several testable hypotheses. One related directly to humility and mental health, which they called the mental health hypothesis. The mental health hypothesis had support from at least five studies. For example, Aghababaei et al. (2016) surveyed five independent samples—422 and 251 Iranian Muslims (in separate samples), 221 and 226 Polish Christians, and 255 Malay Muslims. They correlated humility with mental health variables and religious variables (e.g., intrinsic and extrinsic religiousness). In Christian samples, humility was correlated with only intrinsic religiousness, but in Muslim samples, with both intrinsic and extrinsic religiousness. Humility was related to happiness only in one of the two Polish Christian samples. In three of the five samples (two Muslim, one Christian), humility was related to life satisfaction. In one Muslim and one Christian sample (the only two in which they were measured), humility was related to autonomy, self-acceptance, positive relationships with others, environmental mastery, purpose in life, and personal growth.

Toussaint and Webb (2017) found five studies (Jankowski, Sandage, & Hill, 2013; Kesebir, 2014; Krause, 2014; Quiros, 2008; Rowatt et al., 2006) that support the direct correlation of humility and mental health (see Figure 5.1, Path A). Only one study was experimental. Kesebir (2014) found that humility protected against fear of death when mortality salience is primed (see Figure 5.1, Path G). In fact, priming humility is sufficient to reduce death anxiety (see Figure 5.1, Path A). Three studies found humility and depressive symptoms to be negatively correlated (Jankowski et al., 2013; Krause, 2014; Quiros, 2008). Quiros (2008) found a negative correlation between humility and anxiety. Krause (2014) found that humility was a buffer between stressful interactions with church members and depression (see Figure 5.1, Path G). Rowatt et al. (2006) did not to find a connection between humility and mental health. On the basis of these few studies, we can conclude that humility might reduce depression and anxiety and might moderate the effects of stress on depression and anxiety.

Worthington, Goldstein, et al. (in press) also posed a self-esteem hypothesis: True humility is related to positive self-esteem, but false humility is related to low self-esteem. They found limited empirical support. For example, in

Aghababaei et al. (2016), humility was not related to self-esteem in two of the three samples in which self-esteem was measured. For Chinese participants, Cai et al. (2011) found limited support of the self-esteem hypothesis. Exline and Hill (2012) and Visser and Pozzebon (2013) also found limited support. Baumeister, Campbell, Krueger, and Vohs (2003) showed that stable positive self-esteem is generally associated with positive outcomes, but not so for unstable positive self-esteem, which is often threatened easily.

HEXACO-HH and Happiness

Eight studies—four from the lab of Aghababaei and Arji (2014)—shed light on the direct relationship between humility and happiness (see Figure 5.1, Path A). Aghababaei and Arji used the HEXACO-HH subscale and happiness measures of life satisfaction, subjective happiness, and multidimensional aspects of psychological well-being to study the humility–happiness link. In their work, participants were from Iran, Poland, and Malaysia. HH was consistently unrelated, or at best very weakly related, to subjective happiness. As we described earlier, however, the Honesty–Humility (HH) subscale of the HEXACO measures mostly honesty. Overall, the relationship between humility and happiness appears nuanced at best and perhaps virtually nonexistent.

Humility and Life Satisfaction

Aghababaei and Arji (2014) found stronger associations between HEXACO-HH and psychological well-being (e.g., autonomy, self-acceptance, positive-relations, mastery, purpose, and growth; Ryff & Keyes, 1995) than they found when HEXACO-HH was related to happiness. Two other studies from different labs correlated the HEXACO-HH with life satisfaction. Pollock, Noser, Holden, and Zeigler-Hill (2016) found small, nonsignificant correlations with the HEXACO-HH and life satisfaction. Dangi and Nagle (2015) found HEXACO-HH was related to the subscales of self-acceptance and purpose in life in adolescents from India.

Two studies from other research teams examined humility and life satisfaction, but by using other measures than the HEXACO-HH and happiness (Park, Peterson, & Seligman, 2004; Rowatt et al., 2006). Park et al. (2004) used large Internet samples and the VIA-IS (Values in Action Inventory of Strengths; Peterson & Seligman, 2004) Modesty–Humility subscale to examine the connection between humility and life satisfaction. The associations were small to nonexistent. But again recall that the VIA-IS subscales confound four characteristics. When Rowatt et al. (2006) used a face-valid humility semantic differential scale, they found humility was related to life satisfaction. The correlations between humility and purpose and life satisfaction are small but positive.

Humility, Happiness, and Life Satisfaction and Future Research

The correlation of humility and broader conceptualizations of happiness is stronger, though not strong. Perhaps the investigation of humility and happiness should focus more intently on how humility contributes to a meaningful, satisfying life through such things as autonomy, self-acceptance, positive-relations, mastery, purpose, and growth. It does not seem to relate to momentary happiness. It is important to note, too, that differences in measures and samples have clearly affected results, opening wide the door for additional cross-cultural studies.

HUMILITY AND PHYSICAL HEALTH

Humility has been found to be related to positive physical health. However, the evidence is weaker and more indirect than for the relationship between humility and mental health.

The Physical Health Hypothesis

Worthington, Goldstein, et al. (in press) reviewed the literature and proposed the physical health hypothesis: Humility is related to better physical health. After a review that found no measures of actual physical health, physiological measures, or biomarkers (only self-reports), they concluded that the connection between humility and physical health had not yet been unambiguously investigated empirically. They concluded, though, that there is good reason to believe from theory (and people's self-reported health) that indirect effects will occur. First, humility is hypothesized to be related to more agreeable and conscientious personality characteristics. Agreeableness is likely related to calmer responses to stressors; thus, stress-related disorders are likely to be infrequent. Conscientiousness might be related to better attentiveness to treating health problems. Second, high humility is hypothesized to be related indirectly to better physical health through an indirect path of better mental health. The connection between humility and mental health is well documented, but the humility–physical health connection has not been established. Other connections of humility with mental and physical health have been well documented, so there is reason to expect this will be forthcoming. Third, high humility is hypothesized to be related to better physical health through better relationships. That should result in better and more health-promoting social support and other indirect benefits that good relationships provide to better health.

Humility and Self-Reported Physical Health

Toussaint and Webb (2017) found three studies that address the direct correlation (see Figure 5.1, Path A) between humility and self-reported physical health (Krause, 2010, 2012; Rowatt et al., 2006). Krause (2010, 2012) studied Americans with an average age of 78 from the larger 15-year, five-wave, longitudinal Religion, Aging, and Health Survey. In 2010, Krause found that humility was positively correlated to self-rated physical health. In 2012, Krause found that if humility increases with age, it parallels increases in self-rated physical health. Many potentially confounding variables such as sociodemographics and religiousness were controlled. Rowatt et al. (2006) found that both single-item and semantic-differential-scale measures of humility were negatively related to unhealthy physical symptoms. With few studies to draw from, we can only make the most tentative suggestion that humility is associated with better physical health.

A RECENT LARGE STUDY OF HUMILITY AND FOUR MEASURES OF WELL-BEING

As we have seen in this chapter, recent summaries of research suggest that people who are more humble tend to enjoy better physical and mental health, happiness, and life-satisfaction than individuals who are less humble. In 2016, using a new nationwide survey involving 3,010 respondents, Krause, Pargament, Hill, and Ironson (2016) advanced these findings. Their data suggest that the magnitude of the negative relationship between stressful life events and all four measures of well-being—happiness, life satisfaction, depressed affect, and generalized anxiety—is reduced among people who are more humble. That is, they saw humility as a moderator connecting stressful life events with measures of well-being. They also showed some mechanisms by which any beneficial effects of humility might arise. For example, humility buffers the effects of stressful life events on the four measures of well-being. Thus, the researchers found that for all four measures of well-being, the strength of negative relationship between stressful life events and humility is less for people who are more humble.

We are seeing the beginning of a new wave of understanding of humility and outcomes. These recent studies by this esteemed team of researchers examined mechanisms, not simple correlations.

WHAT CONCLUSIONS CAN WE DRAW?

Toussaint and Webb (2017), at the end of their review of the 14 existing studies they included, offered suggestions. They tentatively suggested that humility might be positively related to both mental and physical health. But they suggested that there is little support that humility is related to happiness. Toussaint and Webb cautioned researchers to consider that virtues and character strengths may not always facilitate positive health, well-being, and (especially) happiness.

We think that the connections of humility to health, well-being, and happiness are weak because an orientation toward the other is often costly. When people are heroically humble, the costs are high. People who serve others, care for others, lift others up at their own expense (like parents with special needs children, caregivers for needy people, or people who sacrifice for an organization like a cherished business or armed services comrades) might find that the costs are so high that they overshadow immediate pleasure or happiness. They might also find that they can be virtuous in situations characterized by loss of basic needs. We recall Viktor Frankl's situation. We note the sacrifices of life and health incurred by people serving their country in military or public service. We hypothesize that humility can buffer psychological problems (e.g., depression) but might be unrelated to happiness. However, our speculation is tentative, based on few studies with limited generalizability potential.

FUTURE RESEARCH IN THE AREA

One piece of good news is that investigating humility and mental and physical health is a wide-open field. Almost any study that addresses these topics will be terra incognita. Methodologically sound studies can contribute to the literature. Some especially potentially fruitful areas cry out for empirical attention.

Measurement

Investigators need to develop brief humility measures for use in health studies. Typically, we seek efficient, psychometrically sound measures that will not burden an already stressed population or will not clutter an epidemiological study. We reviewed some good measures in Chapter 2 (on types of humility), but for health studies, many more are needed.

Health and Physical Measures Instead of Self-Reports of Health

To date, health outcomes have been assessed by self-reports. Self-reports of health can predict physical health outcomes (Idler & Benyamini, 1997). However, both conceptualization and assessment of health could be expanded by developing health surveys, pain assessments, and assessments of impairment and functional status. Measures of health status and health-related quality of life need to be used more often. Health-related behaviors such as eating, nutrition, exercise, sleep, and substance-use have not been included to date. Peripheral physiological measures such as heart rate, blood pressure, heart-rate variability, and skin conductance are needed. Biomarkers such as epinephrine, oxytocin, and cortisol have not yet been tested. Central nervous system assessment has not been used in the study of humility and mental or physical health.

New Samples

Much humility–health data come from college students. Only two studies have come from population-based samples. They were both from Krause's database regarding aging. There are currently no population-based, age-representative studies on humility and health. Twenge (2014) showed that narcissism in millennials has negative health correlates. She also showed that narcissism has extended throughout the developmental span. Together these suggest that population surveys are needed, and some research already suggests this (Reinhard, Konrath, Lopez, & Cameron, 2012). Some populations are ripe for study. For example, much addiction is thought to arise from self-centeredness, and humility is thought to aid recovery (Alcoholics Anonymous, 2001). Empirical investigations of these longstanding, yet anecdotal observations, could affect millions in recovery. Extension to employee assistance programs is fertile soil for study. Encouraging humility among employees is likely to improve relationships but also occupational health. If health were found to be related to humility, then this could lead to enhancing productivity, fewer sick days, and decreased health insurance claims, giving a financial incentive to promote humility.

Cause and Effect

Kesebir (2014) provided the only experimental study on humility's effect on health. Humility was primed and reduced death anxiety. Investigators could build from Kesebir's experiment. Researchers could undertake intervention trials in both healthy and patient samples to study whether promoting humility might affect health.

Mechanisms Relating Humility and Health

Studies need to investigate why humility might be linked to health. Toussaint and Webb (2017) suggested several mechanisms that include social support and stress as mediators. Other potential moderators and mediators include religiousness and spirituality (Krause, 2010), forgiveness (D. E. Davis, Hook, et al., 2011), self-regulation (D. E. Davis et al., 2013), and gratitude (Kruse et al., 2014). Toussaint and Webb also suggested that humility can buffer the deleterious effects of stress on health. For instance, Krause (2014) found that humility buffered against depression that might arise from feeling stress due to interacting with a religious congregation. And, as we saw previously, Krause, Pargament, Hill, and Ironson (2016) provided a study using new data in a nationwide probability sample to begin this needed research focus.

CLOSING THOUGHTS

We are a society focused on health. One of the first questions that journalists ask when interviewing scientists about the study of a new variable (like humility) is, "What are its mental and physical health effects?" It is worth establishing those effects, if any, to provide relevance to a health-conscious society. At this point, there are suggestions from the research that such effects exist, but establishing whether (or not) such effects are real, measurable, large, and enduring needs to be a priority in humility studies.

WHAT DID WE LEARN IN THIS CHAPTER?

1. Humility is not strongly or consistently related to self-esteem. Perhaps this is because self-esteem is about our view of ourselves, but humility is more often other-oriented.
2. Humility seems to be related to positive mental health.
3. Humility does not seem to be related to happiness.

THREE QUESTIONS FOR THOUGHT AND DISCUSSION

1. At this point in the science of humility, there are few studies on humility and mental and especially physical health. Why do you think research has lagged in some other areas?

2. We have speculated on a few mechanisms for why a life of humility might result in better mental and (perhaps) physical health—namely, less stress and better social relationships. Can you think of other reasons why humble people might have better mental or physical health?
3. Think of the five most humble people you know. Write their names down. Think of five people whom you don't think of as humble (but not necessarily those who are arrogant). Compare the two sets of people on mental and physical health. (Yes, this is a limited sample, but can you think of reasons why there might or might not be differences?)

6

HUMILITY, RELIGION, AND SPIRITUALITY

Humility might or might not be good for our physical and mental health. We don't know enough at this point to say. But we can say it is good for our spirit.

SPIRITUAL HUMILITY

Spirituality is defined as closeness or connection with the Sacred (D. E. Davis, Rice, Hook, et al., 2015). People hold numerous things to be sacred. These include God or Higher Powers, which we might call *religious spirituality*. But people also hold humans or humanity sacred, which we might call *humanistic spirituality*. And they can hold nature or environment to be sacred, which we might call *nature spirituality*. Some people hold other things, such as transcendent experiences, the self, or a variety of secular objects (such as one's country), to be sacred.

http://dx.doi.org/10.1037/0000079-007
Heroic Humility: What the Science of Humility Can Say to People Raised on Self-Focus, by E. L. Worthington Jr. and S. T. Allison

Measuring Spiritual Humility

D. E. Davis, Hook, Worthington, Van Tongeren, Gartner, and Jennings (2010) developed a scale that specifically measured spiritual humility, which we described in Chapter 2. They found scores on spirituality to be correlated with amount of similarity of an offender's spirituality to one's own and to trait gratitude. However, scores on spiritual humility were negatively correlated with revenge and avoidance motivations. Scores on spiritual humility were not related to religious commitment.

Some Predictions About Spiritual Humility

After their review of the research, Worthington, Goldstein, et al. (in press) posited the spirituality hypothesis. To the extent that a person has a strong sense of connection to the Sacred, the person will have spiritual humility, and being spiritually humble is thought to be related to predictable outcomes.

The Spirituality Hypothesis

A person who is spiritually humble is hypothesized to be more personally humble, intellectually humble, relationally humble, and culturally humble. However, in spite of the strength anticipated for spiritual humility's influence, the different types of humility (e.g., spiritual, intellectual, relational, cultural) are manifested in different relationships and hence are interrelated but not perfectly correlated. This hypothesis has not been clearly tested.

Spiritual Humility Is Related to Faith

Many studies have related degree of faith commitment to spiritual or general humility. This has yielded a number of investigations finding higher spiritual humility related to higher spirituality and higher spiritual stability (Hopkin, Hoyle, & Toner, 2014). Also, Krause (2014) surveyed 1,154 respondents in a religion, aging, and health study. He found that higher religious commitment was related to humility. In addition, people who scored low on humility tended also to have more negative interactions in their church or place of worship.

Spiritual Humility Is Related to Other Types of Humility

Spiritually humble people are usually more personally, intellectually, relationally, and culturally humble. More spiritually humble people also had more self-regulation, more overt religious practices, better self-ratings of morality, more intellectual humility regarding religion, and less reaction to an author that disagrees on religion. When counselors were more humble spiritually, they had better counseling outcomes for the clients of psychotherapists (Jankowski & Sandage, 2014; Owen et al., 2014).

The Temporal-Effects-of-Spiritual-Humility Hypothesis

To the extent that a person is spiritually humble, other effects that accrue to spirituality and religion (like longer life, better health, etc.) will accrue to the person. Thus, spiritual humility has been found to be related to better mental health, better social and psychological well-being, more prosociality, higher levels of reciprocal altruism, and lower hedonism (Visser & Pozzebon, 2013).

Some Summary Statements

Spiritual humility, being humble before whatever one considers sacred, seems broadly related to a multitude of prosocial outcomes. This concept is bedeviled by the same confounds that make interpreting any religious finding difficult. People who are religious (in this research, usually those who are spiritually humble) do many prosocial and healthful behaviors as a result of their adherence to religion. They belong to a community and thus experience social support. They do not do health-compromising behaviors as often or as frequently as the nonreligious. That is, they do not as often drink, smoke, or do drugs, and thus they do not put themselves at risk as often in bars and neighborhoods where drugs are sold. They do not hang with gangs, rob banks, engage in gunfights, participate in riots, etc. as often as those not affiliated with religion. Thus, people who are spiritually humble (and thus often more religious) are likely to experience many benefits, and it is difficult to sort out what might be due to spiritual humility and what might be due to the concomitants of religion.

RELIGIOUS HUMILITY—HUMILITY AND THE ABRAHAMIC RELIGIONS

In the remainder of this chapter, we adapt portions of a chapter by Porter et al. (2017) with permission from the publisher.[1] Each of the scholars, with commentator Porter discussing the contributions, provided a thorough summary of the position of their own religions on humility. We could not create

[1]From *Handbook of Humility: Theory, Research, and Applications* (pp. 48–60), by E. L. Worthington Jr., D. E. Davis, and J. N. Hook (Eds.), 2017, New York, NY: Routledge. Copyright 2017 by Taylor and Francis. Adapted with permission.

position descriptions nearly as accurately as these scholars, so we direct the reader's attention to the original chapter in *Handbook of Humility: Theory, Research, and Applications* (Worthington, Davis, & Hook, 2017), and we ask that you indulge our abstracting from their separate accounts.

The traditions of Christianity, Judaism, and Islam (the Abrahamic religions) have left an indelible mark on Western civilization. This indelibility likely derives from the spiritual humility (deference to God) that permeates the religions. If truth be told, the permeation of spiritual humility derives from Judaism being born as an oppressed nomadic tribe and Christianity being born in a setting in which Rome ruled with an iron fist and persecuted Christians prior to Constantine during the formative years of the religion's beliefs and practices. Islam was born into a more paradoxical stance. Islam was trying to recover "absolute submission to God," which Muhammad thought had been corrupted in the Christianity and Judaism of the time period when Muhammad was forming Islam. But at the same time, Islam was also a religion of conquest in which Muhammad was in power during the solidification of the religion. In all cases of the Abrahamic religions, though, submission to and humility in the face of God was paramount. So, it is not surprising that a skewed distribution (religious > nonreligious) has derived from Christian influence.

The other philosophic strain that has influenced Western civilization has been the Greco-Roman strain, which emphasized not humility but magnanimity. That strain has typically not preached humility. Humility was seen in classical Greece and during the Roman Empire as a quality of slaves—hence, not admirable but forced on one by one's social circumstances.

But as the two strains have intermingled, the Abrahamic-religion adherents picked up more of the out-front leader-oriented magnanimous characteristics, and their humility became more muted. Simultaneously, the secular strain inevitably responded by incorporating some humility and muting magnanimity.

Judaism and Humility

Moses is the founder of Judaism. The Torah (Num 12:3) emphasizes Moses' humility, describing him as the most humble of people. But it is not until Moses Maimonides that humility receives much attention in Judaism (Porter et al., 2017). Maimonides codified virtue ethics into Jewish law. For Maimonides, most moral truths are aimed at a Golden Mean between two extremes—a nod to Aristotle's influence of Maimonides. But Maimonides (1998) differs from Aristotle with respect to humility. "If a man is only humble, he is not following a good path. Rather, he must hold himself lowly and his spirit very unassuming. . . . [The person must be] 'very humble' and not simply 'humble'." (as quoted in Porter et al., 2017). Maimonides teaches that humility is not utter self-denigration or considering oneself worthless. Other Jewish writers consider humility to presuppose healthy self-esteem and pride in spiritual development (see Porter et al., 2017, for accounts). Low self-esteem is at the root of arrogance. Judaism considers human beings able to grow spiritually, and it demands humility-flavored growth from its believers.

Moses is an exemplar of humility even though he was raised in a royal Egyptian household. His own commission of murder and 40 years of herding sheep and goats shaped him in humility. When God called Moses to return to Egypt to demand that the Pharaoh free the Israelites from captivity, Moses at first demurred. Later, he became an able advocate and representative of God. The Israelites were freed, and Moses became the leader-in-wandering for 40 additional years. His lifetime of brokenness had led him to humility.

Christianity and Humility

Humility is at the core of Christianity. At the outset of Christianity, Christians regarded Jesus's death on the cross as, at once, an act of love, the pathway of God's forgiveness to humans, and an act of humble serving as inspiration and model for Christian believers (Porter et al., 2017). The apostle Paul encouraged Philippian Christians to "do nothing from selfish ambition or conceit, but in humility count others more significant than yourselves" (Phil. 2:3). He claims Jesus's humble incarnation and humble acceptance of death is *the* model of humility that Christians should emulate. Furthermore, it is not just the incarnation that illustrates Jesus's humility. Jesus's incarnation, life, teachings, death, resurrection, ascension, and glory all tell the same story of humility—trust in God, who will bless and work through an empty receptive vessel. Thus, Christians are urged to experience humility before God and to allow that experience to empower a life of service to others.

The importance of humility permeates Christian theologies. However, theologians like Thomas and Augustine differed on their emphasis on humility (Porter et al., 2017). Thomas (ST II-II, 161) suggested that humility tempers our aspirations so that we do not aim beyond our ability. Augustine saw Jesus's humility as the most important principle of ethics and metaphysics. Jesus's humble willingness to become human and serve as a sacrifice for people's sin allows people eternal fellowship with God. For Augustine, humility was necessary for becoming a Christian. Throughout the ages, Christians treated humility toward God as essential and humility toward others as flowing from that. Humility, love, and forgiveness are Christianity's three main virtues.

The primary example of heroic humility in Christian Scriptures is Jesus. His humility was shown throughout his entire life. But let us look also at Paul as a model of heroic humility. Paul is the person who did the most to spread Christianity through the Middle East after Jesus died. Paul was preaching in

Philippi when he was arrested. That night, he was in his cell, singing, and an earthquake sprung the doors of the prison. When the guard saw this, he drew his sword, thinking the prisoners had escaped, and was about to kill himself. Most people would have just allowed the suicide and then walked out of the open prison. Not Paul. He called out that the prisoners had not escaped, literally laying down his life for the jailer. That example of other-oriented humility led the jailer to become a Christian. So, when Paul's later letter to the Philippians addressed humility, his audience had seen Paul's humility with their own eyes. Following Jesus's example of risking death, Paul had laid down his life for others—even a person holding him prisoner. That living out of humility supplemented and complemented Paul's teaching on humility.

Islam and Humility

Humility is a central virtue in Islam (Porter et al., 2017). Within the Qur'ān and in Muslim tradition, humility is opposed to arrogance. Early in the revelation to Muḥammad, we read that people tend to "transgress all bounds," because they are deluded into believing in their self-sufficiency (*istighnā'*) [96:6]. Satan rebelled against God due to arrogance (*istikbār*) [2:34]. And the historical record shows that Pharaoh was overcome by arrogance [28:39]. The Qur'ān notes that *God does not love those who are arrogant, full of conceit* [4:36]. Arrogance is a deal-breaker. One hadith says, "No one in whose heart resides a mustard seed of arrogance shall enter Paradise" (*Muslim*, 1415/1995, 1:89; as quoted in Porter et al., 2017).

Humility begins when people acknowledge that they are dependent on and submissive to God. In fact, the act of *islām* means "humble submission" (Porter et al., 2017). Yet, even believers who seek to be submissive to God might not be humble people.

In Muslim tradition, humility helps people be more perceptive and understanding. God is unlikely to grant those who lack humility keen understanding (Porter et al., 2017). There is a twofold track to develop and maintain humility and make it grow. (a) One must first eschew arrogance by acknowledging God's majesty in light of flawed humanity. (b) One must not allow external forces to despoil whatever humility one experiences. Copying the Prophet, the primary example of humility (*al-Iḥyā'*, N.d., 3:348–58), is the recommended path to humility (Porter et al., 2017).

History reveals many humble Muslims as exemplars, beginning with Muhammad. The prototypical example of Muhammad's humility (and forgiveness) is his triumphant return to Mecca after years of exile. He did not exact vengeance but showed mercy. Another example of heroic humility is Saladin (1137–1193). Salah ad-Din Yusuf ibn Ayyub reigned as Sultan of Egypt (and after conquering it) and Syria from 1174 to 1193. His rise to power was unique. He was a Sunni who was made vizier of Egypt in a Shiite caliphate. He led the Muslims during the Crusades. He is often juxtaposed against British king, Richard the Lionhearted. Despite being at war, Saladin was admired even in Europe as a man of humility, integrity, and honor (Safi, 2010). When Richard the Lionhearted once had a fever, Saladin sent fruits and ice. Saladin was not only religious, a leader, and a warrior. He also founded universities and hospitals, stipulating that they not bear his name. He died in Damascus in 1193, founder of a new dynasty, yet having given away much of his personal wealth to the people under him (Lyons & Jackson, 1982).

RELIGIOUS HUMILITY—HUMILITY AND EASTERN RELIGIONS

Humility is not neglected in the Eastern religions. Hinduism and Buddhism also value humility.

Hinduism and Humility

In Porter et al. (2017), Rambachan summarized humility from a Hindu perspective. He argued that the Bhagavadgītā (13:7), which is usually taken as a pillar of sacred writing within the Hinduism, extols humility. Humility is the first of virtues mentioned by the teacher, Krishna. The Bhagavadgītā also describes a learned person (*paṇḍitāḥ*) as rich in humility (5:18) and a liberated person as without ego (*nirahaṁkāraḥ*). In the Hindu tradition, humility is not self-denigration (6:5).

Humility springs from recognition of our dependence on the universe (Porter et al., 2017). In Hindu tradition, people live as indebted to God, teachers, ancestors, nature, and other people. People can grow in humility and decrease in self-sufficient arrogance by acknowledging our constant debt to others.

Mohandas Gandhi (1869–1948) was a leader of the independence movement in India's struggle against the British, and he became one of the most recognized exemplars of heroic humility. He was born into the Hindu merchant class, trained as an attorney in England, and worked as a civil rights activist in South Africa from 1893 to 1914, where he began to develop his philosophy of nonviolent resistance. In 1915, he returned to India. Amazingly, he had no formal platform of leadership, no presidency, no elected position. Yet, through his moral courage and willingness to take on the powers and argue his case publicly, even suffering many years of imprisonment, he won the hearts of the people. They adopted his principles of nonviolence, and eventually, in 1947, Britain granted India freedom. Gandhi had always worked for religious toleration in an India with a majority of Hindus but Muslim and Christian minorities. However, Britain split off Pakistan as a Muslim state when freedom was granted India. In 1948, he participated in a hunger strike attempting to promote religious harmony between India and Pakistan. Part of that strike was intended to pressure India to repay a monetary debt to Pakistan, and that enraged some extremists, leading to his assassination a few days later.

When asked about his beliefs in 1936, he replied with typical humility.

> I do not want to leave any sect after me. I do not claim to have originated any new principle or doctrine. I have simply tried in my own way to apply the eternal truths to our daily life and problems. . . . The opinions I have formed and conclusions I have arrived at are not final. I may change them tomorrow. I have nothing new to teach the world. Truth and nonviolence are as old as the hills. (Kamath, 2007, p. 195)

Buddhism and Humility

Buddhism has a different take on humility. Humility is seen as freedom from conceit, which is one of the 10 fetters (*saṃyojana*) that prevents beings from being freed from suffering (Porter et al., 2017). Conceit is one of five highest fetters. One can defeat conceit only by achieving the highest level of spiritual development (*arahantship*). At that point, all craving disappears. Buddhist humility involves proper conduct toward people worthy of respect and honor such as parents, and an accurate knowledge of one's limitations (Porter et al., 2017). Buddhist humility involves giving up three conceits—"I am equal, better, or worse" than others. Buddhist humility is interrelated with nonself. The illusion of a permanent self leads to disputes. It is the basis of self-centered, selfish, conceit. To develop humility, the Buddha recommended meditation. The Buddhist is to develop the Noble Eightfold Path (S.V.56) "for direct knowledge of the three kinds of conceits, for their full understanding (*abhiññā*), for their utter destruction, for their abandoning" (as quoted in Porter et al., 2017).

Perhaps the figure who comes to mind readily as a heroically humble exemplar of Buddhist philosophy is the Dalai Lama. He has been a tireless worker throughout the world for peace—both in nations and in individuals. His message is to practice compassionate Buddhism, thus seeking to live out one's compassion toward all.

Syntheses of Eastern Religion and Secular Psychology

Popularizers and synthesizers exist. For instance, Gregory (2014) took a largely Hindu approach to humility, but also drew from Chinese masters (e.g., Lao-tzu, Chuang-tzu, Lieh-tzu, and Confucius), Hindu masters like Krisha and Rama, and Gautama the Buddha. He even drew lessons from Jesus and Muhammad. Modern masters like Sri Ramana Maharshi, Thích Nhat Hanh, and the Dalai Lama were also consulted.

In addition, Whitfield, Whitfield, Park, and Prevatt (2006) drew on a new-age philosophy, transpersonal and recovery psychology, and *A Course in Miracles*, to create a practical amalgam of psychology and religion in their approach to humility. It describes how to handle conflict in three relationships: with self, others, and a Higher Power. It is organized around four levels of triangles. These are Level 1 (conflict; victim, rescuer, and persecutor); Level 2 (co-commitment; empowered self, nurturer, and motivator); Level 3 (co-creator; creativity, love and expansion, energy-movement-vibration); and Level 4 (unity; creator, Christ consciousness, Holy Spirit vibratory bliss). A humility continuum moves from false self to true self to higher self to Higher Power, for the four levels respectively.

RELIGIOUS HUMILITY—HUMILITY AND SECULAR PHILOSOPHY

Taking a position that one does not adhere to a religious belief system is paradoxically a type of religious position. It sets one's ideas as often incompatible with ideas in explicit religious systems and can lead to religious discussions and disagreements.

Humility was not regarded as a virtue by the ancient Greeks. Humility was described as a vice by David Hume and Friedrich Nietzsche. In *Secular Powers*, Cooper (2013) recounted a "received view" of the history of the philosophy of humility, especially in political philosophy. It begins with Aristotle and moves to Augustine and Christian philosophers like Thomas Aquinas, but it majors in the views of Hobbes, who secularizes the understanding of humility and then onward to Hume, Spinoza, Rousseau, and Nietzsche, who send secular philosophy of humility into a progressively descending spiral of disfavor. The view developed that humility was weak at best and pernicious or vicious at worst.

Other more modern philosophers such as Comte-Sponville (1996) have been less negative, seeing humility as something that one might perform as a duty (hence a constraint against freedom) and yet come to enjoy it as a freedom with enough of the right kinds of practice. He tried to find a balance between Kant's observation, "Whoever makes himself a worm cannot complain when he is then trampled underfoot," (Kant, 1964, p. 100) and Comte-Sponville's own rejoinder, "But whoever would make himself a statue—be it for the glory of man or the sake of the law—cannot complain when he is suspected of being hard-hearted or assuming a pose. Better the sublime beggar who washes the sinner's feet" (Comte-Sponville, 1996, p. 145).

Cooper (2013) sought to rethink the history of the philosophy of humility. She attempted to recapture from Hobbes, Spinoza, and Rousseau an idea that she claimed had been lost in the modern and postmodern retelling of their positions. Their acknowledgement of human limitations does not imply weakness, she argued, but in fact is a needed aspect of realizing full power. Unwilling to oppose humility and pride against each other, as Augustine did or to accept that modern philosophy is aimed at the deification of human will, she tried to construct an alternative (to the "received view") history of the philosophy of humility that she dubbed secular power. She claimed that humble awareness of human limitations helps a society become stronger by seeking ways to overcome the limitations. For Cooper, humility is a forgotten, yet promising, road to a more powerful society and, if applied to individuals, more powerful people.

OBSERVATIONS ABOUT RELIGIOUS PERSPECTIVES

In Porter et al. (2017), after each scholar had described his section, Porter drew conclusions. He summarized four insights from the summaries of the religious traditions' views of humility.

First, he observed that humility is recognized and appreciated within all five major religious traditions. However, there was not a common religious motivation to value humility despite all five religions valuing humility (Woodruff, Van Tongeren, McElroy, Davis, & Hook, 2014). Instead, each religion advanced its own reasons to advocate that its adherents embrace humility.

Second, Porter observed that according to the five leading world religions, humility is both important to each and necessary so that believers in each will flourish. Humility was not seen as peripheral or optional. Rather, it is considered to be the fitting posture of humans. Confucius succinctly summarized, "Humility is the solid foundation of all virtues." That insight has been echoed from Augustine to the Buddha. This suggests what we saw in the chapter on humility, virtues, and vices (Chapter 4)—that humility should be expected to be positively correlated with virtues—especially other-oriented ones—and negatively correlated with vices.

Third, the world religions agreed that humility involves an accurate view of self, not one too high or too low. Humility is based on the knowledge that there is something outside of both the self and the universe. That transcendent reality, however it is conceived across religions, gives ultimate meaning to existence. Thus, one owes deference to something beyond the self.

Fourth, all religions suggest that humility might not be fully fostered outside of a religious context. Porter noted that this does not mean that religious people will necessarily be more humble than nonreligious people nor that nonreligious people cannot be humble. Instead, he suggested that religious perspectives argue that humility is coherently located within a religious worldview (see Bollinger & Hill, 2012). We might observe, however, that many philosophers have disagreed (Church & Barrett, 2017; Cooper, 2013; J. G. Murphy, 2017; Roberts & Cleveland, 2017). Most philosophical approaches to humility are grounded in human finitude; the equality of humanity; and the necessity to fit into a large, complex world that often defies human understanding.

WHAT DOES RESEARCH SHOW ABOUT HUMILITY AND RELIGION/SPIRITUALITY?

Leach and Ajibade (2017) recently reviewed the empirical research on humility and its connections with religion and spirituality (R/S). They described the status of research as in its infancy. A systematic search for empirical studies yielded 83 quantitative and qualitative studies. Still, that is almost an order of magnitude more than studies on health and humility.

Humility and R/S

Research has shown that R/S is often correlated with humility (e.g., Exline & Geyer, 2004; Exline & Hill, 2012; Hopkin, Hoyle, & Toner, 2014; Rowatt, Kang, Haggard, & LaBouff, 2014). Exline and Geyer (2004) found humility to be generally viewed as a strength that was associated with more religiousness and better psychological adjustment—in short, as something desirable. Researchers are now studying these relationships in other faith communities, including with Roman Catholics and Muslims. Rowatt et al. (2014) opined that humility in religious teachings might seek to combat self-righteousness. Higher levels of humility have predicted less intense reaction to others' supportive and contrary opinions about one's religious beliefs (Hopkin, Hoyle, & Toner, 2014). Rowatt et al. (2014) also found that increases in self-reported humility, other-rated humility, and self-reported R/S were all three positively correlated.

Krause has repeatedly investigated R/S and humility. In the chapter on health, we reviewed Krause (2010, 2012). Krause and Hayward (2015) used the same data base and found that more frequent church attenders got more spiritual support, leading to more trust in and a closer relationship with God. In turn, that led to feeling awe toward God and thus more spiritual humility.

Also, more religiously committed people were more humble, which supports Worthington, Goldstein, et al.'s (in press) spirituality hypothesis. In addition, people who were less humble tended to have more negative interactions in the church.

Religious people perceive of humility differently and appear to value it more than do nonreligious people. For example, in three studies, Van Tongeren, Davis, Hook, Rowatt, and Worthington (2017) examined whether religious and nonreligious people understood humility differently. In Study 1, 361 students were surveyed. Religious respondents described themselves as more humble than did nonreligious respondents. Van Tongeren et al. used Amazon Mechanical Turk to amass two community samples of 180 and 112, respectively, that they reported in Study 2. Van Tongeren et al. used a prime of humility. The prime affected people differently depending on their religious affiliation. The experimenters criticized the participants. Religious participants primed with humility reported less likelihood of retaliating. Religious respondents more strongly valued being referred to as humble. Using 254 participants in Study 3, Van Tongeren et al. found a main effect for humility in reducing defensiveness—but did not find differences based on religiousness.

Humility, Forgiveness, and R/S

Humility affects relationships in the context of religion. Humble people are supported more by others (Exline, 2012), are more generous to others (Exline & Hill, 2012), and have better relationships with others (Peters, Rowatt, & Johnson, 2011). Like humility, forgiveness can lead to better relationships. We suggest that humble people, who are both other-oriented and have an accurate picture of their own contributions to offenses, might be more forgiving and seek revenge or hold onto grudges less (see D. E. Davis, Hook, Worthington, Van Tongeren, Gartner, & Jennings, 2010). Dispositional forgivingness in Christians acted through humility to produce lower levels of depression (Jankowski, Sandage, & Hill, 2013). Humility was directly related to forgiveness for Christians, and Ayten (2012) found the same for Turkish Muslims. D. E. Davis, Hook, Worthington, Van Tongeren, Gartner, Jennings, and Norton (2010; see also D. E. Davis et al., 2013) found relational humility to be key to forming and maintaining relationships, often acting to repair relationship damage through more likelihood of forgiving. McElroy et al. (2014) found that appraisals of intellectual humility were positively related to parishioners' forgiveness of religious leaders after an offense. Overall, humility and forgiveness seem to be related in religious people, though at this point findings are limited to Christians and Muslims.

Humility, Personality and Social Psychological Relationships, and R/S

Religiousness is usually associated with the high agreeableness [A] and high conscientiousness [C] within the Five-Factor model of personality. However, by adding the HH factor, Ashton and Lee (2005, 2007, 2009) have shown that HH accounts for additional variance in religiousness after variance for A and C have been removed. This has also been found with Iranian Muslims (Aghababaei, Mohammadtabar, & Saffarinia, 2014). Participants higher in humility were more likely to describe religion as important to them, have less negative attitudes toward religious institutions, and more literally adhere to religious institutions and doctrine (Silvia, Nusbaum, & Beaty, 2014). Low humility may affect one's faith—predicting divine struggles, religious guilt, and religious fear (Grubbs & Exline, 2014). But an insecure relationship with God (or others) predicts fear, shame, self-regulation difficulties, and low humility (for reviews, see Worthington & Sandage, 2016).

Intellectual humility around religious beliefs, values, and practices is difficult because religious beliefs are imbued with sanctity by many. Van Tongeren, Davis, and Hook (2014) studied Christians who were challenged on their views of a strongly felt topic by an interaction partner described as an ingroup or an outgroup member. Humility was assessed as less defensiveness, presumably because intellectually humble individuals were assumed to be more open to alternative perspectives. Van Tongeren et al. found that humility could be increased when people had more affirming relationships with others.

In 2016, Aghababaei et al. conducted five studies using a total of 1,375 participants from Iran, Malaysia, and Poland to test whether religiousness was more strongly related to Honesty–Humility than to Agreeableness, which had been previously found. Honesty–Humility was more highly correlated with religiousness than the Big Five, though both agreeableness and conscientiousness were highly related also. Extraversion was somewhat related to religiousness. Aghababaei et al. suggested that the personality characteristics associated with religiousness were relatively consistent across models and measures. Honesty–Humility was consistently related to measures of psychological well-being but not as consistently related to measures of subjective well-being. Given that those constructs are typically strongly correlated, this might have more to say about the sample, which was heavily Muslim, rather than to the measures. Thurackal, Corveleyn, and Dezutter (2016) also examined the Big Five and honesty–humility as predictors of self-compassion. They sampled Roman Catholic and Indian seminarians ($N = 494$) and nonseminarians ($N = 504$). They compared the two samples. Mean levels were higher for seminarians on all variables except neuroticism (e.g., emotional reactivity). Thurackal et al. thus analyzed the samples independently of each other. Consciousness, agreeableness, extraversion, openness to experience, and neuroticism (negatively) were related to self-compassion. Honesty–humility was moderately positively correlated with self-compassion.

Honesty–humility has been repeatedly shown to be a personality disposition related to religiousness. However, once specific beliefs, values, and opinions are considered, things become more complicated. Hoyle, Davisson, Diebels, and Leary (2016) investigated specific religious beliefs and a specific measure of intellectual humility. Religious humility is one type of intellectual humility. Hoyle et al. developed a general measure of intellectual humility that could be modified by inserting words dealing with various specific beliefs—religious, political, scientific, and the like. In Study 1, they reported the development of the scale. In Study 2, they established measurement invariance and provided evidence of both convergent and discriminant validity. In Study 3, they showed that the measure was not just associated with beliefs about religion, but applied to intellectual humility across a broad spectrum of beliefs. It is important to note that they showed that intellectual humility was more specific than merely being related to personality. Rather, it depended also on how extreme the belief or opinion was that one was discussing. The degree of intellectual humility was also based on the foundation of the belief and its degree of evidential support (including the value of different type of evidence).

One reason that religious people might hold a sense of openness in religious sharing of their religious beliefs is that religious humility might be related to reduced prejudice toward outgroup members. Van Tongeren et al. (2016) conducted three studies to test that assertion. They reasoned that part of humility is regulating self-enhancing motives in service of others. They conducted three studies to evaluate the extent to which humility reduced negative attitudes, behavioral intentions, and behaviors toward religious outgroup members. In Study 1 ($N = 159$), humility about one's religious beliefs was associated with more positive attitudes toward people who adhered to other religions. In Study 2 ($N = 149$), Van Tongeren et al. used a hypothetical situation in which people imagined important beliefs to be criticized. Relational and intellectual humility were associated with less aggressive behavioral intentions. In Study 3 ($N = 62$), people were implicitly primed with humility. They gave less hot sauce (a behavioral measure of aggression) to a religious outgroup member who criticized their cherished views relative to participants in the neutral prime condition.

SOME QUESTIONS RAISED BY THE EMPIRICAL LITERATURE

Most research on religion and humility has been published within the past 5 years. Leach and Ajibade (2017) reviewed 83 studies on religion or spirituality and humility that had been published through the end of 2015. Despite that number of published studies, a research agenda is still wide open.

An Abbreviated Research Agenda

Leach and Ajibade (2017) suggested that there is a need to compare religious believers of various faith perspectives with each other. In addition, religious people of various faith traditions should be compared with people who do not embrace religion and with people who consider themselves spiritual but not religious. Leach and Ajibade also recommended a simultaneous consideration of how race and ethnicity affects the comparisons across faith traditions.

A Brief Philosophical Riff

Hopkin, Hoyle, and Toner (2014) explored how people high in intellectual humility respond to messages from others that match or don't match their religious beliefs. Hopkin et al. found religious humility, a form of intellectual humility regarding religious ideas, was illustrated by understanding that religious beliefs might be fallible, practicing discretion in asserting those beliefs, being comfortable with keeping religious beliefs private, and being respectful of others' beliefs. This is a recent shift in understanding of religious humility. Previously, religious humility was thought to involve holding firmly to one's beliefs, values, and practices, being bold in stating them while being respectful of others' right to hold their different beliefs equally strongly. G. K. Chesterton chided this newer view of humility back in 1959.

> What we suffer from today is humility in the wrong place. Modesty has moved from the organ of ambition. Modesty has settled upon the organ of conviction; where it was never meant to be. [People were] meant to be doubtful about [themselves] but undoubting about the truth. This has been exactly reversed. . . . We are on the road to producing a race of men too mentally modest to believe in the multiplication table. (pp. 31–32)

Mouw (2010) in *Uncommon Decency: Christian Civility in an Uncivil World*, provided advice in contradistinction to the findings of Hopkin et al. (2014). Mouw advocated convicted civility. Listeners consider each other empathically. Thus, when people have acted uncivilly, apologies and forgiveness seeking are recommended. Mouw advocated careful hearing and speaking in a way that respects differences. People who follow those recommendations will more likely behave civilly—with "public politeness . . . tact, moderation, refinement and good manners towards people who are different from us" (p. 14). Mouw noted that people do not need to approve of others' views or like them as people. Instead, we commit ourselves to merely listen respectfully. Rather than the *Zeitgeist* revealed in Hopkin et al.—softening one's beliefs because one believes they are fallible, self-censoring expression of one's beliefs by being discrete in their expression or keeping them to oneself, and being respectful of others' beliefs—Mouw zeroes in on respect for others and special care in expressing what we firmly believe.

How did this generally accepted philosophical change occur? As Worthington (2017) argued in an essay on political humility, Charles Taylor (2007) articulated a modern understanding of secularism in *A Secular Age*. How is it, Taylor poses, that in the year 1500, virtually all people were religious, but by the end of the 20th century, almost none were? In 1500 selves were seen as vulnerable to attack by demons, spirits, situations, and powerful human agents. Modernity saw the self as impermeable and disengaged. This is what Chesterton urged against—people who are divorced from their own minds, the world, and others. In the mid- to late-1900s, when modernity was underway but postmodernism had not gained traction, people ordered life without God, not to dethrone God and assume self-sovereignty, but as a protected feeling. People felt that an encapsulated self protects them from attack. For secular people, pride was okay, not a sinful curse with which Augustine had tarred it.

Since Chesterton's (1959) critique, we have moved from modernity to a place where modernity and postmodernity intersect. A postmodern person doesn't believe that people can be completely impermeable and disengaged from their own minds, the external world, and other people. Rather, in postmodernism people live in co-constructed interdependent worlds. They are affected by other cultures, people, and situations (Gergen, 2015), which Taylor (2007) saw as by nature diverse. Because all views are culture bound, Taylor argued that no side can assemble a perfectly evidence-supported case. Being humble is thus a realistic, pragmatic stance. All arguments are vulnerable to critique, so people feel that their own arguments also are fragile. Dogmatic self-assertion is foolish, and humility is likely *the* virtue for the secular age. This fits with postmodern values, which are seen as contextualized within communities. Diversity is embraced, because reality is different in different communities. None is *ipso facto* superior.

A PARTING REFLECTION FOR ALL OF US

In a book on humility and in a chapter on the particular types of intellectual humility focusing on religious and philosophical humility, we cannot resist the temptation to close with one of Jesus's parables from Luke 18: 10–14 (NIV). It is a cautionary tale as we read about the beliefs of other religions and philosophical systems and ponder our own beliefs. We recount this because it reveals our own tendency to judge. Hopefully it will repay our joint reflection.

> To some who were confident of their own righteousness and looked down on everybody else, Jesus told this parable:
>
> "Two men went up to the temple to pray, one a Pharisee and the other a tax collector. The Pharisee stood up and prayed about himself: 'God, I thank you that I am not like other men—robbers, evildoers, adulterers—or even like this tax collector. I fast twice a week and give a tenth of all I get.'
>
> "But the tax collector stood at a distance. He would not even look up to the heaven but beat his breast and said, 'God, have mercy on me a sinner.'
>
> "I tell you that this man, rather than the other, went home justified before God. For everyone who exalts himself will be humbled, and he who humbles himself will be exalted."

Of course, as we ponder this, we see the deeper level of application, for as we hear the parable unfold, we find ourselves thinking, *I am so glad I'm not like that Pharisee*, and we can become convinced that humility really is hard to maintain.

WHAT DID WE LEARN IN THIS CHAPTER?

1. All major religions value and encourage believers to experience humility—both before the Sacred and to other humans.
2. All major religions have a different understanding, context, and emphasis on it.
3. Research on religion and spirituality and humility has suggested that humility is related to many aspects associated with religion and spirituality.

THREE QUESTIONS FOR THOUGHT AND DISCUSSION

1. Are the five major religious perspectives very similar or very far apart on their view of what humility and how to practice it?
2. The five religions argue that humility needs to be contextualized within a religious framework for optimal experience. We observed that there are counterarguments. On which side do you fall?
3. Do you think Charles Taylor's explanation that humility is the virtue for the 21st century is supported by accurate analysis?

7

HUMILITY, SOCIETY, AND LIFE SATISFACTION

On July 18, 1918, in a small village on the banks of the Mbashe River in what is now South Africa, a baby named Rolihlahla was born. In Xhosa, that meant "pulling the branch of a tree," which, colloquially understood, meant "troublemaker" (Hort & Brown, 2006, p. 6). That baby became an exemplar of heroic humility who eventually changed his own society and the world. That was Nelson Mandela.

Mandela's father was a chief who forfeited his position as chief on a matter of principle. He refused to attend court in front of a British magistrate because he did not believe that his tribe was governed by British law. Suddenly poor, Nelson moved with his mother to a poor village and grew up in a mud hut. His father sent him for schooling at a missionary school, generally for White boys. Although Mandela believed at first he would be a star pupil, his lifelong realism—his accuracy of self-assessment—quickly kicked in. "Most of my classmates could outrun me on the playing field and outthink me in the classroom" (Hort & Brown, 2006, p. 14).

http://dx.doi.org/10.1037/0000079-008
Heroic Humility: What the Science of Humility Can Say to People Raised on Self-Focus, by E. L. Worthington Jr. and S. T. Allison

Reaching adulthood, he moved to Johannesburg, entered a law practice, and boxed for 90 minutes every weekday to stay in shape. He became convinced of the evil of apartheid, and he joined the African National Congress (ANC) in spite of its association with communists. As an early leader in the ANC's fight against apartheid, he spent many a night in jail. On December 5, 1956, he was arrested for treason and, after 5 years, declared innocent.

However, in 1962, he was tried again for inciting workers to strike and for leaving the country without a passport. He was convicted, incarcerated first in Pretoria for 6 months, and later transferred to Robben Island, 8 miles off of the coast of Capetown. He was not released for 22 years. Life on Robben Island provided conversations by many political prisoners, especially after the Soweto (a township outside of Johannesburg) Uprising began on June 16, 1976, which eventually left over 1,000 dead. Political prisoners from the struggles against apartheid populated the prison.

As time passed, the pressure on the South African government mounted. Prime Minister Botha offered Mandela a deal: his freedom for the pledge that he would not advocate violence. Mandela sent his reply in writing to his daughter, Zindzi, who read it on February 10, 1985, before a packed stadium in Soweto. He wrote,

> I am not a violent man. Let [Botha] renounce violence. Let him say that he will dismantle Apartheid. . . . I cherish my freedom dearly, but I care even more for your freedom. . . . Only free men can negotiate. Prisoners cannot enter into contracts. . . . I cannot and will not give any undertaking at a time when I and you, the people, are not free. Your freedom and mine cannot be separated. I will return. (Mandela, 1994, p. 523)

On February 11, 1990, Mandela was freed. His freedom speech was humble.

> Friends, comrades, and fellow South Africans. I greet you all in the name of peace, democracy, and freedom for all! Your tireless and heroic sacrifices have made it possible for me to be here today. I therefore place the remaining years of my life in your hands. (Mandela, 1994, pp. 565–566)

Later, as he began to deal with press conferences, he was the essence of modesty. "When asked what role I would play in the organization, I told the press that I would play whatever role the ANC ordered" (Mandela, 1994, p. 568). He was still other-oriented toward the Whites who had kept him prisoner for 22 years.

> I wanted to impress upon the reporters the critical role of whites in any new dispensation. . . . From my very first press conference I noticed that journalists were eager to learn about my personal feelings and relationships as my political thoughts. . . . I nevertheless found their curiosity difficult to satisfy. I am not and never have been a man who finds it easy to talk about his personal feelings in public. (Mandela, 1994, pp. 568–569)

His long-time friend, Oliver Tambo, had been head of the ANC while Mandela was imprisoned. He visited him in Stockholm.

> "Nelson," he said, "you must now take over as president of the ANC. I have been merely keeping the job warm for you." I refused, telling him that he had led the organization in exile far better than I ever could have. It was neither fair nor democratic for a transfer to occur in such a manner. "You have been elected by the organization as the president," I said. "Let us wait for an election; then the organization can decide." Oliver protested. But I would not budge. It was a sign of his humility and selflessness that he wanted to appoint me president, but it was not in keeping with the principles of the ANC. (Mandela, 1994, p. 574)

Ten days before the elections in 1994, de Klerk and Mandela held a television debate and exchanged some sharp criticisms. But, at the end of the debate, Mandela said,

> The exchanges between Mr. de Klerk and me should not obscure one important fact. I think we are a shining example to the entire world of people drawn from different racial groups who have a common loyalty, a common love, their common country. . . . [Mandela looked at de Klerk] "Sir, you are one of those I rely upon. We are going to face the problem of this country together." [Mandela takes his hand] "I am proud to hold your hand, for us to go forward." (Mandela, 1994, p. 617)

A humble leader can change a country. A humble leader can affect the world.

THE SOCIETAL PEACE HYPOTHESIS

Humble societal leaders can affect society and even the world. They are on a grand stage. Can everyday humility affect society? There are a number of indications that it can. The societal peace hypothesis is that a society composed of many humble citizens will likely be less combative (because fewer people will take offense due to awareness of their own limitations), and they will likely present their own position modestly, instead of provocatively. Their orientation toward the good of others will lead to valuing social justice and diversity more. Basically, if social transformation occurs, increasing people's willingness to embrace humility across society, then we anticipate that society itself will be changed. Perhaps the whole will be greater than the sum of its parts. That is, to the extent that social worldviews shift, we might expect that social norms might shift, affecting not just a few individuals but even people who were not originally humble.

Worthington, Goldstein, et al. (in press) located 10 studies that have addressed this hypothesis. Tests of this hypothesis have addressed disparate societal influences. For example, one study related humility to proenvironment attitudes (Hilbig, Zettler, Moshagen, & Heydasch, 2013). Violence is always a problem in societies. Studies have shown that humility in adolescents has resulted in less bullying, responding aggressively, or acting out as delinquents (Book, Volk, & Hosker, 2012). In adults, humility has been related to less likelihood of engaging in workplace deviance (Oh, Lee, Ashton, & De Vries, 2011). Humility has been found to be related to less music piracy (Brown & MacDonald, 2014). Surveying 716 Dutch citizens, Van Gelder and De Vries (2012) found that humility was related to making fewer criminal choices. The evidence supports that highly humble people fit society well.

Like Nelson Mandela, leaders are so often those with the heroic humility to persevere in humility—often into imprisonment (e.g., Jesus, Thomas More, Gandhi, Mandela, Martin Luther King Jr.), or even unto death (e.g., Jesus, More, Gandhi, and King). But, their life is about lifting others up; it is not about their own comfort, or even their own freedom. They have a dream, as Martin Luther King Jr. most eloquently described it in his address at the Lincoln Memorial on August 23, 1963. He closed like this:

> I have a dream today. I have a dream that one day every valley shall be exalted, every hill and mountain shall be made low, the rough places will be made plain, and the crooked places will be made straight, and the glory of the Lord shall be revealed, and all flesh shall see it together. This is our hope. . . . Knowing that we will be free one day. . . . When we let freedom ring, when we let it ring from every village and every hamlet, from every state and every city, we will be able to speed up that day when all of God's children, black men and white men, Jews and Gentiles, Protestants and Catholics, will be able to join hands and sing in the words of the old Negro spiritual, "Free at last! Free at last! Thank God Almighty, we are free at last!" (Safire, 1997, pp. 535–536)

King was born January 15, 1929, and raised in Atlanta. He received a PhD from Boston University in 1955, went to jail often, received the Nobel Peace Prize in 1964, and was assassinated April 4, 1968. A happy life? Probably not one we might seek if we equate happiness with a run of good times—but a life that was societally transforming and ultimately satisfying.

THE ULTIMATE SATISFACTION HYPOTHESIS

The ultimate satisfaction hypothesis is that humility will ultimately help people feel their life is satisfying. Although they might not be temporally happier than others, humility will make people content. Sometimes that will correlate with being happier; sometimes not. Humble people might not seek immediate pleasure. People might reject them. Or they might sacrifice excessively for others (e.g., care of older people with dementia)—but even in those cases, they will rate their lives as more satisfying than others.

A great example of this attitude is Albert Schweitzer (1875–1965). Schweitzer was a polymath—a philosopher, historian, biblical scholar, musician, writer, and adventurer. He was Indiana Jones before there was *Indiana Jones*. He started a theological movement with his *The Quest for the Historical Jesus*. At the peak of productivity, he became a physician in Gabon, West Africa. In 1952, he was awarded the Nobel Prize for his work on reverence for life. He believed that humans were not respecting life and not trying to balance all people's will to live. Of course, he gave the money from the Nobel Prize to establish the Albert Schweitzer Hospital, a leper hospital in Lamboréné (now Gabon). "Only a person . . . who has no thought of heroism, but only of a duty undertaken with sober enthusiasm, is capable of becoming the sort of spiritual pioneer the world needs," he wrote in his autobiography. "There are not heroes of action—only heroes of renunciation and suffering" (Schweitzer, 1998, pp. 88–89).

Earlier, we found that humility is not consistently related to happiness (see Chapter 5). We did not expect a completely null relationship because humility was hypothesized to make people satisfied with their lives, and often that will also correlate with being happier. But not always. Imagine people giving care to elders with dementia, for example. Even in those cases, those humble helpers will rate their lives as more satisfying than others. Those are the "heroes of renunciation and suffering" (p. 88) that Schweitzer spoke of.

Seven studies have presented data that addressed the ultimate satisfaction hypothesis. Although measures of ultimate satisfaction have included things such as academic performance, self-control in exercise, and the like, Visser and Pozzebon (2013) investigated 166 Canadian undergraduate students in one sample and 409 Canadian undergraduate students in another. They found that the Canadian students' humility predicted the positivity of their life aspirations. Not all studies have supported such findings. For example, in Iran, Aghababaei (2013) found that honesty–humility was an important element for understanding social behaviors and interpersonal outcomes, but it was not the most central to personal feelings of happiness and life satisfaction.

Humility is a virtue that draws us to embrace it—as do all virtues—for self-interested reasons. But not merely for self-interested reasons. We have seen in earlier chapters that social and religious or spiritual motives might be the major motivators that pull people to become more humble. But there is a bud of research on societal benefits of humility. And there is a bud of research on ways that humility can contribute to life that is ultimately satisfying, a life that contributes to causes greater than promoting things of temporal importance to us. We would love to see researchers make these two areas a priority for the next wave of humility research.

AN EXAMPLE AFFECTING SOCIETY IN WHICH HUMILITY WAS NOT RELATED TO HAPPINESS BUT TO ULTIMATE SATISFACTION

Lyndon Johnson was not known for his humility. If anything, just the opposite. But he was driven by lifting needy people up, as shown by his Great Society initiatives. Although political conservatives might not evaluate the extreme governmental involvement as a good thing, and might decry the fall-out in increased governmental intervention that has rolled down through the decades since, we don't believe that there are many in the United States who now believe that the effects on promoting equality among all races and groups is a bad thing. In fact, though many believe that there is far more to achieve in terms of racial and ethnic equality, both conservatives and liberals and those in between—the red, blue, and white states, respectively—can look with some satisfaction at the changes since 1963.

One of the people involved in Johnson's programs was Jack Valenti, appointed on the plane to Washington, DC, the day President Kennedy was shot. Valenti was a World War II combat hero from Texas. In 1952, he founded an advertising agency in Houston and got involved with Johnson's political career. Of course, Johnson ran afoul of both left and right during his one elected term of president—the left because of the war in Vietnam, the right because of the heavy governmental involvement in the Great Society programming. Johnson's friends distanced themselves—except for Jack Valenti. After Johnson completed his single term, Valenti became president and CEO of the Motion Picture Association of America. He remained loyal to Johnson. On January 31, 1996, Valenti gave a memorable speech to the Federal Communications Bar Association (for the transcript, see Safire, 1997, pp. 592–595).

Here are some excerpts of the humorous, touching, and wise speech in which he recounted lessons learned in his political life close to the center of power in the United States:

> I learned that in the White House there is one enduring standard by which [everyone] . . . must inevitably be measured . . . "good judgment." . . . Judgment is something that springs from some little elf who inhabits an area between your belly and your brain, who from time to time, tugs at your nerve edges, and says, "no, not that way, the other way." . . . I learned that economic forecasts beyond about two weeks have the same odds of accuracy as guessing the winning numbers in the D. C. lottery. . . . Whenever an economist can't remember his phone number, he will give you an estimate. . . . I learned never to humiliate an antagonist and never desert a friend. . . . I learned that nothing lasts. (Safire, 1997, pp. 592–593)

Then Valenti related his greatest lesson learned. He told of a meeting that he arranged and sat in on between Senator Richard Brevard Russell of Georgia, the man most responsible for Johnson's rise to the presidency, and new President (2 weeks) Johnson. Johnson sat facing Russell and launched in.

> "Dick, I love you and I owe you. If it had not been for you, I would not have been leader, or vice president, or now president. But I wanted to tell you face to face, please don't get in my way on this civil rights bill. . . . I intend to pass this bill, Dick. I will not cavil. I will not hesitate. And if you get in my way, I'll run you down."
>
> Russell sat mute for a moment, impassive, his face a mask. Then he [said] . . . "Well, Mr. President, you may just do that. But I pledge you that if you do, it will not only cost you the election, it will cost you the South forever."
>
> [President Johnson] touched Russell lightly on the shoulder, an affectionate gesture of one loving friend to another. He spoke softly, almost tenderly: "Dick, my old friend, if that's the price I have to pay, then I will gladly pay it." (Safire, 1997, pp. 594–595)

Heroic humility—doing what he thought was right to elevate those who needed elevation, regardless of the personal and political cost. Said Valenti,

> President Johnson in all the years I knew him so intimately never made me prouder than he did that Sunday morning so long, long ago. . . . It illuminated to a blinding blaze the highest point to which the political spirit can soar. I have never forgotten it. I never will. (Safire, 1997, p. 595)

SUMMARY

In Chapter 5, we saw that humility could contribute to better psychological welfare and might be shown in the future to contribute to physical well-being. In Chapter 6, we saw that humility could lead to more religious and spiritual well-being. Is humility related to societal and personal enrichment? In the present chapter, we saw that the small amount of research addressing this issue is clear: Yes, it is. But seeking even the noble hope of ultimate validation for one's life or the hope of a more peaceful society will likely not be a motivation that draws people to want to be more humble. The major motives drawing people to a humble life are likely (a) social attractions of liking people who are humble and wanting to be liked because we are humble and religious or (b) spiritual or inspirational attractions. Humble people inspire and motivate us. Let's look more closely at those who exhibit heroic humility.

WHAT DID WE LEARN IN THIS CHAPTER?

1. Humility can transform society through great exemplars of humility—especially humility so profound it is considered heroic.
2. Many humble people can change society by the weight of their numbers, but there might be a critical mass at which a society can become more humble than just the product of their individual leaders.
3. Sometimes positive psychology seems overly preoccupied by promoting happiness. One counterintuitive finding in studying humility is this: Humility is not always a producer of happiness, but it can produce a long-term satisfaction with life.

THREE QUESTIONS FOR THOUGHT AND DISCUSSION

1. About half of the people who identify as positive psychologists think of positive psychology as the science of happiness. The other half tends to think of it as the psychology of character strength and virtue. Where do you fit? And why?
2. The societal peace hypothesis is dependent on a society in which many people are humble. Is this possible in today's world? What would have to happen for the United States to become a society that had many, perhaps most, people who exhibited humility?
3. Are you on track to be ultimately satisfied with your life? If you do not feel that you are and if you value that as a goal, do you want to make any changes in your life? What would you change?

III

HEROES, HUMILITY, AND HEROIC LEADERSHIP

8

HEROIC HUMILITY AND THE HERO'S QUEST

By foreign hands thy humble grave adorned;
By strangers honored, and by strangers mourned.

—Alexander Pope

We now turn our attention to heroism itself and to the important role of humility in the hero's journey. Scholars have yet to reach a consensus definition of a hero (Allison, Goethals, & Kramer, 2017b). Definitions converge around the idea that a hero is one who (a) voluntarily takes actions that are deemed to be exceptionally good, or that are directed toward serving a noble principle or the greater good; (b) makes a significant sacrifice; and (c) takes a great risk.

Franco, Blau, and Zimbardo (2011) offered this definition: "Heroism is the willingness to sacrifice or take risks on behalf of others or in defense of a moral cause" (p. 13). Allison and Goethals (2011) defined heroism as "doing the right thing at a critical moment," with the right thing involving a combination of "great morality and competence" (p. 9). Merriam-Webster's definition of *hero* also adds that a hero attracts admiration from others, a *recognition* aspect of heroism that most scholars do not include in their definitions. People

http://dx.doi.org/10.1037/0000079-009
Heroic Humility: What the Science of Humility Can Say to People Raised on Self-Focus, by E. L. Worthington Jr. and S. T. Allison

who only serve the greater good when they are being observed are clearly not showing heroic humility. In fact, as we've discussed, the best exemplars of heroic humility are those who do their heroic work without fanfare, even without awareness that what they're doing is heroic, and who continue over time, trials, and temptations to quit.

Allison and Goethals (2011) adopted a subjective approach to defining heroism. They claimed that "heroism is in the eye of the beholder" (p. 196). These scholars observed that people's needs and motives determine whom they choose as heroes. For example, patients with cancer choose cancer survivors as heroes, and soccer players choose soccer stars as heroes. Maturity and development also play a role in hero selection. Younger people tend to choose heroes known for their talents, and older people tend to choose morally virtuous heroes. This suggests that we may be less likely to value humility as a virtue when we're young and full of bravado than when we're older and appreciative of kinder, gentler behavior. As we age and (hopefully) get wiser, our views of heroism evolve toward ideas that transcend mere physicality, an idea captured in the hero subtype of *transitional heroes* proposed by Goethals and Allison (2012). Transitional heroes are heroes that we "outgrow" as we pass through the various stages of life development.

We take the position that heroic humility is evident in people who heroically serve others while enduring great costs for them. As we have briefly seen and will show in more detail in Chapter 10, there is near-universal agreement that Viktor Frankl, Mohandas Gandhi, and Abraham Lincoln, and many similar others are paragons of heroic humility in the way they combined their service to the world with self-effacement. We can better understand these exemplars of heroic humility by reviewing studies of how the general population perceives and defines such heroes. Allison and Goethals (2011) asked over 500 participants to list as many traits as they could that best describe heroes. These traits were sorted by other participants by similarity. The resultant piles were subjected to exploratory multivariate factor analyses and cluster analyses. The resultant factors and clusters revealed the following eight categories of traits describing heroes: *intelligent*, *strong*, *reliable*, *resilient*, *caring*, *charismatic*, *selfless*, and *inspiring*. Allison and Goethals called these trait categories the *Great Eight traits of heroes*. When we examine these eight attributes, we see traits associated with humility, such as caring for others and showing selflessness in one's relations with others.

Kinsella, Ritchie, and Igou (2015b) recently used a prototype analytic approach to discern people's conceptions of heroic traits. Their analysis yielded 12 central characteristics of heroes and 13 peripheral characteristics. Kinsella et al.'s (2015b) central characteristics were *brave*, *moral integrity*, *conviction*, *courageous*, *self-sacrifice*, *protecting*, *honest*, *selfless*, *determined*, *saves others*, *inspiring*, and *helpful*. The peripheral characteristics were *proactive*, *humble*, *strong, risk-taker, fearless, caring, powerful, compassionate, leadership skills, exceptional, intelligent, talented,* and *personable*. This analysis illuminates heroically humble attributes such as self-sacrifice, selflessness, helpfulness, and compassion. Most striking is that humility itself appears as a secondary characteristic of heroism. Kinsella et al.'s (2015b) results represent the first direct evidence that humility is perceived by laypeople to have a significant association with heroism.

Social scientists have proposed several different taxonomies of heroes (Allison, Goethals, & Kramer, 2017a). There are at least two reasons why we might not expect humility to appear in a hero taxonomy. First, given the historic emphasis on heroism as masculine, agentic, powerful, and machismo (see Allison et al., 2017a), we suspect that some of our ancestors might dub "heroic humility" an oxymoron. Second, the three main taxonomies of heroism in the current literature are based on the *situational demands* of the heroism (Franco et al., 2011), the *social influence* exerted by the hero (Goethals & Allison, 2012), and the *social structure* of heroism (Allison & Smith, 2015). None of these taxonomic structures are based on heroic attributes that might implicate the expression of humility from a hero.

We do find that heroic humility comes close to being represented in the *tragic hero* subtype as described in the influence-based taxonomy of Goethals and Allison (2012; see also Allison & Goethals, 2013). If you are familiar with Shakespearean tragedies, then you know the tragic hero all too well. Consider the sorrowful tales of King Lear, Macbeth, Hamlet, and Othello. These great individuals self-destruct because they refuse to be humbled by events that should have humbled them. The ancient Greeks called it *hubris*, an extreme form of pride that has toppled many great people from Tiger Woods and Lance Armstrong in the world of sports to Adolf Hitler and Richard Nixon in the realm of politics. Power, fame, and wealth are not necessarily bad qualities in themselves, but they are dangerous to the human psyche. Our greatest heroes avoid succumbing to hubris and manage to maintain their heroic humility.

THE HERO'S JOURNEY

To understand more about how heroes avoid succumbing to hubris, we turn to the classic hero's journey in mythology, literature, and film. This journey turns out to be a rich source of insights about heroic humility. Hero tales from antiquity to modern times follow the same clear and predictable pattern. The hero is an ordinary person who is summoned on a journey away from her safe, familiar world to a new and special world fraught with danger.

Comparative mythologist Joseph Campbell (1949) described the classic hero's journey in this way:

> A hero ventures forth from the world of common day into a region of supernatural wonder: fabulous forces are there encountered and a decisive victory is won: the hero comes back from this mysterious adventure with the power to bestow boons on his fellow man. (p. 30)

Campbell's Account of the Journey

At the outset of the journey, the hero is missing an important quality, usually self-confidence, humility, or a sense of her true purpose in life. The hero's journey is always a voyage toward self-realization and transformation (Allison & Goethals, 2014, 2017; Allison & Smith, 2015). Receiving assistance from enchanted and unlikely sources, the hero develops remarkable cunning, courage, and resourcefulness to triumph—whatever is needed to build into the missing aspects of his or her character. Once successful, the hero returns to his or her original familiar world ready to bestow a boon to the entire community. In all, the hero's journey describes a transformative process that turns ordinary people into heroic leaders.

For Campbell (1991), acquiring humility is a central feature of the hero's journey. He wrote, "We must be willing to get rid of the life we've planned, so as to have the life that is waiting for us" (p. 18). Commenting on the inevitable fall of the hero, he observed, "It is by going down into the abyss that we recover the treasures of life" (p. 24); "The dark night of the soul comes just before revelation" (p. 24); and "When everything is lost, and all seems darkness, then comes the new life and all that is needed" (p. 39). Paraphrasing Matthew 10:39 in the Christian scriptures, Campbell (1991) noted, "He who loses his life shall find it" (p. 102). He appreciated the metaphorical value of scriptures, arguing that Adam and Eve were the first humans to be heroically humbled in the Garden of Eden. Their "fall" set the stage for transformation and for later heroic resurrection, as "Christ represents the reentry into the Garden" (Campbell, 2001, p. 58).

The hero's journey is the human journey, and it's all about falling, getting humbled, acquiring self-insight, and using these insights to make the world a better place. This journey is evident in Maslow's (1943) hierarchy of needs, which describes difficulties associated with satisfying one's basic motivations. Growth that results from resolving these challenges can lead to transcendent self-actualization. The lifespan developmental stages of Erik Erikson (1994) also fit the hero's journey. With each developmental stage, there is a crisis that is encountered and must be resolved for successful passage to the next stage. The final stages of Erikson's model describe the apex of the hero's journey. People achieve selfless *generativity* and *integrity*.

The powerful allure of the hero's journey is evident in our favorite novels and movies. Storytelling since the dawn of humanity has told of heroes being humbled and using this humility to become forever changed and reunited with the world. Let's explore the psychology of the hero narrative in more depth.

Psychological Benefits of Hero Narratives

Allison and Goethals (2014, 2016) introduced the term *heroic leadership dynamic* to illuminate the ways that heroes and hero stories nourish the human mind and spirit. Central to the heroic leadership dynamic is that hero narratives fulfill important cognitive and emotional needs, such as our need for wisdom, meaning, hope, inspiration, and growth. The heroic leadership dynamic describes how our most basic human needs can account for our thirst for heroes, and how these needs explain why we are drawn to them, benefit from them, stick to flawed ones, and repudiate them only after they have outlived their psychological usefulness.

The principles underlying the heroic leadership dynamic draw from the abundance of research underscoring the psychological significance of narrative storytelling (McAdams, 1997; Sternberg, 2011). Stories crystallize abstract concepts and endow them with contextual meaning. McAdams (1997) argued that personal self-narratives shape life trajectories and the maintenance of subjective well-being. Stories are rich, emotionally laden capsule summaries of wisdom for which the human mind was designed (McAdams, 1997). According to Price (1978), "a need to tell and hear stories is essential to the species Homo sapiens—second in necessity apparently after nourishment and before love and shelter" (p. 3).

One could argue that the main function of hero stories is to teach us the value of humility. Nearly every main character in fiction must be humbled before he or she can become a hero. According to Jerome Bruner (2002), "Narrative is a recounting of human plans gone off the track, expectations gone awry. It is a way to domesticate human error and surprise" (p. 31). This taming of the ego is essential for protagonists in stories to undergo heroic growth.

Because stories exert such a strong psychological impact, they can be misused to support destructive norms and promote oppressive dictatorships. Adolf Hitler's rise to power was largely based on his use of narratives that justified nationalistic pride and arrogance, which we know led to military aggression and the extermination of Jews, Catholics, gays, gypsies, and other groups (Rosenbaum, 2014). The policies and agendas of countless leaders with dubious moral legacies have been inspired by heroic narratives. Hero stories can be twisted to serve the psychological needs and goals of both leaders and followers (cf. Frimer, Schaefer, & Oakes, 2014). Many nations have waged wars against each other, with leadership on each side proclaiming the morally (and heroically) superior upper hand. So we see that hero stories can tap into the dimension of pride versus humility, inspiring people to do either great good or great harm.

The Epistemic Function of Hero Stories

> The path to wisdom is paved with humility.
>
> —Tim Fargo

Stories of heroic action impart wisdom by supplying mental models, or scripts, for how one could, or should, lead one's life. Martin Luther King Jr. based his strategy of nonviolent resistance on stories of similar tactics used successfully by Gandhi (S. H. Bennett, 2003). Heroic narratives also teach us how we should behave in crises (Allison & Goethals, 2011, 2014; Goethals & Allison, 2012). The heroic actions of Wesley Autrey, which we summarized in Chapter 1, offer a compelling example of the wisdom imparted by hero stories. Autrey was the construction worker who received international acclaim when he rescued a complete stranger from an oncoming New York subway train in 2007 ("The Hero in the Subway," 2007). Autrey provided a script for heroic action to millions of New York citizens hungry for such a script. Heroes such as Autrey are role models who perform behaviors that affirm our most cherished worldviews (Kinsella, Ritchie, & Igou, 2015a; Solomon, Greenberg, Schiel, Arndt, & Pyszczynski, 2014).

Another function of hero stories is their ability to shed light on meaningful life paradoxes. Most people have trouble unpacking the value of paradoxical truths unless the contradictions contained within the paradoxes are illustrated inside a good story. One paradox inherent in hero tales is the idea that to be humbled is to be empowered.

Consider one of Joseph Campbell's (1949) most famous quotes:

> We have only to follow the thread of the hero-path. And where we had thought to find an abomination, we shall find a god; where we had thought to slay another, we shall slay ourselves; where we had thought to travel outward, we shall come to the center of our own existence; and where we had thought to be alone, we shall be with all the world. (p. 18)

Campbell (1949) unraveled these paradoxes by first observing that all mythic hero stories involve a necessary departure into a new, dangerous world that will require a descent into hell before an ascent into enlightenment. For the hero, "the way down is the way up" (Rohr, 2011, p. 18). As we have noted, all human beings face painful challenges that are a necessary path toward personal growth. "Where you stumble," wrote Campbell, "there lies your treasure" (p. 75).

Campbell (1988) often used dragon slaying as a metaphor for describing how the confrontation of our fears is necessary for later redemption. When heroes summon the courage to face their challenges, they enter the dragon's lair, and only when they defeat the monster is their personal transformation complete. When we slay our dragons, we are slaying our false or former selves, thereby allowing our true heroic selves to emerge. The journey away from the comforts of home and into unfamiliar darkness is a counterintuitive yet necessary element of heroism and of life (Campbell, 1988). Embarking on this pilgrimage is a sure path to growth and transformation, and hero stories teach us that all of us, whether we are heroes or not, must leave our safe, familiar worlds to find our true selves (Levinson, 1978).

Hero narratives also promote the development of emotional intelligence, which refers to our ability to identify, understand, manage, and use our emotions (Caruso, Fleming, & Spector, 2014; Mayer, Salovey, Caruso, & Sitarenios, 2001). Humility grounds us emotionally. When we are humbled, the need to "feel" pride is removed, and we gain a sense of peaceful union with our fellow humans. Psychoanalyst Bruno Bettelheim (1976) identified the role of heroic fairy tales in helping children understand emotional experience. The heroes of fairy tales usually experience dark, foreboding experiences, such as encounters with witches, evil spells, abandonment, neglect, abuse, and death. Listeners to these tales experience these dark stimuli vicariously, which allows them to develop strategies for dealing with challenges and becoming humbled by them. Bettelheim believed that even the most distressing fairy tales, such as those by the Brothers Grimm, add clarity to confusing emotions and increase people's purpose and meaning. The darkness of fairy tales allows children to grow in a humble awareness that they are not always in control and that life is difficult. This recognition cultivates emotional intelligence and prepares children for the challenges of adulthood.

Benefits of Being Humbled Through Suffering

Carl Jung (1970) once wrote, "There's no coming to *consciousness* without *pain*" [italics added] (p. 74). In fact, people's efforts to avoid pain just bring about even greater pain. Setback and suffering, and the humility that follows, are all part of the human equation. There is nothing noble per se about suffering. Sometimes it simply eats people's will, indeed their very lives. But while we need not look for suffering out of some masochistic attempt to better ourselves, suffering will find all of us if we live long enough. And one of our principal life tests often comes in how we deal with suffering when it does find us. On the hero's journey, almost no one can avoid suffering, but suffering can be fuel for growth. Given that it is virtually inevitable in life, let's look at some potential benefits.

One benefit of suffering is humility, which every hero must develop. Kurtz and Ketcham (1992) wrote, "The main benefit of struggle and failure is that it helps protect against the ultimate bane of all spirituality—conceit, the self-centeredness that claims absolute self-sufficiency, the pride that denies all need" (p. 52). Lack of humility is what cast Lucifer out of heaven. Augustine observed, "It was pride that changed angels into devils; it is humility that makes men as angels" (p. 188).

Psychological Benefits

Psychologists believe that psychological "wholeness" depends on realistic self-appraisal. Such accurate self-conceptions are rare, however. The vast majority of people harbor the illusions—even if unconsciously—that they are better, more moral, fairer, and more competent than others (Goethals, Messick, & Allison, 1991). Suffering occurs when our pink clouds are burst, when our self-serving illusions are undermined by irrefutable evidence that we are flawed and limited beings who are no better, and often worse, than others. Spiritual traditions tell us that "pruning" is needed to keep us "right-sized." In Daniel 11:35 of the Hebrew scriptures, we learn that "some of the wise will stumble, so that they may be refined, purified and made spotless." In John 15:2, Jesus said, "every branch in me that does not bear fruit, He takes away; and every branch that bears fruit, He prunes it so that it may bear more fruit." In the end, Jesus' humility before God (i.e., spiritual humility) brought him to accept his suffering rather than reject it, as the crowds urged him to do (Mark 15:29–32, Matthew 27:39–44). He understood that suffering is necessary. Indeed, some degree of pain and suffering seems necessary to keep us all humble.

Spiritual Benefits

Spiritual traditions from around the world emphasize that although life can be painful, a higher power is at work using our circumstances to humble us and to shape us into what the Sacred wants us to be. C. S. Lewis (1940) once noted, "God whispers to us in our pleasures, speaks to us in our conscience, but shouts in our pains: It is His megaphone to rouse a deaf world" (pp. 57–58). Theologian Richard Rohr (2011) opined that suffering "doesn't accomplish anything tangible but creates space for learning and love" (p. 64). Suffering rouses us from our inherent spiritual laziness and opens us to growth and maturity. Suffering reminds us that we are not God, thus making us more receptive to the divine. Spiritual leaders teach us, often by example, that suffering serves the purpose of humbling us and waking us from the dream of self-sufficiency.

Benefits Identified in Recovery Movements

Humility is a major step toward "recovery" in the many twelve-step programs. Step 1 asks participants to admit their total powerlessness over their addiction. The spiritual principle at work here is the idea that victory is only possible through admitting defeat. Rohr (2011) argued that only when people reach the limits of their private resources do they become willing to tap into the "ultimate resource"—God, Allah, the universe, or some power greater than themselves. Pain, misery, and desperation become the keys to recovery. Step 7 later asks program members to "*humbly* ask God" [italics added] to remove personal defects of character. This humility can only be experienced by admitting defeat and by accepting that one cannot recover from addiction without assistance. Twelve-step programs begin by focusing on defeat and suffering (Step 1), the possibility of a higher power being the solution (Step 2), trust in that higher power (Step 3), personal self-improvement with God's help (Steps 4–9), and service to others (Step 12), which is the step of spiritual leadership. Mentoring others through the steps is central to maintaining one's own sobriety and recovery.

Allison and Setterberg (2016) identified ways that heroic humility borne of suffering can benefit us. These benefits include that heroic suffering (a) has redemptive qualities, (b) signifies important developmental milestones, (c) elevates compassion, (d) encourages social union and action, and (e) provides meaning and purpose. Let's look closer at these benefits.

Suffering Can Be Redemptive

Spiritual traditions emphasize the redemptive value of suffering (for some accounts from different religious and spiritual traditions, see Chapter 6). Buddhism's four noble truths focus on the inevitability of suffering, the source of it, the elimination of it, and the path one must take to free oneself of its ravages. Buddhism points to, and offers antidotes for, the unavoidable suffering of birth, old age, sickness, and death. Centuries later, Sigmund Freud (1930) wrote about the inevitability of physical suffering as endemic to the human condition, noting that our fractious relations with others are an additional painful source of suffering. Buddhism teaches the potential for spiritual awakening, but it requires willingness to use suffering as a catalyst for further spiritual journey. The Buddha cautioned that the desire for awakening asks much from those who seek it. One must turn *toward* the suffering to conquer it.

Christianity, and Catholicism in particular, emphatically embraces the redemptive value of suffering. Foremost in the Judeo-Christian tradition is the idea that all human suffering stems from the fall of humanity (Genesis 1:31). The Hebrew scriptures also emphasize that people reap what they sow, with suffering serving as the natural consequence of rejecting God (in the Christian scriptures, see Galatians 6:7–10). We witness such suffering when David commits adultery (2 Samuel 11:1–5), when Solomon ignores God's caution about marriage (1 Kings 11:1–5), and when the Israelites experience consequences of rejecting God (Numbers 14:41–45).

For Christians, God imparts value into suffering for its own sake, and not as a judgment against sin. For instance, Peter states, "it is commendable if someone bears up under the pain of unjust suffering because they are conscious of God" (1 Peter 2:19). The centerpiece of suffering in the Christian scriptures is, of course, the passion of Christ described in the Synoptic Gospels. For Christians, Christ's redemptive death is the ultimate illustration of God's grace. Jesus's suffering served the purpose of redeeming no less than the entire human race. Pope Francis suggested that the suffering of Christ redeems all of our suffering by allowing the sufferer to share in the redemptive sacrifice of Christ:

> To suffer is to take the difficulty and to carry it with strength, so that the difficulty does not drag us down. To carry it with strength: this is a Christian virtue. Saint Paul says several times: Suffer, endure. This means do not let ourselves be overcome by difficulties. This means that the Christian has the strength not to give up, to carry difficulties with strength. Carry them, but carry them with strength. It is not easy, because discouragement comes, and one has the urge to give up and say, "Well, come on, we'll do what we can but no more." But no, it is a grace to suffer. In difficulties, we must ask for [this grace]. (Kaczor, 2007)

The redemptive value of suffering is evident in many striking examples of leadership both within and outside the realm of traditional religions. Suffering plays a central role in illuminating the hero's missing qualities that must be recovered, or discovered, for the hero to achieve his or her heroic transformation. Martin Luther King Jr. once said that he would not permit suffering to defeat him or engender bitterness. Rather, King wrote that his goal was to "transform the suffering into a creative force" (King & Armstrong, 2007, p. 97). King understood that the redemptive and transformative power of suffering occurs at two different levels. At the individual level, heroes are personally transformed by their suffering (Campbell, 1949). Heroic leaders then use this personal metamorphosis to transform the society to which they belong (Allison & Smith, 2015; Goethals & Allison, 2016).

Suffering also transformed Nelson Mandela, who endured 27 years of imprisonment before assuming the presidency of South Africa (for an extended account, see Chapter 7). While imprisoned, Mandela and other inmates performed hard labor in a lime quarry. Prison conditions were harsh; prisoners were segregated by race, with Black prisoners receiving the least rations. Political prisoners such as Mandela were kept separate from ordinary criminals and received fewer privileges. Mandela has described how, as a D-group prisoner (the lowest classification), he was allowed one visitor and one letter every 6 months. Mandela's ability to prevail after such long-term suffering made him an inspirational hero. His remarkable triumph over adversity, occurring before his presidency, propelled him to international fame and admiration. When asked to reflect on Mandela's ordeals, Desmond Tutu opined that "the suffering of those 27 years helped to purify him and grow the magnanimity that would become his hallmark" (Perry, 2013).

In the field of positive psychology, scholars have acknowledged the role of suffering in the development of healthy character strengths (Hall, Langer, & McMartin, 2010). Positive psychology recognizes beneficial effects of suffering through the labels of posttraumatic growth, positive adjustment, positive adaptation, stress-related growth, and adversarial growth. A study of character strengths measured before and after the September 11, 2001, terrorist attacks showed an increase in people's "faith, hope, and love" (Peterson & Seligman, 2003). The redemptive development of hope, wisdom, and resilience as a result of suffering is said to have contributed to the leadership excellence of figures such as Helen Keller, Aung San Suu Kyi, Mohandas Gandhi, Malala Yousafzai, Stephen Hawking, Franklin D. Roosevelt, Shiva Nazar Ahari, Oprah Winfrey, J. K. Rowling, and Ludwig van Beethoven, among others.

Suffering Signifies a Necessary "Crossover" Point in Life

As we have noted, psychologists who study lifespan development have long known that humans traverse through various stages of maturation from birth to death. Models of human development include transitional events that mark the close of one developmental stage and the launching of another. Notable theories include Bowlby's (1969) theory of emotional development, Kohlberg's (Kohlberg & Hersh, 1977) theory of moral development, Gibson's (1991) theory of perceptual development, Piaget's (1972) theory of cognitive development, and Erikson's (1994) theory of psychosocial development. Erikson believed that people do not navigate through a developmental stage until they successfully negotiate a specific crisis that corresponds with that stage. If prolonged or mishandled, the crisis can produce suffering, and it is this suffering that serves as the necessary catalyst for progression to the subsequent stage.

From this perspective, suffering can be a significant stimulus for human growth and development. To illustrate, consider the transition from middle adulthood to late adulthood. Erikson was the first psychologist to describe important late-life stages, and in fact, he was the first to address the causes and consequences of the "midlife crisis." According to Erikson (1994), middle-aged people often struggle to find their purpose or meaning in life, particularly after their children have grown and left the house. Erikson surmised that the unhealthy resolution of this struggle is a descent into a life of meaningless, narcissistic self-absorption.

Suffering borne of isolation and stagnation is the inevitable result of this choice. The only way to move forward is to carve out a life of selfless *generativity*. A generative individual is charitable, communal, socially connected, and willing to selflessly better society. Generativity is the antidote to the midlife crisis. Middle-aged and older adults who are able to model healthy generativity serve an important leadership role for their peers and for younger adults. Generative individuals are among society's most valuable human assets—often called society's "elders."

Spiritual masters all say that we must die, or some part of us must die, before we can live or at least move forward. This process of going down to go up is counterintuitive and thus fiercely resisted by most people. Some type of dying is a natural prerequisite for living. If we resist dying—and most every one of us does—we resist what is good for us and hence bring about our own suffering. Carl Jung observed that "the foundation of all mental illness is the avoidance of true *suffering*" [italics added] (Allison & Setterberg, 2016). The paradox here is that if we avoid suffering, we avoid growth. Perhaps the great Cistercian monk, Thomas Merton, summed it up best: "The truth that many people never understand, until it is too late, is that the more you try to avoid suffering the more you suffer because smaller and more insignificant things begin to torture you in proportion to your fear of being hurt" (Merton, 1999, p. 91). People who resist this type of dying and the necessary suffering are ill-equipped to serve as the society's leaders. Our most heroic leaders have been "through the fire" and have gained the wisdom and maturity to lead wisely. Notable examples include Franklin D. Roosevelt, who overcame polio; John F. Kennedy, who underwent a near-death experience during World War II and battled life-long illness; Nelson Mandela, who endured imprisonment; and Helen Keller, who overcame deafblindness.

Suffering Stimulates Compassion

Suffering invokes compassion for those who are hurting. Virtually all spiritual traditions emphasize the importance of consolation, relief, and self-sacrificial outreach for the suffering. Buddhists advocate *karuna*, which is the willingness to bear another's pain and practice kindness, affection, and gentleness toward sufferers. Buddhists also use *metta*, which is altruistic kindness and love free of selfish attachment. The expression of these values is crucial to leading a holy life and attaining nirvana. Vietnamese Zen Buddhist monk Thích Nhất Hạnh (1999) emphasized how suffering builds compassion: "When another person makes you suffer, it is because he suffers deeply within himself, and his suffering is spilling over. He does not need punishment; he needs help. That's the message he is sending" (p. 198).

Scriptural references to compassion abound for Christians. According to James 1:27, "Religion that is pure and undefiled before God, the Father, is this: to visit orphans and widows in their affliction." And in Mark 6:34, "When he went ashore he saw a great crowd, and he had compassion on them, because they were like sheep without a shepherd. And he began to teach them many things." In 2 Corinthians 1:3–4,

> Blessed be the God and Father of our Lord Jesus Christ, the Father of mercies and God of all comfort, who comforts us in all our affliction, so that we may be able to comfort those who are in any affliction, with the comfort with which we ourselves are comforted by God.

For Jesus, compassion for the poor, the sick, the hungry, the unclothed, the widowed, the imprisoned, the sinful, and the orphaned was at the core of his heroically humble leadership.

One fascinating finding in psychology is that wealthy individuals may be challenged in their ability to show empathic responses to others. In a series of clever studies, Kraus, Piff, and Keltner (2011) observed drivers at a busy four-way intersection. Drivers of luxury cars were more likely to (a) cut off other motorists rather than wait their turn at the intersection and (b) speed past a pedestrian trying to use a crosswalk than to let the pedestrian cross the road. Wealthy people, compared with lower and middle-class people, showed little heart-rate change when watching a video of children with cancer. These data suggest that powerful and wealthy people are less likely to show humble, compassionate responses to the weak and the poor.

Wealthy and powerful people may also be more likely to act unethically. Over the past decade, numerous executives at Goldman Sachs and other high-powered financial corporations have been convicted for illegal activity borne of excessive greed (Grewal, 2012). Research shows that wealthy individuals are more likely to agree with statements that greed is justified, beneficial, and morally defensible (Piff, Stancato, Côté, Mendoza-Denton, & Keltner, 2012). Those with the most resources seem to be motivated to give the least and to take the most from the poorest among us. Heroically humble leaders somehow are able to guard against letting the power of their position compromise their values of compassion and empathy for the least fortunate.

Suffering Promotes Social Union and Collective Action

Toward the end of his life, Freud became preoccupied with the social aspects of his psychoanalytic theory. His groundbreaking *Civilization and Its Discontents* in 1930 addressed the harsh realities of intergroup conflict and its role in producing unhappiness and suffering in humans. Freud wrote, "We are never so defenseless against suffering as when we love, never so forlornly unhappy as when we have lost our love object or its love" (Freud, 1930, p. 57). Freud viewed social relations as the cause of suffering. A spiritual view of suffering suggests the opposite: Namely, suffering is actually the cause of good social relations. Suffering brings people together and is better than joy at creating bonds among group members (Rohr, 2011).

Social psychologist Stanley Schachter discovered this in a series of laboratory experiments he reported in his 1959 book, *The Psychology of Affiliation*. Schachter told his research participants that they were about to receive painful electric shocks. Before participating in the study, they were asked to choose one of two waiting rooms in which to sit. Participants about to receive shocks were much more likely to choose the waiting room with people in it compared with the empty room. Schachter concluded that misery loves company. He then asked a different group of participants, also about to receive the shocks, if they would prefer to wait in a room with other participants who were about to receive shocks, or a room with participants who would not be receiving shocks. Schachter found that participants about to receive shocks much preferred the room with others who were going to share the same fate. His conclusion: Misery doesn't love just any kind of company; misery loves miserable company.

Effective leaders intuitively know how to use suffering to rally people behind a cause. Winston Churchill and Franklin D. Roosevelt were masters at capitalizing on the suffering of British and American citizens to bolster resilience and ingroup morale. Suffering can be the glue that binds and heals after everything has seemingly shattered. This has been evident in the Christian scriptures (see Romans 12:15–16), but support groups, self-help groups, and twelve-step programs are also designed to achieve these aims. And there is some evidence suggesting that group therapy can sometimes achieve a higher rate of efficacy than individual therapy (Corazinni, 2011). Misery doesn't just love miserable company; misery helps alleviate the misery in that company.

Suffering can mobilize people. Mobilization can occur when suffering inspires the emergence of spiritual leadership needed to ameliorate the suffering. Good leaders can invoke suffering as a noble means for achieving a greater end. Franklin D. Roosevelt used the suffering of impoverished Americans during the Great Depression to justify his New Deal policies and programs. During World War II, both he and Winston Churchill cited the suffering of both citizens and soldiers to justify rationing. In North America, African Americans were subjugated by European Americans for centuries, and from this suffering emerged the leadership of Rosa Parks, Martin Luther King Jr., and John Lewis, among others. Suffering of women inspired Susan B. Anthony, Elizabeth Cady Stanton, and many activists to promote women's suffrage.

Three days after the September 11, 2001, terrorist attacks, George W. Bush used the suffering of America to galvanize support for military involvement in Afghanistan. Standing amidst the rubble of the fallen twin towers, Bush grabbed a bullhorn and shouted to the grief-stricken crowd, "I can hear you. The rest of the world hears you. And the people who knocked these buildings down will hear all of us soon" (Glover, 2001, p. xi). The crowd roared approval and, for better or for worse, Bush secured American military involvement in the Middle East. In our previous work, we have argued that heroism is in the eye of the beholder (Allison & Goethals, 2011, 2013, 2014; D. J. Davis, Burnette, Allison, & Stone, 2011; Goethals & Allison, 2012, 2014, 2017). The policies and agendas of countless leaders who have invoked spiritual principles, from George W. Bush to Osama Bin Laden, suggest that spiritual leadership may also be in the eye of the beholder. If heroically humble leadership serves a higher moral purpose, as we contend here, then we must be mindful that morality can be twisted to serve the psychological needs and goals of the beholder. Sadly, many God-loving nations have waged wars against each other, with leadership on each side proclaiming the spiritually superior upper hand.

Jonathan Haidt (2012) argued that human morality is governed by primitive righteous minds that focus on achieving three main goals. The righteous mind wants to divide the world into "us" versus "them"; it tells us that "our" group is morally superior to "their" group; and it blinds us to the truth—that, of course, there is no "us" and "them," only humanity, and that acquiring humility is the best way to overcome the social destructiveness of the righteous mind.

Suffering Instills Meaning and Purpose

The fifth benefit of suffering resides in the meaning and purpose that suffering imparts to the sufferer. Many spiritual traditions underscore the role of suffering in bestowing a sense of significance and worth to life. In Islam, the faithful are asked to accept suffering as Allah's will and to submit to it as a test of faith. Followers are cautioned to avoid questioning or resisting the suffering; one simply endures it with the assurance that Allah never asks for more than one can handle. This philosophy is not unlike that of Christianity.

Both suffering and divine comfort in the context of suffering mobilize the Christian's identification and connection with Christ.

Friedrich Nietzsche (1886/1992) once observed that "to live is to suffer, to survive is to find some meaning in the suffering" (p. 110). This drive for meaning as a coping mechanism for suffering has been explored by many scholars, including Diehl (2009), Egnew (2005), and Frankl (1976). Frankl suggested that a search for meaning *transforms* suffering into a positive, life-altering experience:

> In some way, suffering ceases to be suffering at the moment it finds a meaning, such as the meaning of a sacrifice. . . . That is why man is even ready to suffer, on the condition, to be sure, that his suffering has a meaning. (p. 145; for more on Frankl, see Chapter 5, this volume)

Diehl (2009) listed "an inability to experience and grasp some meaning of life" among eight primary potentials for human suffering (p. 37). Thus, the search for meaning not only alleviates suffering; the absence of meaning can cause suffering.

The legendary poet William Wordsworth must have been intuitively aware of the meaningfulness of suffering, sacrifice, and the infinite when he penned the following line: "Suffering is permanent, obscure and dark, and shares the nature of infinity" (quoted in Gill, 1989, p. 132). Campbell (1972), moreover, connected the dots between suffering and people's search for meaning. According to Campbell, the hero's journey is "the pivotal myth that unites the spiritual adventure of ancient heroes with the modern search for meaning" (p. 112).

WHAT DID WE LEARN IN THIS CHAPTER?

1. Kinsella et al. (2015b) conducted a prototype analysis of heroism and found that traits associated with heroism included primary attributes like self-sacrificing, protecting, selfless, saves others, and helpful, and also peripheral characteristics like humble, caring, compassionate, and leadership skills. These seem to suggest that an orientation toward others is a prerequisite for heroism, as it seems to be for humility.
2. On the basis of Campbell's and others' analyses of hero myths, it seems that one main function of hero stories is to teach the value of humility. Most fictional protagonists must be humbled by setback before they can become heroes.
3. Suffering is not something we should seek, but if we respond well to it, it can be redemptive.

THREE QUESTIONS FOR THOUGHT AND DISCUSSION

1. In this chapter, we provided two reasons they think that humility does not often appear as a quality associated with heroism. After you review their reasons, can you think of others?
2. We enumerated, at length, many benefits of suffering. If it is so beneficial, should people seek out experiences that can possibly lead to suffering?
3. Should we each seek to take a hero's journey, or is that something that special people are "called" to? If we are to seek the possibility of a hero's quest, how do we decide whether we are doing the right thing or simply being foolhardy or adrenaline junkies?

9

TRANSFORMATION TO HEROIC HUMILITY

The hero's transformation is essential for the hero to achieve his or her goal on the journey. Describing the transformation, Campbell (1972) wrote that "ineffable realizations are experienced" and "things that before had been mysterious are now fully understood" (p. 219). The ineffability of these new insights stems from their unconscious origins. Jungian principles of the collective unconscious form the basis of Campbell's theorizing about hero mythology. As Le Grice (2013) noted, "myths are expressions of the imagination, shaped by the archetypal dynamics of the psyche" (p. 153). Ultimately, the hero's outer journey reflects an inner, psychological journey that involves "leaving one condition and finding the source of life to bring you forth into a richer or mature condition" (Campbell, 1988, p. 152). Heroic humility describes that mature condition.

Initiation rituals, common in nearly all human societies, are designed to produce a transformation toward humility. Campbell (1959) wrote that initiation rituals "suppress as much as possible the sense of ego and develop

http://dx.doi.org/10.1037/0000079-010
Heroic Humility: What the Science of Humility Can Say to People Raised on Self-Focus, by E. L. Worthington Jr. and S. T. Allison

that of participation" (p. 82). During initiation rituals, "The crude energies of the young human animal are to be cowed, broken, recoordinated to a larger format, and thus at once domesticated and amplified" (p. 90). Suffering plays a big role here. Throughout the world, "the rituals of transformation from infancy to manhood are attended with, and effected by, excruciating ordeals. Scourgings, fastings, the knocking out of teeth, scarifications, finger sacrifices, the removal of a testicle, cicatrization, circumcision, subincision, bitings, and burnings are the general rule" (p. 117). The human body "is transformed by the ordeals into an ever-present sign of a new spiritual state" (p. 117).

Despite intense suffering, ritualistic transformation has a positive purpose. Campbell (1959) emphasized that rituals are "progressive, not regressive" (p. 91). Specifically, "Ritual is mythology made alive, and its effect is to convert men into angels" (p. 118). According to Campbell (1988), ritual and myth "grab you somewhere down inside" and "inspire the possibility of the realization of your perfection, the fullness of your strength" (p. 183). Rituals and myths "provide a field in which you can locate yourself" (Campbell, 2004, p. xvi) and they "carry the individual through the stages of life" (p. 9). In short, becoming humbled from your hero's journey is a sign that you are growing and on the right path to becoming your best self.

THE ROLE OF TRANSFORMATION TO HEROIC HUMILITY

Transformations, including those toward heroic humility, serve five purposes (Allison & Goethals, 2017). First, they foster developmental growth. The hero's journey is seen as a metaphor for successful passage through the various stages of life from birth to death. As we have seen, human societies have long recognized the value of initiation rituals in promoting the transition from childhood to adulthood (Allison, 2015). Coming-of-age stories are common in mythic hero tales about children confronting dangerous new worlds that must be conquered for entry into later developmental stages. A second purpose of transformations toward humility resides in their ability to promote healing. The simple act of sharing stories about hero transformations can foster self-awareness, relieve stress, and cultivate a sense of meaning. Third, humble transformations deepen spiritual and cosmic understanding. Campbell (1988) observed that the hero's transformation involves learning "to experience the supernormal range of human spiritual life" (p. 152). Hero myths, he said, "bring us into a level of consciousness that is spiritual" (p. 19). A fourth purpose of a transformation toward humility lies in its ability to cultivate social unity. Campbell (1972) argued that hero transformations "drop or lift [heroes] out of themselves, so that their conduct is not their own but of the species, the society" (p. 57). The transformed individual has moved "from the lesser, secondary knowledge of himself as separate from others" to "the greater, truer truth, that we are all one in the ground of our being" (p. 151). Transformed humble leaders are "selfless, boundless, without ego." No longer isolated from the world, transformed individuals enjoy a feeling of union with others. In describing the hero's journey, Campbell (1949) wrote, "where *we had thought to be alone, we* shall be with *all the world*" [italics added] (p. 25). The fifth purpose of humble transformations is to advance society. The culmination of the hero's journey is the hero's boon, or gift, to society. This gift is what separates the hero's journey from a mere test of survival. For the voyage to be heroic, the protagonist in myth must use her newly acquired humility to better the world.

During the hero's journey, heroes are humbled by their "fallings and failings" (Rohr, 2011, p. xv). Joseph Campbell (2004) acknowledged that not all heroic quests end with glorious, heroic success. He said, "There is always the possibility for a fiasco" (p. 133). Such fiascos can serve as the grist for a larger transformative mill, producing a kind of suffering needed to humble us and fuel a greater hero journey.

As we have seen in the previous chapter, transformation requires that we undergo a series of trials during our journey. Campbell (1988) believed that "trials are designed to see to it that the intending hero should be really a hero. Is he really a match for this task?" (p. 154). The point of greatest danger for the hero is when he or she enters the belly of the whale (Campbell, 1949). The belly can be entered literally as in stories of Jonah and Pinocchio, but usually the belly is a metaphorical place along the journey in which the hero's darkest inner demons must be "disempowered, overcome, and controlled" (p. 180). For Campbell, the hero's journey truly is an inner task of conquering one's fears and slaying one's dragons. In the 16th century, Saint John of the Cross referred to this ultimate trial as the *Dark Night of the Soul*, which describes a state of spiritual desolation that we are called to overcome and is at the heart of the road to enlightenment (Johnson, 1991). Positive psychologists today refer to this transformative process as posttraumatic growth, during which people convert the worst thing that ever happened to them into the best (Rendon, 2015).

Transformational Patterns

There are three patterns that characterize the transformational arc toward heroic humility (Allison & Goethals, 2017). First, there is a shift in mindset from *egocentricity* to *sociocentricity*. According to Campbell (1988), "when we quit thinking primarily about ourselves and our own self-preservation, we undergo a truly heroic transformation of consciousness" (p. 155). Campbell believed that one of the central functions of hero mythology is to connect one with the greater social world. In most hero narratives, the hero begins the journey as a disconnected, self-centered, prideful individual whose sole preoccupation is establishing identity, career, and material goods. The primary goal of the heroic leader's journey is to awaken the hero to the larger, deeper task of thinking beyond herself, to developing communion with everyone and with everything. In short, the heroic life is one that nurtures a compassionate and humble unification with all of humanity.

A second pattern of transformation toward humility can be described as a shift from *dependency* to *autonomy* (Allison & Goethals, 2017). Campbell (1988) believed that Western cultures promote dependency by emphasizing a preoccupation with safety, security, socioeconomic well-being, and entertainment. People's behavior and identity are steeped in consumerism, materialism, competition, violence, and nationalism. This emphasis on the lower-level needs in Maslow's (1943) hierarchy stunts people's transformative growth. A person's willingness to deviate from the dominant cultural pattern is essential for heroic transformation. Heroes do the right thing, and do what they must do, regardless of authority, tradition, and consequence. Maslow called this characteristic *autonomy*. "There are the 'strong' people," wrote Maslow, "who can easily weather disagreement or opposition, who can swim against the stream of public opinion and who can stand up for the truth at great personal cost" (p. 379). Fulfillment of the lower needs in the pyramid is essential for autonomy to develop in individuals. The world's most heroically humble leaders have been fearless in their autonomy. Examples of leaders we have not already mentioned include Joan of Arc, Malcolm X, and Harvey Milk.

The third heroic transformation toward humility is the change from *stagnation* to *growth*. One can be sociocentric and autonomous but not necessarily growing and stretching toward realizing full potential. The hero must leave home and venture out to obliterate a status quo that is no longer working. The pretransformed hero resists change, and severe setbacks may be her only impetus to grow. Without a prod, she will remain comfortable in her stagnation, oblivious to the idea that anything needs changing. For this reason, many spiritual traditions call the hero's journey an awakening to one's true calling in life, also described as the death of the false self and the birth of the true self. Campbell (1988) described the process as "killing the infantile ego and bringing forth an adult" (p. 168). This adult is always humble and in union with the world.

FACTORS THAT TRIGGER TRANSFORMATION TO HEROIC HUMILITY

Both internal and external factors can set off a cascading transformation to heroic humility. Painful as it can be, often it is failures and changes in the environment that lead to suffering that can initiate movement toward a life stance characterized by humility.

Internal Causes of Transformation

Internal factors that trigger a humble transformation include our mistakes and transgressions. Rohr (2011) observed that "failure and humiliation force you to look where you never would otherwise" (p. 66). Rather than get stuck in a cycle of shame and guilt about our errors, we can use them as fuel for transformation. Contemporary philosophy Leszek Kolakowski (2007) wrote, "the sacred is revealed to us in the experience of our failure" (p. 42). Carl Jung wrote extensively on the importance of learning from our *shadow*, that part of our personality that we deny but somehow holds the key to personal growth. Capitalizing on the dark side to ourselves, and using our mistakes to grow, has been called a spirituality of imperfection (Kurtz & Ketcham, 1992). No wonder Jean-Pierre Cuassade (2005) implored us to "Rejoice every time you discover a new imperfection" (p. 58).

Another way we internally transform to heroic humility is through our suffering, and from the sacrifices we make in life. We have already discussed the role of suffering in producing transformations to heroic humility. A related phenomenon is that of sacrifice, which is acknowledged to be another pivotal aspect of the hero's journey (Franco, Blau, & Zimbardo, 2011). When we choose to sacrifice for others, and when we give to others out of love and compassion, we have experienced our heroic humility.

External Causes of Transformation to Heroic Humility

Changes in the external environment can be exposure to magnificent sights, sounds, and experiences. Those can be transformative. But, as impressive as the magnificence of creation can be, it is the social environment that provides the most transformative possibilities. That is because of the sheer variety of social interactions we encounter.

Physical Environment

Psychologists have only recently begun to appreciate the transformative experience of *awe* in response to one's environment (Piff, Dietze, Feinberg, Stancato, & Keltner, 2015). Campbell (1972) believed that wonder and awe are keys to understanding the appeal of hero mythology. A central function of myth, he argued, is to "waken" the person and instill him or her with awe. "Nature, as we have seen, is tough. It is terrible, terrific, and monstrous" (Campbell, 1972, p. 215). Maslow considered the awe to be a main characteristic of self-actualized individuals. A sense of awe activates a sense of the humble self. "Wonder makes us fall to our knees," wrote St. Gregory of Nissa (Fell, 2011, p. 215).

Another, less appealing source of humility stemming from the environment are the obstacles we all face, and many of which we cannot surmount. Sacred texts have described transformative obstacles as goads. An ox goad was a sharp iron stick used to prod the oxen when plowing. Farmers would prick their animals to steer them in the right direction. At times the animal would rebel by kicking out at the prick, and this would result in the prick being driven even further into its flesh. In short, the more an ox rebelled, the more it suffered. We all have our goads that we can be tempted to rebel against. Our goads are something or someone that forces us to do what we would never do willingly. Loss, suffering, and difficult people can be our goads. According to Rohr (2011), goads "dethrone our own narcissism" (p. 34).

Social Environment

Many types of social events can trigger a heroic transformation toward humility, but we will focus on two: death and mentorship. The loss of a loved one may be life's most humbling experience. It has been said by many that the grave is a great equalizer. Perhaps this is one reason why we are so reluctant to criticize the dead. In fact, there is a tendency to elevate the dead to heroic status, and this "heroification" may arise from humbling effects of death (Allison, Eylon, Beggan, & Bachelder, 2009).

Another reason we are humbled by the hero's journey is because it underscores our need for help from others. None of us can do our life journeys, or our hero journeys, alone. One of the most essential social events of the hero's journey is the arrival of the mentor figure (Allison & Smith, 2015). In classic myth, the mentor is often a magical outsider, an elder, an exotic person or creature whom one would least expect to possess the wisdom needed for the hero to succeed. The majority of people who are asked to name their heroes mention a mentor or coach who had a transformative effect on them (Allison & Goethals, 2011). As legendary football coach Tom Landry observed, a mentor is someone "who tells you what you don't want to hear, who has you see what you don't want to see, so you can be who you have always known you could be" (Farcht, 2007, p. 294). Famous mentors in hero tales include Merlin the Magician who led King Arthur to develop the knowledge to rule England, Yoda who helped Luke Skywalker defeat Darth Vader, and Mr. Miyagi who trained the Karate Kid.

Good mentors equip the hero with what he or she needs, but there can also be dark mentors who steer the hero down a sinister path of self-destruction (Allison & Smith, 2015). Examples of dark mentors include the serpent in Genesis 3:4, Sauron in *Lord of the Rings*, Terence Fletcher in *Whiplash*, and Tyler Durden in *The Fight Club*. Good mentors humble us with their wisdom; dark mentors humble us by serving as the goad that we kick against.

The temporal sequencing of mentorship is an important element of the hero's journey. Mentors help heroes become transformed, and later, having succeeded on their journeys, these transformed heroes then assume the role of mentor for others who are at earlier stages of their quests. In short, "transformed people transform people" (Rohr, 2014, p. 263). Mentors can have a transformative effect with their words of advice, with their actions, or both. Words can fall on deaf ears but one's actions, attitudes, and lifestyle can leave a lasting imprint. St. Francis of Assisi humbly conveyed it this way: "You must preach the Gospel at all times, and when necessary use words" (p. 263).

WHAT TYPE OF TRANSFORMATION IS MOVING TOWARD HEROIC HUMILITY?

Allison and Smith (2015) argued that heroic transformations can be moral, mental, emotional, physical, or spiritual. We believe that a transformation toward heroic humility has elements of four of these types of transformations: moral, mental, emotional, and spiritual.

Moral Transformation

The moral transformation portrayed in countless stories is the protagonist's evolution from an immoral to a moral character. One of our favorite examples is found in Bill Murray's character, Phil Connors, in the 1993 film, *Groundhog Day* (Albert & Ramis, 1993). In this movie, Connors evolves from arrogant jerk to humbled altruist. Piff et al. (2015) noted that experiencing a sense of a "small self" is linked with generosity and heightened moral consciousness. In other words, transformations toward humility and selflessness appear to be linked.

Mental Transformation

Mental transformations refer to a lead character's change in intelligence, creativity, or some fundamental knowledge about the world. Our hero in *Groundhog Day*, Phil Connors, develops significant insight about life's priorities and about what kind of person he truly is. His transformation toward humility is not just moral; it represents a fundamental change in his mental outlook and worldview.

Emotional Transformation

Heroes often have to face emotional challenges that forever change them. In *The Hobbit* (Tolkien, 1937), Bilbo Baggins must face his fears and show grit and self-confidence. Louis Zamperini in *Unbroken* (Hillenbrand, 2010) is also a dramatic example of heroic growth in emotional strength, courage, and resilience. These characters are humbled by adversity, yet paradoxically, by being knocked down a peg, they are also elevated emotionally.

Spiritual Transformation

Spiritual transformations occur when characters undergo a change in their beliefs about the nature of God or the mysteries of the universe. Some spiritual transformations are about finding God, but not all. In the 2014 film *Interstellar* (Thomas, Orbst, & Nolan, 2014), Matthew McConaughey's character, an astronaut named Joseph Cooper, undergoes painful trials that forever alter his beliefs about the nature of the universe. His newfound humility, accompanied by insights about the glue that holds the cosmos together, can be considered a spiritual revelation.

THE PROBLEM OF TRYING TO "WILL" HEROIC HUMILITY

Psychologists, philosophers, and spiritual gurus are all in agreement that heroic humility is not something that you can decide to have. Rather, it is something that happens to you. Psychologist Leslie Farber (1966) is best known for his work on identifying the psychological problems that arise when people try to transform themselves rather than allowing the transformation to occur naturally. Farber recognized two realms of will. One realm is the domain of *objects*, which is under our control and consists of activities such as acquiring knowledge, going to bed, doing good deeds, and acting meekly. The second realm of will is the domain of *goals*, which are not under our control, although we would like them to be. So although we can choose to acquire knowledge, we cannot choose to be wise; although we can lie down, we cannot choose to fall asleep; although we can do good deeds, we cannot choose to become a hero; and although we can act meekly, we cannot choose to become humble.

The problem of trying to become humble is not unlike the elusive challenge of finding happiness. As Eleanor Roosevelt once said, "Happiness is not a goal; it is a byproduct." We argue that humility is also a byproduct of the vicissitudes of the life journey, the hero's journey. As Rohr (2011) noted, "Any attempt to engineer or plan your own enlightenment is doomed to failure because it will be ego driven" (p. 39). He added, moreover, "Once you can get 'out of the house,' your 'castle' and comfort zone, much of the journey has a life—and death—of its own" (p. 21). In short, "We cannot rush the process" (p. 24).

The hero's journey, replete with obstacles, setbacks, and transformation, remains one of the only true ways to acquire humility. A classic Islamic tale underscores this truth: A man approached an Islamic cleric and asked him to teach the man humility. The cleric responded, "I cannot do that because humility is a teacher of itself. It is learned by means of its practice. If you cannot practice it, you cannot learn it" (Kurtz & Ketcham, 1992, p. 185).

In this same vein, Farber (1966) provided clues about the genesis of heroic humility. If we cannot "will" it, then it can only emerge from challenging circumstances, when "we are mercifully free of self-consciousness, when our senses, and beyond our senses, our very being, are alert to the situation itself, ready to meet it, not to force it" (B. J. Moore, 2001, p. 1). Just as courage cannot be willed and only arises when dangerous circumstances force it out of us, humility cannot be willed and only arises when painful situations strain and tame our egos. Afterwards, our friends may infer that we have been courageous, or that we have developed humility, but to seek to acquire courage or humility directly is impossible. As Moore described it, "We are most free precisely at such moments of surrender, when the clamors and claims of self will are subordinate to the situation itself" (p. 1).

French philosopher George Bataille once noted, "Words have something of quicksand about them. Only *experience* [italics added] is the rope that is thrown to us" (Vande Kappelle, 2015, p. 107). Enlightenment and transformation cannot happen by reading books. We cannot decide to be enlightened and transformed; they are unplanned and often unsought. Psychologist Dan Gilbert was asked the secret of career success. His reply: "Get lucky. Accidentally find yourself at the right place and the right time" (Tesser, 1993). Gilbert's point is that although we would like to think of ourselves as the architects of our own destiny, we are more the product of situational forces beyond our control than we would like to think. Gilbert went on to explain this idea more fully in his best-selling book, *Stumbling on Happiness* (Gilbert, 2007).

Farber (1966) believed that many mental and emotional disturbances are caused by people trying to "will" goals that are unwillable. There are psychic costs to seeking happiness, courage, and humility, when these things cannot be wrested from life. The costs are often anxiety and depression, which have reached epidemic proportions today. Farber argued that we live in "The Age of Disordered Will" (Masters, 2010, p. 34). Campbell (1959) called our age "The Age of Anxiety" (Gerzon, 1998, p. 255) for the same reason. He wrote, "The failure of mythology and ritual to function effectively in our civilization may account for the high incidence among us" (p. 255) of anxiety and malaise. The hero's journey in storytelling and in our own lives makes transformation to heroic humility possible.

Media strategist Ryan Holiday (2016) believes that speakers at commencement ceremonies are misguided in urging graduates to "change the world." These speakers assume that such transformative actions are possible by simply deciding to do so. Author Nassim Taleb calls this tendency the *narrative fallacy* and explains that "narrativity causes us to see past events as more predictable, more expected, and less random than they actually were" (p. 1). People can harbor a simplistic understanding of events, causes, and effects—and this naiveté can undermine progress toward heroically humble transformation.

HEROIC HUMILITY DESCRIBES THE AUTHENTIC SELF

Perhaps no other film better captures all the essential elements of the hero's journey than *The Wonderful Wizard of Oz* (Baum, 1900). The hero, Dorothy, is sent on a dangerous journey against her will and is forever transformed by her experience. As with many heroes on their journeys, Dorothy is given the goal of finding home. Almost every hero's journey, either literally or metaphorically, is a journey homeward. And when they return home, as poet T. S. Eliot (1942) wisely observed, we "know the place for the first time" (p. 13). Such is the inevitable consequence of transformation. We gain new eyes—or at least adjusted vision.

The journey homeward is always an interior journey toward self-discovery. Joseph Campbell (1995) wrote, "The goal of the hero's journey is yourself, finding yourself" (p. 154). Kurtz and Ketcham (1992) observed,

> Home is the place where we can be ourselves and accept ourselves as both good and bad, beast and angel, saint and sinner. Home is the place where we can laugh and cry, where we can find some peace within all the chaos and confusion, where we are accepted and, indeed, cherished by others precisely because of our very mixed-up-edness. Home is that place where we belong, where we fit precisely because of our very unfittingness. Humility allows us to find the fittingness of our own imperfection. (p. 191)

The words *home*, *human*, and *humility* share the same root: the ancient Indo-European *ghom*, translated in English as humus, which is dirt, or earth. Thus to be humble is to be down to earth, rightsized, on level ground with everything else—in other words, right at home. Earlier, we noted that a transformation toward humility was a type of spiritual metamorphosis, a transformation toward "one-ness" with the world. Spirituality "involves a continual falling down and getting back up again" (Kurtz & Ketcham, 1992, p. 193). Spirituality "goes on and on, a never-ending adventure of coming to know ourselves, seeing ourselves clearly, learning to be at *home* [italics added] with ourselves" (p. 193).

Campbell (1991) argued that "true" human nature, the authentic self, is found only at the end of the hero's journey. Spiritual masters such as Eckhart Tolle speak of true human nature as consisting of a vast transformed intelligence, with all humanity occupying a single consciousness. The German philosophy Arthur Schopenhauer called it the "truer truth" that "we are all one" (Campbell, 1972, p. 151). According to Kurtz and Ketcham (1992), pride is "the root of all deviation and distortion from our *true* [italics added] being" (p. 171).

In Buddhism, the transformed mind, called the *bodhicitta*, is humanity's "true nature and condition" (Landaw, 2014, p. 3). It is an "impulse toward perfect altruism and self-forgetting" (p. 4). In Buddhism,

> the transcending of the notion of ego itself and the understanding that, in the final analysis, the existential barrier dividing self from others is totally unreal, a mere mental construction. Once this barrier has been crossed, the Bodhisattvas realize the unreality of the distinction between self and other, the sufferings of others become as real to them as their own. (p. 18)

The Bodhisattva takes "pleasure in the practice of humility" (Landaw, 2014, p. 71).

According to Buddhist tantra, "The more we train ourselves to see the basic equality of everyone—having overcome our habitual tendency to stick them rigidly into categories of friend, enemy, and stranger—the more our heart will open, increasing immeasurably our capacity for love" (Landaw, 2014, p. 54). This represents "the full realization of the bodhicitta" (p. 54). "In the clear space of the fully relaxed mind there is no distinction between your fundamental reality and my fundamental reality. One is not better than the other; one is not worse than the other" (p. 77).

One of Campbell's (1988) most celebrated quotes is "A hero is someone who has given his or her life to something bigger than oneself" (p. 151)—which we have talked about throughout as being "other-oriented to lift others up." The paradox here is that a transformation to becoming heroically humble means both finding oneself and also transcending oneself. This idea is pervasive in our culture. Mike Sullivan, head coach of the 2016 Stanley Cup champion Pittsburgh Penguins, said, "When you're part of something that's bigger than yourself, it's a special feeling" (Gentille, 2016, p. 1). The fictional character Professor Charles Xavier of the X-Men tells his students, "Here you have the chance to be part of something much bigger than yourself" (Donner et al., 2011). Norman Vincent Peale said, "The more you lose yourself in something bigger than yourself, the more energy you will have" (Dickerson, 2015, p. 115).

If you take the time to search the Internet for quotes about the transformative power of being part of something bigger than yourself, you will find many pithy sayings from both luminaries and laypeople. Our brief search yielded quotes on this topic from Barack Obama, Rachel Wolchin,

Jaireck Robbins, John Zorn, George Alexiou, Jim Rohn, Shimon Perez, John McCain, Walter Isaacson, Steve Jobs, Rex Harrison, and Jose Antonio Vargas, to name a few.

Martin Seligman (2011) himself, the founder of the field of positive psychology, wrote in his book *Flourish* that "the life committed to nothing larger than itself is a meager life indeed" (p. 284). We agree. Our friend and University of Richmond Chaplain Craig Kocher (2016) wrote that people's life purpose is discovering "a sense that one's life has a larger significance" (p. 184). Acquiring a humble sense of one's self as but a small part of something grand is not only part of life's journey, but it may also be the very centerpiece of the journey.

CONCLUDING THOUGHTS

When people embark on the hero's journey, they "undergo a truly heroic transformation of consciousness," requiring them "to think a different way" (Campbell, 1988, p. 155). The shift toward humility is one such metamorphosis, and it provides a new "a map or picture of the universe and allows us to see ourselves in relationship to nature" (Campbell, 1991, p. 56). Buddhist traditions and twelve-step programs of recovery refer to transformation as an "awakening." In a similar manner, Campbell (2004) described the journey's purpose as a much-needed voyage designed to "wake you up" (p. 12).

The world's most revered leaders have traveled the hero's journey of personal transformation and, in turn, have used their gifts to transform others. Martin Luther King Jr. came from humble origins to organize the American civil rights movement. He transformed himself and then heroically transformed others, as evinced in his famous quote: "Life's most persistent and urgent question is: what are you doing for others?" (Carson, 2001, p. 3). The hero's journey also characterizes the lives of indirect leaders such as Helen Keller. Born with illness that left her without sight or hearing, Keller overcame her severe disability to achieve a life of extraordinary philanthropy and humanitarianism. She said, "I long to accomplish a great and noble task, but it is my chief duty to accomplish humble tasks as though they were great and noble" (Wallis, 1983, p. 240). Keller's personal transformation toward heroic humility played an inspiring role in transforming the world.

The heroic leader's journey is the human journey, characterized by struggle, growth, learning, transformation, and ascendency from followership to heroic leadership (Goethals & Allison, 2016). Those who are compelled to transform by their journey grow into fully developed human beings ready, willing, and able to transform others. The transformed hero represents the pinnacle of human maturity, the state of well-being that allows people to flourish (Seligman, 2011) and experience *eudaimonia* (Franco, Efthimiou, & Zimbardo, 2016).

For Buddhists, the highest state of enlightenment is *nirvana*, a state of bliss when one is reborn into a new life and is free from all suffering. For Hindus, this ultimate state of bliss is *ananda*, and for Muslims it is *taqwa*. Peterson and Seligman (2004) identified six universal human character virtues—wisdom, courage, humanity, justice, temperance, and transcendence—that closely match Campbell's (1949) description of the transformed heroic leader. As a result of their journeys, heroic leaders acquire wisdom about themselves and the world, develop the courage to face their inner dragons, are in union with humanity, pursue justice even at a cost to themselves, become humbled and tempered, and use their acquired gifts to unify the world.

WHAT DID WE LEARN IN THIS CHAPTER?

1. There are three transformations toward heroic humility: from egocentricity to sociocentricity, from dependency to autonomy, and from stagnation to growth.
2. The four types of transformations we encounter in moving to heroic humility are moral, mental, emotional, and spiritual.
3. Trying to will ourselves to become heroically humble might be an exercise in humility, yet if one seeks to develop character strength throughout life, if one does have an opportunity for humble heroism, one is prepared.

THREE QUESTIONS FOR THOUGHT AND DISCUSSION

1. The authors say that most societies have initiation rituals aimed at guiding people toward developing humble characters. If this is so, why aren't more societies characterized by humble attributes?
2. Joseph Campbell (1995) wrote, "The goal of the hero's journey is yourself, finding yourself" (p. 154). But much of what the authors have written throughout this book is more about transcending the self by have others' betterment as our focal goal, not finding ourselves as the focus of our attention and energy. Of course, it is possible to help others while focusing on finding ourselves and also to find ourselves while focusing on helping others. Which one do you believe *should* be our goal?
3. If part of heroic humility is finding something "bigger than ourselves" to dedicate our lives to, how do we find that bigger cause? Have you found such a cause in your life?

10

EXEMPLARS OF HEROICALLY HUMBLE LEADERSHIP

> To be a great champion you must believe you are the best. If you're not, pretend you are.
>
> —Muhammad Ali

We begin this chapter with a very unhumble sounding quote from the late, great Muhammad Ali, a man whose cockiness belied his nature. Calling himself "The Greatest" early in his career, Ali alienated many who were turned off by the bragging of "The Louisville Lip" or "Gaseous Cassius." Now people realize that his braggadocio was always part of the act, something that enabled him to perform at his best in the ring. When Ali's image appeared on a box of Wheaties cereal, the citation credited his impact in sports and beyond: "He was a courageous man who fought for his beliefs" and "became an even larger force outside the ring with his humanitarian efforts." Indeed, Ali "devoted his life to helping promote world peace, civil rights, cross-cultural understanding, interfaith relations, humanitarianism, hunger relief, and the commonality of basic human values" ("Muhammad Ali," 2016).

In the present chapter, we profile some exemplars of heroic humility. These individuals have gone above and beyond everyday humility to acquire

http://dx.doi.org/10.1037/0000079-011
Heroic Humility: What the Science of Humility Can Say to People Raised on Self-Focus, by E. L. Worthington Jr. and S. T. Allison

a more highly developed heroic form of humility. Oversimplifying, there are two general types of heroes. There are those who respond to a particular situation, act into the danger inherent in the situation to promote or protect the welfare of others, and might (or might not) emerge with a changed character. They might have wonderfully humble characters, or not. But basically they are responding to situations. Their humility is largely incidental, and their heroism in response to danger is the key. There are other heroes, though, who commit themselves to costly actions, maintain their commitment across many hardships, and usually have humility shaped within their souls. They might have some characteristics that are not necessarily the most humble—consider Muhammad Ali. But they have a deep sense of humility from responding to struggles they have met head-on. Their humility is heroic humility.

A friend of ours once remarked with irony, "Fictional heroes are the only true heroes." What he meant, of course, is that fictional heroes can be counted on—more so than real-life heroes—to produce heroic results and display heroic traits. Allison and Goethals (2011) found that people rated fictional heroes as more extremely good than nonfictional heroes, and fictional villains as more extremely bad than real-life villains. Fictional heroes and villains are created to be vividly moral and immoral, respectively, and thus they can be considered "true" to us.

Myths and other fictional hero stories reveal basic truths about how to live a good life, and how a culture sees itself and would like to see itself. In constructing heroic tales, fiction writers are no doubt trying to entertain us. But hero stories also educate and inspire. Consider the ubiquitous nature of children's fairy tales. Vivid fables about heroes and villains, intended for children, are found in almost all human cultures. What is the point of these stories? For one thing, they teach us valuable lessons for living. The story of the three little pigs teaches us to plan ahead, to take precautions against danger. The third little pig clearly becomes the hero of the story by thwarting the wolf attack and protecting his siblings. The tragic fate of the other two pigs teaches us the danger of not having humility. Although we mention only a few fictional heroes next, we commend them as a great source of inspiration.

FICTIONAL HEROES OF HUMILITY FROM LITERATURE AND MOVIES

Atticus Finch

Heroically humble people are also morally courageous. They have the willingness to do the right thing even at great risk to their own well-being. In the novel *To Kill A Mockingbird* (H. Lee, 1960), Atticus Finch demonstrated great moral courage. He defied group pressures, put his family in danger, and stood by his belief in racial equality as a prominent lawyer who put the community's racist beliefs aside when he agreed to defend an African American named Tom Robinson. When the trial began, an angry mob of White men tried to lynch Robinson, but Atticus defused the situation.

Atticus was one of the few people in his small Southern town who believed in racial equality. It took courage to challenge the racist climate. It would have been easier for him to align with the majority than to fight for the rights of one Black man. Atticus showed his children firsthand a hard lesson about right and wrong and that sometimes the unpopular road is the right road. Witnessing their father's actions, Jem and Scout learned to stand up for truth and justice regardless of the consequences. Atticus spread moral courage without realizing it. His bold actions of moral courage showed that it didn't matter whether people viewed him as a hero. What mattered was the lesson, the example he set for his own children, and his bravery in going against his entire town to defend one man's rights. His action reflected the qualities of a truly moral lawyer and remarkable human being. Atticus Finch is an admirable hero of humility.

George Bailey

In the 1946 film *It's a Wonderful Life* (Capra, 1946), the lead character George Bailey emerges as one of the most saintly and selfless characters in movie history. As a child he saves his brother's life and stops the local pharmacist from accidentally poisoning a customer. As a young adult, he sacrifices his own life plans to save the town of Bedford Falls from falling into the hands of Mr. Potter, a greedy slumlord as evil as Bailey is good.

But it isn't George Bailey's heroic battle with Mr. Potter that makes him unforgettable. What moves us most about Bailey's character is the fallout from a mistake by Bailey's uncle. He misplaced cash that Bailey owed the bank. The cash inadvertently fell into Mr. Potter's hands. He issued a warrant for Bailey's arrest rather than return the cash.

The prospect of prison time prompted Bailey to consider suicide. However, a guardian angel (Clarence) appeared and showed Bailey what the world would be like had Bailey not lived. Bailey was stunned to learn that without him the world would be a grim place with thousands of lives lost or ruined. In this alternative timeline, Bailey was devastated to discover that his many friends were either dead or unrecognizably scarred, and that even his family did not exist.

Clarence then returned the distraught Bailey to the original timeline. Recognizing that he has had a wonderful life, Bailey rushed home a happy man despite being informed by authorities that he is under arrest for misappropriating funds. The prospect of imprisonment means far less to him than seeing his family again. But dozens of Bailey's friends and neighbors arrived to help him. Hearing that he is in financial trouble, they happily gave him money while joyously recounting the times Bailey saved them. The cash given Bailey is many times what he owes. So, the warrant for his arrest is dismissed. In an ironic reversal of the usual hero storyline, the hero Bailey has been saved by the town's citizens. *It's a Wonderful Life* is a rare example of the heroic humility of a protagonist being matched by the heroic humility of the supporting characters.

SPIRITUAL FIGURES WHO WERE HEROES OF HUMILITY

Jesus of Nazareth

Jesus embodied three important elements of heroic humility. First, he suffered terribly on the cross. His Roman executioners made sure that there was no more painful or grisly way to die. As we have seen in Chapters 8 and 9, suffering is strongly associated with heroic humility. Although not a rigorous rule, usually the more that heroes suffer for their cause, the higher the pedestal on which we place them.

Second, Jesus made the ultimate self-sacrifice. He died to save the world. The circumstances of his death are largely responsible for the formation of the Christian faith. As with other great heroes (e.g., Socrates), Jesus could have saved himself from his gruesome death by saying the right things to the authorities. But he stood by his principles.

Third, he transformed society, inspiring and elevating people to higher morality. Historian and author H. G. Wells wrote,

> I am an historian, I am not a believer, but I must confess as a historian that this penniless preacher from Nazareth is irrevocably the very center of history. Jesus Christ is easily the most dominant figure in all history. (Hodge & Patterson, 2015, p. 77)

Mohandas Gandhi, a Hindu, had nothing but praise for Jesus, describing him as "a man who was completely innocent, offered himself as a sacrifice for the good of others, including his enemies, and became the ransom of the world" (Steels, 2011, p. 241). Referring to Jesus' death at the cross, Gandhi said, "It was a perfect act" (p. 241).

Confucius

Some heroes have wisdom so timeless and profound that they are able to shape the moral philosophy of an entire society for millennia. Confucius fashioned a philosophy of virtuous living that is embraced today by hundreds of millions of Chinese, Japanese, Koreans, and Vietnamese. Confucius believed that people are teachable, improvable, and capable of great morality. He preached honesty, hard work, and learning by example. He communicated his wisdom by conversation, by asking questions, and by imploring students to find their own answers. Confucianism encourages the development of humility. One of his better-known aphorisms is "Real knowledge is to know the extent of one's ignorance" (Hult, 2006, p. 124). Confucius prepared his students for public service, to develop compassion, and to respect others. His philosophy emphasized justice, sincerity, and morality in personal life and government.

Confucianism exhorts people to strive for the ideal of the "perfect person" (Bakic-Miric, 2012, p. 23). An apt description of perfection is combining "the qualities of saint, scholar, and gentleman" (p. 23). Perfect people display morality, piety, and loyalty. They cultivate humanity, or benevolence. They champion strong familial loyalty, ancestor worship, and respect of elders by their children. According to Confucius, strong family values and relationships are the key to a stable society. Mutual respect and devotion to family are central to his teachings. In promoting all these virtues, Confucius proved himself to have heroic humility.

HISTORICAL FIGURES WHO WERE HEROES OF HUMILITY

John F. Kennedy

Kennedy served as America's president for less than 3 years but was rated as the sixth greatest president in a 2009 survey of historians, and the Kennedy magic is still strong to many Americans. A half-century after his death, he is still a hero across the country and around the world, especially in Boston. What accounts for Kennedy's status as a hero to so many people after such a long time?

He became a champion of public service and emphasized altruism and sacrifice, possibly more than any other president. Very few passages from presidential inaugural addresses are recalled or even recognized. But aside perhaps from FDR's "the only thing we have to fear is fear itself" (Houck, 2002, p. 4), Kennedy's call to service is the most familiar line from any inaugural address: "Ask not what your country can do for you, ask what you can do for your country" (Schlesinger, 2008, p. 32). Kennedy is positively associated with the Peace Corps, with the successful resolution of the Cuban missile crisis, and with the introduction of what became the 1964 Civil Rights Act. To many, Kennedy is one of America's great heroes of the 20th century. He was humbled by the Bay of Pigs fiasco and used the lessons learned from this humility to save the world from nuclear confrontation during the Cuban missile crisis.

Mother Teresa

Earlier we described the Great Eight traits of heroes—*smart, strong, selfless, caring, charismatic, resilient, reliable,* and *inspiring*. Which of these eight attributes is most central to heroism? Allison and Goethals (2011) asked participants to rank the Great Eight list in order of importance. One trait emerged as the most important: *selflessness*. Heroes, it seems, are strongly characterized by service to others, consistently placing the welfare of other people ahead of their own well-being. Devotion to service is the essence of heroic humility.

In modern culture, perhaps no other individual is more strongly associated with the trait of selflessness than Mother Teresa. As a young woman, she felt the call to serve God. At 18, she left home in Macedonia and joined the Sisters of Loreto, a community of nuns with missions in India. In 1931, she took her vows and joined a convent in Calcutta. At that time, she experienced what she later described as *the call within the call*. "I was to leave the convent and help the poor while living among them," she said. "It was an order. To fail would have been to break the faith" (Jacobs, 1994, p. 20).

Mother Teresa obtained permission to leave the convent and work among the poorest of the poor in the slums of Calcutta. In 1950, she founded the Missionaries of Charity to care for "the hungry, the naked, the homeless, the crippled, the blind, the lepers, all those people who feel unwanted, unloved, uncared for throughout society, people that have become a burden to the society and are shunned by everyone" (Goll, Goll, & King, 2016, p. 98). Missionaries of Charity began with 13 members. Today it has 5,000 nuns running orphanages, AIDS hospices, and charity centers that care for refugees and the blind, disabled, aged, alcoholics, poor and homeless, and victims of floods, epidemics, and famine. During her lifetime, she became an international symbol of love and service to others. Although she championed the cause of helping the poor in India, she was deeply concerned with the emotional and spiritual well-being of people residing in the more affluent Western world. "I found the poverty of the West so much more difficult to remove," she said.

> The poverty in the West is a different kind of poverty—it is not only a poverty of loneliness but also of spirituality. There's a hunger for love, as there is a hunger for God. The hunger for love is much more difficult to remove than the hunger for bread. (Teresa, 1995, p. 46)

The overarching theme of Mother Teresa's life was simply loving others. "Not all of us can do great things," she said. "But we can do small things with great love" (p. 47).

POLITICAL FIGURES WHO WERE HEROES OF HUMILITY

Besides our treatment of Nelson Mandela in Chapter 7, we can mention again George Washington (for more on Washington, see Chapter 4). As a young man, he served bravely and was an obvious choice to lead the first Continental Army starting in 1775, at the age of 43. He won the war mostly by not losing decisively and by not letting the British destroy his army. Quite remarkably, he resigned from the army after the war, though he easily could have become a military dictator or even king.

George III asked what Washington would do after the war. When told that he would go back to his farms, the king said that if he did so, he would be the greatest man in the world. That is exactly what Washington did, demonstrating remarkable heroic humility. After just a few years back at Mount Vernon, Washington was convinced to attend the constitutional convention in Philadelphia in 1787 and served as its president. Everyone knew that Washington would be the first American president and that he would conduct the office honorably and effectively. He was elected unanimously for two terms, the only man to be so chosen. He left office exhausted 2 years before his death, but he succeeded in establishing firmly our system of government.

During his lifetime, Washington developed deepening doubts about the morality of slavery. In his final act, Washington did all that he could to steer the country in the right direction: He freed his own slaves. Unfortunately, few others followed. It would take another great president with heroic humility, Abraham Lincoln (for more, see Chapter 10), to oversee the end of American slavery.

PUBLIC FIGURES WHO WERE HEROES OF HUMILITY

Grace Kelly

Winning an Academy Award at the age of 24, Grace Kelly[1] became Her Serene Highness Princess Grace of Monaco at age 26. But neither of these accomplishments made her a humble hero. An incident that took place in 1951 at the Stork Club in New York City revealed Grace Kelly's humble and heroic character.

[1]Our summaries of Grace Kelly's and Mae Jemison's heroic humility are based on excellent contributions from Rick Hutchins to Scott Allison's heroes blog (http://www.blog.richmond.edu/heroes). We are grateful to Rick for these insights.

At the time, the Stork Club was a popular hangout for celebrities from both Hollywood and Washington. As she dined with some friends and colleagues one night, she was witness to what was an all-too-common event in those days—a woman being refused service because of the color of her skin. That woman turned out to be Josephine Baker, an internationally famous singer and exotic dancer (herself a hero of World War II and the civil rights movement), who, at that time, was a far bigger celebrity than Grace Kelly.

With no thought to the possible consequences to her own career, Kelly left her dinner, took Baker by the arm, and departed for more welcoming pastures. (To their credit, her companions followed suit.) She vowed never to return to the Stork Club, and she kept that promise. From that night onward, Grace Kelly and Josephine Baker were lifelong friends. Throughout her short life, Kelly proved herself a true philanthropist, always using her fame and wealth and status to promote the betterment of mankind, work that still continues today through the Princess Grace Foundation. However, nothing exemplifies her heroic character more than that one selfless act of friendship to a stranger, in the days when that was all she had to offer.

Mae Jemison

Not all heroes are created in a moment of crisis or deadly peril. Sometimes a life will simply grow to heroic proportions. Mae Jemison is just such a hero, a polymath who has dreamed great dreams and made them come true and, in so doing, has shown us the greatness inherent in us all.

Mae Jemison, MD, is best known as the first female African American astronaut. If this were Jemison's only notable contribution, she would still be a hero worthy of the record books. However, this Renaissance woman's life was remarkable long before her historic shuttle flight and continues to be remarkable to this day. As a little girl, she was enamored of the arts and sciences. As early as kindergarten, she assumed that she would one day travel in space and that she would grow up to be a medical doctor. After completing her medical degree, Jemison spent 2 years in Liberia and Sierra Leone as a medical officer with the Peace Corps.

Following her historic career at NASA, Jemison started her own company, the Jemison Group, which develops science and technology for use in daily life. She also founded the Dorothy Jemison Foundation for Excellence, named for her mother, which promotes various projects, such as international science camps for children and adults. Several years later, she founded BioSentient Corp, a company that is working to commercialize a patented NASA biofeedback technology. She has also served on the board of directors of Gen-Probe Inc.; as an honorary member of Alpha Kappa Alpha, a sorority founded in 1908 at Howard University to promote scholarship among black women; as a professor-at-large at Cornell University; and as a professor of environmental studies at Dartmouth University.

To put it briefly, she has lived a life devoted to bettering humanity through the arts and sciences. Since her historic mission on the Space Shuttle Endeavor in 1992, Jemison has touched the lives of millions of Americans and given inspiration to countless women, minorities, and young people. However, just as there have been no limits in her own life, there are no boundaries to the dream she represents, and she has been a role model for people all around the world. She is the embodiment of the humble spirit that will take us to the stars.

SPORT FIGURES WHO WERE HEROES OF HUMILITY

John Wooden

John Wooden called the gymnasium his classroom. Wooden's primary goal never wavered: He taught his students how to succeed, not just in basketball but in life. To him, success was simple, unique, and refreshing: "Success comes from knowing that you did your best to become the best that you are capable of becoming," he said (Lindsey, 2010, p. 1).

Always a humble man, Wooden would recoil at mention of his accomplishments as a coach. But we would be negligent not to point out that his UCLA Bruins won more basketball championships than any other NCAA Division I team in history. He was a living legend for more than half his life. President George W. Bush also awarded him the Presidential Medal of Freedom, the nation's highest civilian honor.

Wooden had only a few team rules, and they were strictly enforced. Never be late. Be neat and clean. No profanity. And never criticize a teammate. He developed a seven-point creed by which to live one's life, and he followed it to the letter:

1. Be true to yourself.
2. Make each day your masterpiece.
3. Help others.
4. Drink deeply from good books, especially the Bible.
5. Make friendship a fine art.
6. Build a shelter against a rainy day.
7. Pray for guidance and give thanks for your blessings every day.

For Wooden, success was never about winning games. It was reaching one's potential. He taught his players that the final score of a game doesn't matter. "If you make an effort to do the best you can, the results will be what they should be," he said (Allison & Goethals, 2013, p. 85).

Wooden was most proud of witnessing dozens of his players become doctors, dentists, attorneys, and teachers. "I taught them that they were there to get an education," he said. "Basketball was second" (Allison & Goethals, 2013, p. 85). When Wooden passed away in 2010 at the age of 99, his former players and colleagues were effusive in their praise for the man they all called "Coach." Kareem Abdul Jabbar recalled that Wooden "really wanted us to get our degrees and learn what it meant to be a good citizen, good parents and husbands, and responsible human beings" (Allison & Goethals, 2013, p. 85). John Wooden was proof that coaches and teachers with heroic humility can impart those qualities to others.

Roberto Clemente

Roberto Clemente was a rare and extraordinary person who fit almost everyone's definition of hero. Nearly 4 decades after his death, Clemente's charisma, accomplishments, and selflessness make him unforgettable. Former major league baseball commissioner Bowie Kuhn once said of Clemente, "He had about him the touch of royalty" (Powell, 2014). Schools, hospitals, parks, and baseball fields bear his name today.

We won't delve into details of Clemente's genius on the baseball field. People who knew him argue that as great as he was a player, he was an even better human being. When traveling from city to city as a player, he routinely visited sick children in local hospitals. He spent much time in Latin American cities, where he would often walk the streets with a large bag of coins, searching for poor people. When he encountered needy strangers, he would ask for their name and inquire about their well-being. He would hand them coins until his bag was empty. Clemente once said, "Any time you have an opportunity to make things better and you don't, then you are wasting your time on this Earth" (Ford, 2005, p. 6).

To this day, Roberto Clemente's death at the end of 1972 still brings people to tears. He was carrying relief supplies to earthquake victims when his plane crashed after takeoff. News of his death spread quickly. In Puerto Rico, New Year's Eve celebrations ground to a halt. "The streets were empty, the radios silent, except for news about Roberto," said long-time friend Rudy Hernandez. "All of us who knew him and even those who didn't wept that week" (Allison & Goethals, 2013, p. 138). Another friend summed it up like this: "It was the night the happiness died" (p. 138).

ENTERTAINMENT FIGURES WHO WERE HEROES OF HUMILITY

Fred Rogers

About 20 years ago, a friend of ours was in the throes of a major depression. As she lay listlessly on the couch one day, feeling the weight of the world on her shoulders, she flipped through the television channels and came across the classic children's television program *Mister Rogers' Neighborhood.* Struck by the show's gentle, loving host Fred Rogers (see also Chapter 4), our friend penned a letter to him, expressing her grief and hopelessness but also her appreciation for his briefly lifting her spirits with his message of love and hope. A week later, to her great surprise, she received a handwritten letter back from Rogers, who thanked her for writing and gave her encouragement and support. To this day this framed letter from Rogers hangs on the wall of our friend's home, and she remains deeply grateful to him for reaching out to her during the most difficult time in her life.

Not surprisingly, Fred Rogers wrote many such letters to fans. In an age when celebrity misbehavior and drug use capture headlines, Rogers was a true gentleman whose primary mission in life was to enrich the lives of other people, especially children. Rogers developed a show in 1968 that helped children build self-esteem, conquer their fears, and love others. *Mister Rogers' Neighborhood* encouraged children to become happy and productive citizens.

Jimmy Fallon

When one of us (Scott) was a young boy, his mother often mentioned that actor and singer Pat Boone was the celebrity she most admired. The reason? "He's genuinely a nice guy." More than 30 years later, one of our daughters, at age 14, became a fan of actor and comedian Jimmy Fallon. The reason was familiar: "He's genuinely a nice guy," she said.

In a time when celebrities routinely make the news for their bad behavior, it is refreshing to find examples of decency and virtue. These rare shining lights in the entertainment industry are heroes to many young fans who are thirsty for positive healthy role models. Fallon began his career doing stand-up comedy, but he achieved fame during a 5-year stint as a cast member on *Saturday Night Live* (SNL). Well-liked by both his fans and costars, Fallon cultivated a reputation for being a genuinely good guy, almost generous to a fault, always available to fans. Fallon eventually left SNL, appeared in a few successful movies, and was then given his own show on NBC, *Late Night With Jimmy Fallon.*

All along his professional climb upward, Fallon has remained modest and likeable. He recently appeared on the cover of *Rolling Stone* magazine in

2011 with the caption "The eternal sunshine of Jimmy Fallon: Can anyone really be this nice?" And he is modest. "The fact that I get to work in TV is beyond belief," he said (F. Moore, 2010, p. 1). As befitting a hero, Fallon devoted both his time and money to many charitable causes, including the Food Bank for New York City, Stand Up to Cancer, AIDS research, and Robin Hood's antipoverty programs. To millions, Fallon sets a great example for how to treat people, conduct oneself, and handle success.

SOCIAL ACTIVIST HEROES WHO WERE HEROES OF HUMILITY

Bayard Rustin

Bayard Rustin was an accomplished tenor vocalist, a renowned scholar, and a versatile athlete. But Rustin's most important contribution to the world may have been his life-long devotion to defending the rights of oppressed groups of people across the globe, especially in the United States during the civil rights movement of the mid-20th century.

As a young man in the 1940s, Rustin helped convince President Franklin D. Roosevelt to eliminate racial discrimination in defense industries and in federal agencies. He traveled to California to protect the property of Japanese Americans who had been wrongly imprisoned in internment camps. In the Deep South, Rustin was arrested for violating segregated seating laws on buses, a crime for which he served 22 days on a chain gang. Between 1947 and 1952, Rustin made frequent trips to India and Africa to meet with practitioners of Gandhi's teachings about nonviolent protest philosophies. His subsequent influence on Martin Luther King Jr. was unmistakable. When Rosa Parks was arrested for bravely defying Jim Crow laws in Montgomery, Alabama, Rustin advised King to practice nonviolent protest.

But Rustin was limited in the help that he could offer King. A gay man, Rustin lived when homosexuality was unacceptable to most Americans. During the Montgomery boycott, a reporter threatened to undermine King's cause by exposing Rustin's sexual orientation. King and Rustin agreed that their civil rights crusade would be best served if Rustin distanced himself from King. Rustin was so careful not to undermine King's work that he fled Montgomery at night in the trunk of a car. Still, Rustin continued to advise King and influence the civil rights movement in significant ways from a distance that kept King safe from that criticism.

Rustin devoted his life to promoting human rights, not only in North America but in Haiti, Poland, Zimbabwe, and elsewhere. When asked to summarize his philosophy, he said, "The principal factors which influenced my life are nonviolent tactics; constitutional means; democratic procedures; respect for human personality; and a belief that all people are one" (Finkelman, 2009,

p. 144). As with many humble heroes, Rustin showed a courageous willingness to sacrifice his own well-being for a noble principle—equality—an illustration of other-oriented warmth toward people.

Malala Yousafzai

Malala Yousafzai grew up in the Khyber Pakhtunkhwa province of northwest Pakistan. This area was a dangerous and problematic part of Pakistan. The local Taliban went to great lengths to prohibit girls from attending school. Defying Taliban oppression, Malala (showing other-oriented humility) wanted to let the world know of this injustice. She blogged about life under Taliban occupation, their threats to control the country, and her views on education for the girls in Swat Valley. Malala's popularity grew, leading to interviews and a documentary film about her life. The Taliban took notice.

On October 9, 2012, a gunman shot Malala three times as she was boarding her school bus. She was in critical condition, but she survived. Despite Pakistan's effort to protect her and her family, the Taliban kept making assassination threats. These murderous threats only gave further visibility to the issues that Malala promoted. Malala's painful hero's journey led to a United Nations petition demanding that all children be in school by the end of 2015. Pakistan has now ratified their first Right to Education Bill. Malala's courage and selfless humility bettered the world. Today, she delivers speeches worldwide, writes blogs, and oversees the Malala Education Foundation, which enables girls living in poverty to attend school.

Malala's father, Zia Yousafzai, made the following statement, demonstrating his own heroic humility: "When Malala was shot, she was reborn. Now she's leading and I'm one of her supporters. I have found her more successful than me, wiser than me, and more resilient than me. I have learned from her many things" (Sanchez, 2016, p. 1).

MILITARY HEROES WHO WERE HEROES OF HUMILITY

Pat Tillman

Pat Tillman, whom we mentioned briefly in Chapter 4, didn't start out with dreams of serving in the U.S. military. Playing football was his passion. He was a star defensive safety for Arizona State University from 1994 to 1997, where he was an honor roll student. Believed to be too small to compete in the NFL, Tillman nevertheless made it to the Arizona Cardinals and made headlines for his ferocity. He made *Sports Illustrated*'s 2000 NFL All-Pro team and married his high school sweetheart, Marie. His future looked bright. It was not to be.

The September 11, 2001, terrorist attacks altered Tillman's priorities. Shortly after the attacks, Tillman turned down a multimillion dollar contract offer from the Arizona Cardinals. He enlisted in the U.S. Army to honor the sacrifices of others. "My great grandfather was at Pearl Harbor and a lot of my family has fought in wars," he said. "I really haven't done a damn thing as far as laying myself on the line like that. So I have a great deal of respect for those who have" (Cascio, 2011, p. 26). Tillman served his country with distinction until April 2004. He was killed in Afghanistan, 25 miles from the Pakistan border.

Tillman's self-sacrificing actions demonstrated the other-oriented nobility of character that drove his life. Millions of dollars and a life of luxury were less important to him than finding the terrorists who brought down the World Trade Center on September 11. Consistent with other heroes of humility, he was willing to die fighting for a just cause.

Dakota Meyer

On September 8, 2009, U.S. Marine Sergeant Dakota Meyer was in Afghanistan when he heard of an ongoing Taliban attack on a nearby village. Members of his unit and allied Afghan fighters were being bombarded. He repeatedly asked his superiors for approval to aid those under attack. Requests denied. It was too dangerous. Meyer was heavily outnumbered.

Defying orders, Meyer headed into the besieged village, where he encountered several wounded allied Afghan fighters. He transported them to safety and headed back into battle. Over several hours, Meyer entered the "kill zone" five times, rescuing 23 Afghans and 13 Americans. He was under heavy enemy fire the entire time from a numerically superior foe. Despite receiving shrapnel wounds to his arm, Meyer killed at least eight Taliban while evacuating people to safety. During one trip into the village, he stumbled across the bodies of four of his teammates killed by gunfire. "I checked them all for a pulse. Their bodies were already stiff," Meyer said (Walling, 2015, p. 87). He decided to bring his friends back home. Bleeding from his shrapnel wound and still under fire, he carried their bodies back to a Humvee with the help of Afghan troops. Meyer said that he expected to die that day. He also remains humble about his heroism, focusing instead on his guilt and pain of not being able to save the lives of the four men whose bodies he collected. "It's hard getting recognized for the worst day of your life," Meyer said. "There's not a day—not a second—that goes by when I don't think about what happened that day. I didn't just lose four [colleagues] that day; I lost four brothers. I went in there to get those guys out alive, and I failed. So I think it's more fitting to call me a failure than a hero" (Allison & Goethals, 2012, p. 1).

During the Medal of Honor ceremony, President Obama addressed Meyer's obvious heartache. "Dakota, I know that you've grappled with the grief of that day; that you've said your efforts were somehow a failure because your teammates didn't come home," Obama said. "But as your commander-in-chief, and on behalf of everyone here today and all Americans, I want you to know it's quite the opposite. You did your duty, above and beyond, and you kept the faith with the highest traditions of the Marine Corps that you love. Because of your honor, 36 men are alive today" (Kummer, 2015, p. 326).

SCIENTIFIC FIGURES WHO WERE HEROES OF HUMILITY

Albert Einstein

Scientists are often humbled by the complexity of the natural forces that they attempt to understand. Albert Einstein once said, "I have no special talents. I am only passionately curious" (Calaprice, 1996, p. 29). *Time* magazine, in awarding Einstein the Person of the Century award, noted the following: "Einstein taught the greatest humility of all: that we are but a speck in an unfathomable large universe" (Qazi, 2014, p. 62).

If anyone had reason not to be humble, it was Einstein. By the age of 26, he had revolutionized the field of physics, publishing four seminal research papers on the special theory of relativity, the Brownian motion theory, the photon theory of light, and the equivalence of mass and energy. In a single year! A decade later he published a paper on general relativity, unifying Newton's law of gravity and special relativity. Yet he knew that there was far more to learn about our physical world than what he had discovered.

Einstein was offered the presidency of Israel in 1952, but he declined the honor. His focus was on transforming society's perceptions of scientists. From his writings it is clear that he believed that scientists have a moral responsibility to improve humanity. He was an outspoken advocate of pacifism, international cooperation, democracy, and improving the quality of human life. He helped reshape the image of the scientist from a private specialist to a public personality deeply committed to improving the fate of humanity. His heroic humility in his career might well have been as profound as any of his theoretical advances in physics.

Joseph Campbell

Ironically, the first psychological analysis of heroism wasn't penned by a psychologist. We have referred to Campbell many times in this book; he was a comparative mythologist who mostly studied medieval literature and world religions. In 1949, he published *The Hero With a Thousand Faces*, one of the most influential books of the 20th century.

Campbell proposed that the Jungian hero archetype can explain the pervasiveness of the hero monomyth found across time and geography. Human beings, in effect, may have a biological readiness to encounter heroes and to resonate to hero stories that fit the Campbellian monomythic structure. George Lucas, creator of *Star Wars*, admits that he based *Star Wars* on the hero monomyth. Disney movies such as *Aladdin*, *Beauty and the Beast*, and *The Lion King* also have been influenced by Campbell. Musical artists such as Bob Dylan, Jim Morrison, and Jerry Garcia of the Grateful Dead have all produced work based on Campbell's hero monomyth.

Always humble, Campbell lived most of his life believing that very few people would ever read his work or be influenced by it. His first attempt to publish *The Hero With a Thousand Faces* was met with failure. The publisher was convinced there would be no audience. The unprecedented success of *Star Wars* in the 1970s propelled Campbell's work into the cultural mainstream, catching him by surprise. No doubt, if he were alive today, he would greet his pivotal role in developing a new field of heroism science with the same humble spirit.

EVERYDAY PEOPLE AS HEROES OF HUMILITY

Corrie ten Boom

People are moved by powerful tales of heroism in defiance of the Holocaust during World War II. Corrie ten Boom was a leader of the Dutch resistance during the Nazi occupation of the Netherlands. She helped an estimated 800 Jews avoid Nazi concentration camps during the war. Ten Boom's father, Casper, played a critical role in shaping her values and worldview. The ten Booms lent a helping hand to people of all faiths. When Casper was asked whether he knew he could die if he were caught helping Jews, he replied, "It would be an honor to give my life for God's chosen people" (Edensor, 2015, p. 1).

To hide Jews in their home, the ten Booms built a secret room in Corrie's bedroom, located on the top floor. Eventually an informant reported the ten Booms' activities to the authorities. The entire ten Boom family was shipped to concentration camps. Corrie was released from Ravensbruck on New Year's Eve of December 1944. She later learned that her discharge was due to a clerical error and that all the women her age were sent to the gas chamber.

After the war, in 1947, she was approached one day by a cruel Ravensbruck guard. "Will you forgive me?" he asked, and held out his hand. Ten Boom recalled the moment:

> I stood there and could not. Betsie [Corrie's sister] had died in that place. Could he erase her slow terrible death simply for the asking? It could not have been many seconds that he stood there, hand held out, but to me it seemed hours as I wrestled with the most difficult thing I had ever had to do. We then grasped each other's hands, the former guard and the former prisoner. I had never known God's love so intensely as I did then. (D. Bennett, 2014, p. 50)

Corrie ten Boom taught us that forgiveness may be one ultimate reflection of heroic humility.

Randy Pausch

Some heroes move us by the way they live, and some by the way they die. Randy Pausch was a hero who did both. Pausch was a professor of computer science at Carnegie Mellon University in Pittsburgh who, at the age of 46, was diagnosed with untreatable pancreatic cancer. With only months to live, Pausch was invited by Carnegie Mellon to give *The Last Lecture*—a speech in which eminent professors impart their final words of wisdom as if it were their last chance to do so. In Pausch's case, it was true.

The lecture, given September 18, 2007, was entitled "Really Achieving Your Childhood Dreams." As befitting a hero, Pausch imparted wisdom. "Never give up," he said. "Brick walls are there for a reason: they let us prove how badly we want things. Don't bail" (Zaslow, 2007, p. 1). Pausch emphasized the importance of helping others, nurturing relationships, and remaining loyal to friends. "Do the right thing," he said. "If you lead your life the right way . . . [your] dreams will come to you" (Zaslow, 2007, p. 1). At the end of his lecture, Pausch received a lengthy standing ovation from a tearful audience.

Pausch succumbed to his illness in July 2008 at the age of 47. After his diagnosis, no one would have blamed him if he had simply spent private time with his family. Heroes, however, shun the easy path. They humbly share their time, their wisdom, and their love for others in an effort to make the world a better place. Pausch surely did that, and more.

HUMBLE HEROES WHO OVERCAME GREAT ADVERSITY

Helen Keller and Anne Sullivan

Adversity often gives rise to the greatest and most humble heroism. Helen Keller, whom we mentioned briefly in Chapter 8, is a striking example.

When she was 19 months old, she contracted an illness that left her blind and deaf. She was imprisoned in a dark, silent world. No one in her family could reach her. Her parents hired 20-year-old Anne Sullivan to educate Keller, a seemingly hopeless task. Sullivan was visually impaired herself, and she was empathic, patient, resourceful, and persevering.

Thanks to Sullivan, Keller was transformed into a bright, curious, lovely young woman who was destined to make a positive mark on the world. The bond between Keller and Sullivan grew into a 49-year friendship. Keller was the first deaf-and-blind person in America to graduate from college. She later became a prolific author and an advocate for people with disabilities. The 1962 film *The Miracle Worker* inspired millions of people with its story of her triumph over disability and Sullivan's selfless devotion to helping her fulfill her vast potential. In addition, Anne Sullivan deservedly acquired the reputation as a legendary teacher. Keller and Sullivan are forever linked as heroes of humility who brought out the best in each other.

Lois and Bill Wilson

There is a deep humility at work when one admits to having an addiction and is willing to do the necessary work to address the problem. Bill Wilson, the central founder of Alcoholics Anonymous (AA), knew that he was dying from the disease of alcoholism and began experimenting with a new method of treatment. He and cofounder Dr. Bob developed the Twelve-Step recovery program of AA that bears a striking resemblance to the hero's journey. Bill's wife, Lois, developed the Al-Anon Family Groups after experiencing many years of emotional heartache and financial ruin while living with Bill. Lois was among the first to recognize that alcoholism is a family disease that has adverse emotional effects on every member of the alcoholic's family.

The story of Lois and Bill is poignant. After marrying Bill in 1918, Lois saw him and their marriage spiral down because of the ravages of the disease of alcoholism. During the 1920s and 1930s, Bill's drinking problem destroyed his career, his relationships, and his health. Lois tried, but there was nothing she could do to stop him from drinking. While her husband attended AA meetings, Lois would socialize with family members of other alcoholics and became aware of the devastating effects the disease had on spouses and children. In 1951, she established the Al-Anon Family Groups, a program of recovery for families and friends of alcoholics.

What are the core tenets of AA and Al-Anon? First, it is humility—no one can put an end to a drinking problem except a Higher Power. AA members focus on physical sobriety, and Al-Anon members focus on enriching their own moral and spiritual lives and on not contributing further to the alcoholic's disease. During the early years of Al-Anon, Lois spoke to many groups, sharing her wisdom and inspiring tens of thousands of people. She was instrumental in developing Al-Anon books, pamphlets, manuals, and guidelines.

Both Bill and Lois showed a deep heroic humility. Bill acknowledged that AA "is a terribly imperfect society because it is made up of very imperfect people. I know because I constantly fall short" (Kurtz & Ketcham, 1992, p. 203). Lois always gave Bill unconditional love, even during the worst moments of their marriage. She exuded a positive attitude, which has its imprint all over Al-Anon's principles of recovery. "The world seems to me excruciatingly, almost painfully beautiful at times," she said, adding that "the goodness and kindness of people often exceed that which even I expect" (White & Lindsey, 2017).

A CHAPTER-ENDING THOUGHT

In the Tate Modern hangs a picture, "The Boyhood of Raleigh," by Sir John Everett Millais. An animated bronzed Genoese sailor and storyteller is pointing to the vast open sea as future explorer Sir Walter Raleigh and another boy, then 10 years old, watch spellbound. If one is to achieve the adventure and discovery that Raleigh did as an adult, it is important to learn how to sail, navigate, and construct and repair ships. But often it is the stories that capture the heart and start the journey toward our life's work. We hope that the stories of heroic humility in this chapter and throughout the book capture your heart.

WHAT DID WE LEARN IN THIS CHAPTER?

1. Humility is exemplified by many inspiring humble heroes from fiction and various walks of life. They include spiritual figures, historical figures, political figures, public figures, sport figures, entertainment figures, social activists, military heroes, scientific figures, everyday heroes, and people who fought to overcome great adversity. There were many reasons for sharing these stories.
2. As these stories show, regardless of what your vocational or personal activities are, you can become a heroically humble person if you wish and if you prepare yourself for opportunities that might come available.
3. Stories often capture the heart—sometimes more than facts and figures. This chapter is a necessary complement to the scientific approach.

THREE QUESTIONS FOR THOUGHT AND DISCUSSION

1. Did you identify any particular people who resonated with you and might become (or already are) your heroes of humility?
2. Virtually all of these heroes were highly devoted to a cause. Is it necessary to have an overarching cause to be heroically humble? How might we find a cause worth expending our lives for? Do our friends and family members represent such a cause?
3. Carnegie Mellon professor Randy Pausch was invited to give *The Last Lecture*, which is a tradition in which eminent professors impart their final words of wisdom as if it were their last chance to do so. If you could give a graduating class of university students and their parents a last lecture, what would you say to them?

IV

APPLICATIONS OF THE SCIENCE OF HUMILITY TO 21ST-CENTURY LIFE

11

LIFE LESSONS FROM HEROES OF HUMILITY

In Part IV of this book, we draw together some observations about humility and describe what psychological science has told us about what humility is, how to nurture it, and—if one wishes—how to become a more humble person. We also describe how one might help others become more humble, if asked.

First, though, having now discussed heroic humility and told the stories of a number of heroically humble people, we pause in the present chapter to try to discern some life lessons from the various exemplars of humility and the research that has been conducted on humility. In Chapter 12, we examine what stands in the way of people deliberately succeeding at becoming more humble. Some of it is generational—the *Zeitgeist* of Generation Me, as Twenge (2014) called it. Some is what the field of social cognition has taught us over the last 20-plus years: We are self-interested creatures, and much of that bias seems to be woven into the fabric of our nature. With those

http://dx.doi.org/10.1037/0000079-012
Heroic Humility: What the Science of Humility Can Say to People Raised on Self-Focus, by E. L. Worthington Jr. and S. T. Allison

cautionary tales in mind, we tackle in Chapter 13 a review of the efforts to date and, for those available, scientific studies of their efficacy. We speculate on how one of these programs might use our findings of this book to improve people's deliberate efforts to become more heroically humble. In Chapter 14, we draw on organizational psychology's studies of leaders and consider how to help people become more heroically humble leaders. In Chapter 15, we consider the themes we have developed in the book.

What can we conclude about heroes of humility? From our base of understanding of what humility is, how we can measure it, and what its effects are on relationships, on mental and physical health, on spirituality, on society, and on ultimate satisfaction, we have observed many heroically humble people. We can draw a number of conclusions from both the science and examples we have seen.

A FEW LESSONS IN BEING A HEROICALLY HUMBLE PERSON

We begin with a caution. As we noted in Chapter 10, Farber's (1966) work suggests that we cannot "choose" to become heroically humble. That doesn't mean we are helpless in cultivating virtues such as humility. But we can only choose to work to shape our lives toward humility, and we can't determine the actual outcome. So here are some suggestions.

Avoid the Easy Way

Humble heroes avoid the smooth and easy path of pursuing pleasurable self-interest. They climb and claw up mountains and cliffs (think Edmund Hillary), hack through gigantic jungles (think Albert Schweitzer), break rocks in the sweltering sun (like Nelson Mandela on Robben Island), and trudge through stinging snowstorms (think George Washington at Valley Forge or Aleksandr Solzhenitsyn in exile in Russia) to help others.

Heroes can suffer horrific hurts and hardships and survive. We have mentioned just a few. It is clear that the longer we live, the more likely we are to experience life's "slings and arrows of outrageous fortune" that provide challenges to youthful pride and opportunities to develop humility. Humility starts to develop early. Hagá and Olson (2017) had children ages 4 to 11 years evaluate people who were intellectually humble or intellectually arrogant, and they could tell the difference from middle childhood onward. But the development of humility accelerates when people are old enough to experience suffering. Those life challenges offer opportunities to become more humble. Obviously, not everyone accepts those opportunities over a lifetime, but many do. This has become obvious in recent large-scale work that supplements the longitudinal work by Krause that we have profiled in many chapters in the book. For example, Milojev and Sibley (2017) studied patterns of change in personality traits across the lifetime of adults ages 19 through 74 years. They found support in their longitudinal, six-wave sample of 10,416 New Zealand adults that the period of young adulthood to about the age of 30 was a crucial period for development of personality traits. However, they also found continuing change throughout the adult lifespan. Although the changes in the Big Five were interesting, they also found that honesty–humility showed a pronounced and consistent increase across the adult lifespan. This same trend was found in the work of Ashton and Lee (2016), who used an online multinational cross-sectional sample of around 100,000. Honesty–humility gradually increased by about one standard deviation between ages 18 and 60. Kawamoto (2016) investigated age differences in personality in Japanese middle adults ($N = 2{,}000$; $M = 40.94$ years, $SD = 5.35$, range 30–49; 1,000 women). After controlling for demographics, Kawamoto found that Honesty–Humility increased with age. Kawamoto suggested that personality development, in general, may differ slightly between Western and non-Western countries, but in Honesty–Humility, the patterns were virtually the same as in Western countries. Wherever we are, life invites us—whether we want or not, whether we accept or not—to develop humility, and suffering is often the invitation card.

Humble heroes don't wear that suffering on their sleeves. Perseverance through the long, difficult journey of those who suffer for the good of others without seeking recognition and reward makes them humble heroes. Humble heroes save others from suffering, and sometimes they even struggle to save themselves from suffering.

Humility does not always develop through suffering and privation. Holding a baby in one's arms can fill people with awe, a sense of their limitations, a desire to be teachable, a sense of modesty, and an orientation toward someone who needs care. The same experiences can happen with marriage, grandparenthood, and even promotion to a position of leadership.

Humility Does Not Always Look the Same

As we've seen from the many examples throughout the book thus far, humility can be different in different relationships. Different events trigger humility. Different relationships make it more or less likely to be practiced. That is also what the research tells us. Humility involves accurately assessing oneself and placing the needs of others over one's own and acting to promote the other's interests. People can be humble in one act but never again, can be humble in a particular setting because the conditions just seem to align but not in any other setting, and can be humble in some relationships but not in others.

For most of us, humility is impossible to successfully maintain through one's self-control, and ironically, the only way to defeat pride, self-focus, and ego is to focus on something greater than oneself. That makes it distinctly a spiritual quality because all four major forms of spirituality (religious, humanity, nature, and transcendent) focus people on things greater than they are. But while the spiritual nature of humility allows it to soar, it must, in the end, return to the *humus*, be grounded in helping others (even if that is motivated by a desire to serve God).

Seeing the many different ways that people have been humble gives us (Ev and Scott) hope that perhaps we can find other ways. Each person has a unique life, and each will find his or her own path to heroic humility if that path is being sought.

Lasting Humility Grows From an Acorn and Becomes a Mighty Oak

Lasting humility that has been grown into one's character is a virtue. A *virtue* is a lasting, acquired way of being in many relationships as a moral person. Moral acts go beyond mere dispositions by being oriented at least in largest measure toward seeking the good (for self and others), doing right, acting well, and thus benefiting others (even though a secondary consequential pleasure from doing good might occur). Moral character is not born full-blown. One does not assume a CEO position and then find the next day that he or she is humble. Humility is sown as an acorn. It grows into a flexible whippiness during the adolescent years of experimenting with one's personality. It firms up during the college years, and its trunk thickens and its roots deepen until it is a mighty oak during adulthood. Unlike the physical body, which gradually loses strength each year of adulthood after a certain point, humility stands firm until at last age allows it to lie down and take its rest.

Abraham Lincoln is on everyone's list of the top three American presidents (Lichtman, 2000, Lecture 1). He is an icon of humility. That humility was born of a harsh boyhood. We know the stories about being raised in poverty in a log cabin, educating himself by reading borrowed books, walking 10 miles to return a borrowed book, and losing loved ones. His biographer, David J. Bobb (2013), wrote,

> Hardship sometimes has a way of pressing humility on a person. The poverty into which Lincoln was born, and in which he languished for the first half of his life, made him more aware of its sting in the lives of others. The powerlessness he felt early in life, too, shaped his own conscience and heightened the attention he would show later in life to the plight of the powerless. His loss of love and loved ones reminded him of the even deeper loneliness suffered by widows and orphans. (p. 137)

Indeed, hardships sometimes will crush character qualities like ambition—which Lincoln had in spades in his young adulthood—and arrogance. Hardships can put tension in the bow and aim humility at the soul. Whether the aim is true and whether the arrow sticks are different matters. When the arrow of humility begins to pierce the soul, it is like an arrowhead of gas is inserted into the soul. Like gas, it spreads to fill every square inch of the soul. Unfortunately, arrogance is also like a gas, one that can poison the soul. Lincoln learned that reverence—for God, for the law—helps govern unruly passions. Reverence for the good things builds humility, and "humility helps us govern our passions," said Bobb (2013) about Lincoln:

> The lower parts of the soul must be controlled by the higher, and humility helps to order the passions by restraining the most tyrannical of them. . . . As a virtue, humility has an ordering quality to it. Arrogance has the opposite effect, as it loosens the grip of self-control and throws a human soul into disorder. (p. 131)
>
> Humility for Lincoln came first by hardship and then by habit. His early experiences without privilege, power, or prestige gave him an appreciation of how hard-won success is. It impelled him to fight so that others might have the opportunity he found. (p. 138)

Near the end of the Civil War, he thought a lot about these themes that had developed from the acorn years—privilege, privation, power, prestige, passions, and Providence. Although he was not a religious man until near the end of his life, he thought a lot about Providence. Lincoln's secretary preserved a private memo that lets us into his mind as the Civil War began to enter its last years. Lincoln wrote,

> The will of God prevails. In great contests, each party claims to act in accordance with the will of God. Both may be, and one must be, wrong. . . . In the present civil war it is quite possible that God's purpose is something different from the purpose of either party. (Basler, 1959, p. 237)

What was that secret purpose? By his second inaugural address, on March 4, 1885, just 37 days from the war's end and 42 days from his death, Lincoln had been given some light, which he shared in his second inaugural address:

> The Almighty has his own purposes. . . . He gives to both North and South this terrible war as the woe. . . . Fondly do we hope, fervently pray that this mighty scourge of war may speedily pass away. Yet if God wills that it continue . . . until every drop of blood drawn with the lash shall be paid by another drawn with the sword, as was said three thousand years ago, so still it must be said "the judgments of the Lord are true and righteous altogether." (Safire, 1997, p. 471)

This could have turned many toward retribution. In fact, it did in the reconstruction period after Lincoln's death. But it did not turn Lincoln to retribution. It turned his heart back to poverty, powerlessness, and privation, and he concluded the address with his plea for reconciliation:

> With malice toward none, with charity for all, with firmness in the right as God gives us to see the right, let us strove on to finish the work we are in, to bind up the nation's wounds, to care for him who shall have borne the battle and for his widow and orphan, to do all which may achieve and cherish a just and lasting peace among ourselves and with all nations. (Safire, 1997, p. 471)

The Path to Virtue

One becomes more humble first by glimpsing the goal of the good that one wishes to exert effort toward. This requires preconditions—to discern what is good (Sophia), to have the prudence (practical wisdom) to discern the best means to the good, and to have the courage to overcome fear of failure and other fears to pursue the good. Second, one works until doing good becomes a habit of the heart. Third, one practices perfectly. In doing so, one tests the virtues through self-control and deals with life's trials through wisdom, prudence, and courage. Fourth, one experiences meaningful happiness (which might or might not involve temporal happiness) that comes from a virtue acted out.

Glimpse the Goal

Glimpsing the goal requires cultivating wisdom, prudence, and courage. Wisdom sees the value of outcomes. Prudence sees consequences and ways to devise alternate paths to different consequences. Courage involves the will to act to achieve the right or good outcomes. As a premise, people are naturally self-interested and have a self-serving bias. They also are naturally group-oriented creatures with a desire to promote the group. Glimpsing the goal is keeping the benefit of others more important than one thinks is the self-benefit. Because one's mind is organized by System 1 thinking, which is inherently self-interested, we will usually underestimate how much self-interest and self-serving bias is governing. Thus, the virtuous person will elevate all the more the benefit of others. Often, it is hearing the stories of others that kindles the spark of humility within and sets us up for fanning the flame.

Habituate the Heart

Habituating the heart requires (a) assaying the self to find instances of relational humility in various relationship, (b) enhancing relational humility systematically in each of those relationships (using a solution-focused method of seeking a gradual, step-by-step improvement), and (c) seeking to generalize learning to new relationships until most relationships and most of the time one is behaving humbly. This sounds cognitive. It isn't. The process is one of training the will and emotions rather than training the intellect. The intellect usually acts subservient to the will and emotions and behavior, justifying what one has done or desires to do. So, if we train the will and emotions, the assaying, enhancing, and generalizing become more natural to develop. Habituating the heart is more about retraining through repetition the rhythms and rituals of everyday life than about willing the heart to change. It is repeated humble acts that characterize us—that is, those acts build into our being a humble character.

"Practice Doesn't Make Perfect; Perfect Practice Makes Perfect"

This is a quote from the legendary coach of the Green Bay Packers, Vince Lombardi (n.d.), during the years of the Packer dynasty. Practicing perfectly involves both devising tests of humility that one can succeed at and meeting life's trials. Both require recognizing the test as a challenge—humility is placed under strain when the ego is challenged (i.e., times of success, times of failure and threatened loss of esteem, times of disagreement). Both require strategies for facing the test—we must consult wisdom, exercise prudence, and act in courage. Meeting both self tests and life tests requires humble action.

Generate Generativity

Experiencing satisfaction in humility requires contenting oneself, even if one is not happy or is suffering. This requires taking pleasure in the success of others and quelling the demands of ego. It requires generativity rather than ambition.

Venerate the Virtues

The research clearly tells us a number of things. We have learned (see Chapter 5) that in general, humility is related to other prosocial virtues, and it is negatively related to vices like narcissism, Machiavellian manipulation, and antisocial acts. Also, humility takes many bumps out of close relationships, helps people heal breeches in those relationships, and provides the social oil to make new relationships function well (Chapter 4). This provides a self-reinforcing spiral that leads to good mental health, and, it is hypothesized, good physical health (Chapter 6). Spirituality is heightened to the extent that one is humble in the face of the Sacred (Chapter 7). Societal peace is promoted to the extent people can cooperate humbly (Chapter 8). Finally, humility leads to a sense of ultimate well-being or purpose (Chapter 8).

Lead With Heroic Humility

Humble leaders can help those whom they are leading. A humble stance makes relationships smoother, as we will see in Chapter 14 from research on individual leader, team, and organizational humility by Brad Owens and his colleagues at Brigham Young University (A. S. Wallace, Chiu, & Owens, 2017). Furthermore, as the social bonds hypothesis (D. E. Davis et al., 2013) and other social hypotheses show us (see Chapter 3), humility is socially attracting. Groups led by humble people cohere, and group cohesion promotes good working relationships. Of course, humility in a leader without clear direction and vision for the future might just promote a cohesive group that wanders aimlessly and does not achieve goals. Thus, humility is not an end-all. But it might be, like the relationship in psychotherapy, a great jumping-off point. Success is not impossible if the leader is not humble, but the odds are stacked against the nonhumble leader.

There might be times, too, when simply being humble is not enough for the leader. There might be times in which a heroic humility (see Chapters 8, 9, and 10) is demanded for optimal success. Two types of heroism are possible. One is a long-standing moral courage, such as Gandhi exhibited in persuading India to expel Great Britain from rule in India. The other is the quick, and sometimes very costly, self-sacrifice of a humble leader—such as when Lee Iacocca, CEO of Chrysler Corporation in the 1980s, turned the car company's fortunes around when he made a public declaration that he would not take a salary until the fortunes of the company improved. Drawing on the wisdom of Margaret Mead, he said, "We are continually faced by great opportunities brilliantly disguised as insoluble problems."

Humility Is Not WEIRD

We have used many examples from the United States. But that does not mean that we believe that humility is particularly WEIRD—Western, Educated, Industrialized, Rich, and Democratic (Henrich, Heine, & Norenzayan, 2010). We have instead chosen examples from many cultures, religions, nations, genders, races, and ethnicities. In Chapter 13, we tackle the cultural pressures for and against humility head-on. We do so by reviewing social psychological research that suggests that humility is not something natural in Western culture. However, we find an equal array of evidence suggesting that cultural pressures, even in the West, might push people toward and not just away from humility. The bottom line is that humility is not something antithetical to Western psychology, but even to the extent people are in the West, humility is possible, even among those who are uneducated and are from nonindustrialized nations, are not rich, and are not from democratic political systems.

WE LEARN FROM EXAMPLES

Throughout the book, we have integrated examples within our summaries of science and our expositions of theory. We believe that people learn much through observing and emulating admired examples. We don't see this as social learning in the sense of copying behaviors. Rather, we learn the goals, the values, the driving forces that motivate and energize—not merely the behaviors. This has certainly been true in our lives.

A Significant Example Who Influenced Ev

I (Ev) was born into a working poor family. Both parents were out of the East Tennessee mountain coal mining region. And our fierce Appalachian twang sounded like it, too. I was always saying, "I reckon I'll go to the store" and "I'm a-fixin' to get my work dunn." (It's a wonder I actually ever got around to doing anything.)

My father was brilliant, but life and poverty conspired against him—denying him a college education when the doctor whose office he cleaned during his growing-up years died before he could help Dad attend college. He worked all his life as a railroad brakeman and later freight conductor, reading voraciously, and spewing bitterness. He was out of town 3 of every 4 days, and on his day in town he grabbed some sleep and then was on call. When I reached the eighth grade, his drinking became a problem. After that, I rarely saw him sober, and when he was drinking, he was mean. He would play us children off against each other, telling me, "Why can't you be smart like your brother? He read Charles Dickens in the fourth grade. You're in the eighth and all you read are sports books." But he would tell my brother, "How come you can't make all As like your brother. You're just lazy and triflin', boy." Mike and I never figured out what "triflin'" meant, but we knew it wasn't a good thing.

My mother was a nurse who worked in the Philippines during World War II as an army nurse. After returning to the United States, she was a stay-at-home mother until I (the oldest of three) was a high school junior. She returned to nursing, but slipped a disc in her spine that led to surgery and shortened her career. She battled unipolar depression and was hospitalized and received electroconvulsive therapy on at least three occasions.

I loved school. It got me out of the home. I got a small scholarship in engineering to the University of Tennessee, Knoxville (UTK). As an engineering student, I took mostly technical classes, so with my lower SES background, self-absorbed defensiveness, and nose-to-the-grindstone study habits, I was locked up inside myself. My career goals, adopted uncritically from a statement my father once casually made, were to get a master's from MIT and an MBA from Harvard Business School and become CEO of a large engineering firm.

My life-changing experience with humility happened after I graduated from UTK. I was holding a national fellowship in nuclear engineering to MIT and working the summer at the Atomic Energy Commission in Oak Ridge, Tennessee. In the Planning and Power Division, my boss was St. George Tucker Arnold III—Tuck. Tuck made regular trips to Washington, DC, to present to the administration and to Congress and to the AEC leadership. But he did not let the halls of power shape him. He was perhaps one of the most personally humble people I ever met. Tuck was genuinely interested in each of the people who worked for him. He made each of us an actual expert in something. (He had to work very, very hard to make me, a new grad, an expert in anything. But he did it.) The turning point came at an end-of-the-year dinner at Tuck's home. After the meal, we pulled the chairs around in a circle, had coffee or tea, and talked (no one cracked off-color jokes, and no one put anyone else down). Tuck and his wife treated each person as if that person were the most important person on earth—even me. It was embarrassing. But it showed me a different world than I had been raised in—one that valued people instead of one that tried to one-up people. It was a game changer. I wanted to be like that!

Significant Examples Who Influenced Scott

I (Scott) was raised by two good parents, but there have been many "guardian angels," as I'd like to call them, who went beyond the call of duty to nurture, mentor, and put up with me. Don't laugh—the "putting up with me" part was a serious part of my learning, and looking back, it demonstrated their humility. They let me be me, at whatever immature stage of life I was suffering through. These heroic angels were patient, always loving, and terrific role models.

Foremost was my grandmother on my mother's side, Claire Bergvall. Never have I met such a humble, caring person. Many times when I acted selfishly around her (or should I say, many, MANY times), she would point her finger at me and say, simply, "Others, others, others, others." This was her shorthand way of shaking me out of my default egocentric way of viewing the world. My grandmother cared about others more than herself, it seemed.

She spoke of the problems of hunger, poverty, and disease in the world, and she expressed deep concern about the plight of physical and emotional misfortune facing others. Her empathy and compassion for others was vast, and it fed my soul.

During a particularly tough period in my childhood, my grandmother was there for me, spending hours doing things with me that I know she probably didn't enjoy doing. Boy stuff. But she was there for me—feeding, nurturing, comforting, and passing along wisdom. Most of us are fortunate to have had glimpses of this kind of love, this level of selfless devotion to others. I am eternally grateful. And much of this "attitude of gratitude" comes from her as well. Even when drinking a glass of water, my grandmother would stop halfway and thank God for the water that was quenching her thirst.

Although she grew up surrounded by Jim Crow laws, she never had an ill word to say about anyone based on color or creed. She loved everyone unconditionally. And everyone loved her. It was a crushing blow to lose her, but when someone leaves such a lasting impact, they aren't lost at all. She's with me and with everyone whose hearts and souls she touched. My grandmother exuded humility because she knew she was no better than anyone else. And she knew that the world desperately needed a mind-set of equality, compassion, and peace. I'm still striving to grow up to be like her, and I'd settle for having a fraction of her humility.

DO OUR LESSONS LEARNED TRANSFER TO MODERN CULTURE?

Heroic stories about heroically humble people are mostly about people from the past. It is a fair question to ask: Does this have relevance in today's social media, selfie culture?

WHAT DID WE LEARN IN THIS CHAPTER?

1. People exhibiting heroic humility have found the balance between effort and willpower in seeking to better themselves and traveling a hero's path that often is a quest that seems almost thrust on someone.
2. Preparation of character moves through a predictable path of glimpsing the goal, practicing faithfully, meeting trials and suffering with one's head up, and experiencing ultimate satisfaction even if not temporal happiness.
3. Humility is possible even in the highly individual-centered Western culture.

THREE QUESTIONS FOR THOUGHT AND DISCUSSION

1. Can one will oneself to be more humble, even heroically humble?
2. How much control does one have in following a path of virtue?
3. We suggest that humility is possible in Western culture. But aren't people in Western culture so self-centered that this is a pipe dream?

12

BUCKING THE TREND—BEING HUMBLE IN AN AGE OF SELF-FOCUS

It isn't easy seeking to become more humble than one is now. We looked at classical virtue theory in the previous chapter and saw that the transformation involves glimpsing the goal, habituating the heart, and practicing perfectly. We also showed in Chapter 10 that the road to heroic humility is even more arduous.

Why is it so hard to change? First, recall Solzhenitsyn's quote about the line between good and evil passing through every human heart. So, feeding the good or virtuous side of the heart is not easy. With humility, little victories just make us proud. But our failures energize us to do better. Both sides of our human heart seem to always be active.

Beyond this, though, we want to explore two other barriers to change. The first comes from work on social cognitive psychology (summarized admirably by Kahneman, 2011). Van Tongeren and Myers (2017) recently applied this specifically to humility, and we draw to some degree on some of

http://dx.doi.org/10.1037/0000079-013
Heroic Humility: What the Science of Humility Can Say to People Raised on Self-Focus, by E. L. Worthington Jr. and S. T. Allison

their observations. The second type of barrier is external. It has to do with the social norms. We live in an age tinged by narcissism. Christopher Lasch (1979) and Tom Wolfe (1976) were among the first to bring this to public awareness. Those external normative expectations are hard to buck. We review some of the evidence suggesting that humility is in fact an unnatural act. But that's not the end of the story, as we shall see.

HUMILITY IS AN UNNATURAL ACT

Among some of the best-documented findings in social and cognitive psychology have been the varieties of self-enhancing strategies in which people engage. Some of the strategies are cognitive and mostly implicit. Others are behavioral, and often we are not aware fully of why we are acting as we are. Yet, behind each is a desire to enhance our standing in our own eyes and in the eyes of others. This might have survival advantage because we are salient within a group when it comes to distributing resources (McCulloh, 2009).

We Usually Want to Think Positively About Ourselves

Social psychology shows that we usually want to hold a positive view of ourselves (Baumeister & Exline, 2002). This is particularly salient in most Western individualistic countries, so much so that we might conclude that humility is an unnatural act. For example, in the West, there are numerous cultural pressures to promote the self at the cost of the other in a presumed zero-sum situation, a construal of life as individualistic, and a strong motive to maintain self-esteem even when doing so is costly (see Crocker, Canevello, & Lewis, 2017).

Narcissism in the United States has increased in recent years (Twenge, 2014). Two theories of social psychology address positive self-concept (Van Tongeren & Myers, 2017). *Sociometer theory* (Leary, Tambor, Terdal, & Downs, 1995) holds that our sense of belonging to a group is captured by our self-esteem, which is rooted in evolution because group membership usually increased survival and reproductive fitness. *Terror management theory* (TMT; Pyszczynski, Greenberg, Solomon, Arndt, & Schimel, 2004) suggests that when people sense their own mortality, they are anxious, and to manage the anxiety, people bolster their sense of self-esteem to feel worthwhile.

This strong pull to maintain a positive self-regard not only works against humility, it also results in a number of cognitive distortions (Kahneman, 2011), which also make cognition more efficient because they are shorthand heuristics for decisions and problem-solving instead of protracted algorithms. As Haidt

(2012) argued, these distortions are largely intuitive, rooted in System 1 cognition, and we often use logical, rational System 2 cognition to justify what our intuition has demanded. Haidt used the example of a rider (rational System 2 cognition) on an elephant (intuitive System 1 cognition). The elephant leans left (i.e., toward a cognitive distortion) and the conscious rational mind leans left too (providing a rationale for why the rider "really" wanted to go left). This is outside of people's conscious awareness.

Biases That Make Humility Hard

Humility involves an accurate self-assessment. But unconscious implicit biases can make it almost impossible to accurately assess ourselves. Cognitive scientists like Kahneman (2011) have detailed many of these. The self-serving bias is a double-edged self-protective weapon. When people are told they have succeeded at a task, they often accept credit and claim that the success is based on their ability and effort. But when people are told they failed at a task, they blame failure on external factors like an unfair teacher, a too-hard task, or just plain old bad luck. In the *better-than-average effect*, people almost always rate themselves more competent, better looking, or more ethical than others. People regularly overestimate their own capacities or abilities. As scientists know, all papers that we submit we believe are almost certain to get accepted by journals with 90% rejection rates. We also believe that we are more unique than others and that more people agree with our opinions than usually do in reality. Ironically, we actually are biased about how unbiased we are. Pronin, Lin, and Ross (2002) made people aware of their biases. Did that help them become less biased? No. Informed people concluded that they were less biased than others and thus could control their biases better. The bias blind spot makes becoming more humble harder. Freud suggested that our ego defenses motivate self-protection. Arrogant people have too high an estimation of themselves. So they are motivated to perceive things selectively.

The upshot of these biases is that people may think they are way more humble than average (D. E. Davis, Worthington, & Hook, 2010). People in the middle of the humility trait normal distribution will be subject to some bias and likely to overestimate their humility a moderate amount. People with true high humility might be sensitive to social pressures for modesty, and they might overestimate their humility by a small amount. But there are also people with low self-esteem that is unrealistic. They might actually say and believe they are less humble than others see them. They might be just as inaccurate as arrogant estimators, but in a different direction, but they are just as fiercely motivated to maintain their self-perception as the highly arrogant jerk.

HUMILITY IS NOT AN UNNATURAL ACT

At this point, it looks as if humility is simply not natural. But as many infomercials say, "But wait! There's more!" (And no, it does not involve amazing Ginsu knives for only $19.99.)

Social Functions of Humility

Van Tongeren and Myers (2017) observed that there are also motivational pressures to view oneself as humble. (Whew!) Those pressures come not from the cognitive and perceptual side of motivation but from the social side. Humility serves many social functions, many of which push people toward wanting to be more humble. Van Tongeren and Myers observed that those motives are just as driven by evolutionary pressures as are cognitive motives. They identified four cognitive motives: self-regulation, relational bonding, orientation toward others, and reducing prejudice.

Self-Regulation

Humility helps regulate the ego. Regulating the ego can improve evolutionary fitness, from regulating diet and exercise, to work achievement, to presenting an attractive face to potential mates (see Baumeister & Tierney, 2011). Self-regulation also affects bonding and other-orientation because it is not easy to set aside one's own self-interests.

Bonding

Humility can allow social bonding to occur between friends (D. E. Davis et al., 2013), romantic partners (Van Tongeren, Davis, & Hook, 2014), and work colleagues (Owens, Rowatt, & Wilkins, 2011). We reviewed the bonding hypothesis in Chapter 3.

Other-Orientation

When people act humbly, it signals that they value the well-being of others. That suggests that a humble person might be safe to interact with because the humble person is perceived to be attuned to others' needs and not just to his or her own needs. Thus, perceiving the humble person to be other-oriented, one is more likely to forgive mistakes by humble people. And the other-orientation also means humble people also are more willing to forgive (Burnette, McCullough, Van Tongeren, & Davis, 2012). More willingness to forgive could build cooperation in groups. Humble people also tend to be more helpful, altruistic, and generous (Exline & Hill, 2012). In short, they display the range of prosocial acts that we reviewed in Chapter 4. Being focused on others makes positive social interactions likely. Therefore, humble people are highly desirable group members.

Nonprejudice

Humility is associated with lower intergroup prejudice and greater group harmony (Van Tongeren & Myers, 2017). The other-orientation, accuracy of self-perception, teachability, and modesty lead humble people to value and seek out the opinions of others and to acknowledge their own weaknesses. They show more tolerance for and acceptance of people with different beliefs and values. They also view people in outgroups more positively, helping to promote positive intergroup interactions.

More Good News From an Ecosystem View of Relationships

Crocker et al. (2017) noted that although many hold an *ego*system viewpoint, others perceive relationships to be more of an *eco*system. Ecosystem motivation promotes behaviors that are good for both oneself and others. With ecosystem motivation, people view their relationships as thriving when people's needs are met. They assume that supporting others benefits the relationship. This is consistent with the understanding of humility we have advanced—that humility requires an orientation to build others up. Crocker et al. showed that when people see themselves as contributing to a relationship, they increase their non-zero-sum beliefs and strengthen their lay theory of relationship. But when people act competitively in a relationship, the opposite occurs: They increase their zero-sum beliefs, which weakens their lay theory of the relationship.

Situational Pressures That Affect Humility

Let's round out the picture. Besides cognitive and social motives to be humble (or not), there are situational pressures affecting humility. Although personality traits are strong predictors of behavior, some situations can shift ordinarily humble people toward arrogance. But they can, as we claim in the following chapter, also guide people toward more humility. We know that life involves the interaction of situations, personality, genetics, and choice. So, it is worthwhile to consider situational pressures that might affect humility.

Van Tongeren and Myers (2017) discussed three of those. First, situations that reward humility make it easier to be humble. Second, situations that focus on humility make it hard to practice (D. E. Davis, Hook, et al., 2011; D. E. Davis et al., 2013). They heighten social pressure to act humbly, whether that reflects one's usual motives. For example, humility predicts generous allocations to strangers in some decision-making games (e.g., Hilbig,

Thielmann, Hepp, Klein, & Zettler, 2015). When situations prime humility, people do not respond aggressively as often (Van Tongeren & Myers, 2017). Situations that prime self-interest are likely to move people to act less humbly. Third, when situations shift attention externally—that is, away from a self-centered focus—then people act more humbly simply because they are not thinking as much about themselves. Thus, situations that call for gratitude to those who have helped (i.e., the focus is on what the person did to help) or seeing needy people whom one might reasonably help (i.e., the focus is on the other person's need) or mentoring people less experienced (i.e., the attention is on what might be done that would help the mentee improve) might instigate humility.

CONTEXT FOR HUMILITY

Cultural currents in the United States and the modern world make humility harder today. Many people value themselves more than they value other relationships or institutions. Twenge (2014) acquired a massive amount of data supporting this increase over the past few decades.

Can Humility Exist in This Self-Absorbed Age?

Twenge (2014) dubbed the millennial generation "Generation Me," continuing a theme set forth earlier by Tom Wolfe (1976) and Christopher Lasch (1979), who called the baby boomers' culture a culture of narcissism. Wolfe called baby boomers the "me generation" in an article in *New York Magazine*, which he ended as follows:

> they discovered and started doting on Me! They've created the greatest age of individualism in American history! . . . One only knows that the great religious waves have a momentum all their own. . . . And this one has the mightiest, holiest roll of all, the beat that goes . . . *Me* . . . *Me* . . . *Me* . . . *Me* . . .

New York Times columnist David Brooks (2015) called attention to the shift since World War II away from a crooked-timber vision of humanity's development of moral excellence. He drew on Kant (1797/1964), who said, "Out of the crooked timber of humanity, no straight thing was ever made." Kant presupposed that people are inherently flawed. In the crooked timber tradition, people own their limits and make moral adjustments to protect others. Instead, Brooks claimed that modernity has embraced a Romantic tradition, which assumes people are inherently good and that moral excellence occurs if human innocence can be sheltered from a corrupt society.

Three Potential Solutions

Cultural currents today make self-focus normal. Is there room for humility as a virtue?

Return to Crooked-Timber Philosophy

Brooks (2015) argued that to correct the inherent bent-ness of humanity, a crooked-timber view of humans makes it essential to cultivate humility. Romanticism, he said, leans toward self-focus that adores and trusts the self. Too much.

Not everyone agrees with Brooks's (2015) analysis. Charles Taylor (2007), in *A Secular Age*, argued that humility is in fact demanded by our epistemological lack of certainty (recall our little "philosophical riff" from Chapter 6).

Return to Idealistic Social Transformation

We are in a time when much of the Western world is self-focused. The generation of the 1960s rebelled socially on the basis of idealism. The population bubble of the boomers has made that theme dominant in culture by the sheer weight of numbers. Recently, Generation Me—people from adolescence through their mid-to late-30s today—has begun to outnumber the boomers, and the gap will grow as boomers die at a faster clip than Generation Me adults. GenMe has been raised on a steady diet of self-esteem building, often divorced from real accomplishment. Yet, the irony is that a generation that was taught to pursue their dreams, and (by the way) to dream big, increasingly has found that jobs are not available, especially not dream jobs, and that costs for housing, health care, and higher education have placed them in debt. Two incomes are necessary to purchase necessities (including communication plans and foodie plans). There simply is not enough time, money, or energy to reach those goals. Thus, GenMe is dissatisfied with GenMe constraints. Yet, there has not yet been a cultural GPS navigation system to guide people into the future.

Engage Individuals in Deliberately Becoming More Humble

Humility might be a step in the right direction. It gets people's attention off of themselves and orients them to helping others. The idealism of doing something that matters can be fed, even without a dream job. But cultivating humility requires swimming against the cultural tide. It requires not just humility but heroic humility. And if people are to do things that matter, it will require heroic humble leadership to nurture and guide others. But how can people become more humble? It is easy to find heroes to look to for inspiration, but how can everyday people become more humble?

FOREWARNED IS FOREARMED, BUT IS FOREARMING ENOUGH TO MAKE A DIFFERENCE?

If we seek deliberately to become more humble, it helps to know what we are up against. But knowing might not guarantee success. I (Ev) know a lot about losing weight. But, late at night, the peanut butter calls to me in a siren song to lure me onto the rocks of eating calories and fat, and I haven't the courage to get my wife to lash me to the mast to resist its call.

In psychotherapy, we can help people with problems in self-control, but the path is arduous. Psychotherapy is, in social psychological terms, a strong situation in which—like a benevolent Milgram study—people work with the psychotherapist toward their own goal. About 85% of those people succeed. In the following chapter, we examine some treatment programs that have emerged to help people develop humility if that is their goal.

WHAT DID WE LEARN IN THIS CHAPTER?

1. Humility is not natural. It requires going against implicit cognitive biases.
2. Humility is not natural. It also requires bucking recent social evolution toward increasing self-focus.
3. Numerous commentators argue that the world is becoming increasingly self-focused. To combat this trend, some voices advocate a return to a crooked-timber view of humanity or an ideal-informed social revolution. We suggested seeking to interest people in deliberately becoming more humble.

THREE QUESTIONS FOR THOUGHT AND DISCUSSION

1. Are we indeed as a culture becoming more self-focused? If we are becoming more self-focused, is this a bad thing?
2. Brooks (2015) championed a return to a crooked-timber view of humanity as inherently flawed but as responsibly trying to

accept our limitations and build the best society that can be constructed from the crooked timber. Is it possible to return to such a view? Which do you think is more true? (a) New context means we cannot go back; or (b) There is, after all, nothing new under the sun when it comes to human nature.

3. Do you think it is possible for people to build a humble character by some psychological intervention? Do you think only life's exigencies can transform character?

13

BECOMING MORE HUMBLE—DELIBERATELY

Trait humility is not achieved. In fact, in the face of a successful act of humility or experience of a successful state of humility, the pursuit of humility must resume very quickly. It cannot be maintained.

At first, this might seem discouraging, but it is similar to life's breath. Immediately on inhaling, one must exhale. It is not discouraging that we continually need our next breath. It is a fact of existence. Similarly, if we try to hold onto humility, it is like holding our breath. We cannot take in the next needed breath without exhaling the old. The oxygen has nurtured our blood, and the old air, now carbon dioxide saturated, must be expelled. A humble act or state nurtures our soul, but the more we hold it in, revel in it, and seek to retain it, the more it pollutes and prevents growth in virtue. However, that doesn't mean we throw up our hands and shrug our shoulders in oh-well futility. We can change our level of humility even if the sloshing bobs back and forth around that mean level.

http://dx.doi.org/10.1037/0000079-014
Heroic Humility: What the Science of Humility Can Say to People Raised on Self-Focus, by E. L. Worthington Jr. and S. T. Allison

SOURCES OF LEARNING ABOUT HUMILITY

As you have seen from our book, we are recapturing an ancient virtue but with a new, scientifically informed spin. There are few recent resources available for people who wish to become more humble—even fewer if we make randomized controlled trials a *sine qua non* for giving an approach credibility. But there are numerous resources to fuel our practice of humility. We look at learning from the practitioners of humility now and from the past and also from science.

Humility practitioners are important—perhaps the most important—sources of learning. Observing heroically humble models (see Chapters 8, 9, and 10, this volume, especially) and inhaling their attitudes can help you become more humble. Some heroically humble people are public figures, and others are workaday folks from all corners of life. Many of the public figures have written books. Books can give practical advice about being more humble. Likewise, reading biographies and histories can also give you good ideas about how to cultivate, practice, and test the virtue of humility.

There are a few time-tested programs of humility. Benedict of Nursia put forth his 12-step rule (see Chapter 7 of *The Rule of St. Benedict*) for climbing the ladder of humility in the 12th century. Its success at passing the test of time provides valuable empirical evidence that aspects of the rule work. Even if we are not Roman Catholic, Christian, or even religious, St. Benedict's ladder might help if we approach it with intellectual and religious humility.

Science gives us another slant. A few have attempted to create scientifically tested programs to promote humility. We look at them and suggest other as-yet-untested interventions.

LEARN HUMILITY FROM THE PRACTITIONERS AND THE PAST

Humility Books Can Help

Most of the books that have been written on humility are Christian trade books. Some are about general humility, and most have at least one self-help chapter. The major approaches have been information, inspiration, and exhortation.

Advice From Transpersonal Psychology Practitioners

One predominantly self-help book was by Whitfield, Whitfield, Park, and Prevatt (2006), *The Power of Humility: Choosing Peace Over Conflict in Relationships*. This book was overtly aimed at transpersonal psychology approaches, including alternative spirituality like New Age religions and

A Course in Miracles. It taught principles and exercises consonant with the authors' practice and was based on their clinical work and personal experiences.

Practical Advice on Modest Self-Presentation From a Leader

C. Peter Wagner (2002), chancellor of the Wagner Leadership Institute in Colorado Springs, has given much practical advice about humility, but I will summarize his advice on making a modest self-presentation. He is a leadership practitioner. In many ways, his book *Humility* deals with what we might call the forms of humility—that is, the external behaviors within which the internal trait of humility can grow. Wagner's advice about modest self-presentation provides a way of acting that has a good chance of allowing humility to grow inside of the person. Humility, as we've argued throughout this book, has both intrapersonal (i.e., knowing one's limitations, cultivating a teachable spirit, and being oriented to building others up) and interpersonal (i.e., behaving in ways to solicit advice and new information, modest self-presentation, and using one's power under control to build others up and not put them down) aspects. Wagner deals with both, but more thoroughly with the external aspects. Here are some bits of advice he offers.

- *Deal modestly with your successes and value your gifts.* Celebrate successes with a first response of gratitude. Reject flattery. Accept praise and credit when it is due. Don't make a big deal of it. If you are not recognized for your accomplishments, do not get resentful. Recognize and value your gifts. Build them into ever-stronger strengths instead of resting on natural ability.
- *Look for others' contributions to you and the organization.* Give credit to others. In fact, look for opportunities to praise and honor others. That will keep you focused on others. Be alert for ways that your gifts and theirs can build on each other.
- *Correct weaknesses and mistakes.* Discern your weaknesses. Listen nondefensively to critics. Empathize to determine where they are coming from. Take the criticisms seriously. Express gratitude for sharing. Do not devalue, criticize, or argue with the critic. Let criticisms sit. Fix problems, not blame. Discern what needs to be changed, plan steps to change, and act. Monitor your progress. Adjust the plan or your behavior if you do not make sufficient progress.
- *Take measured risks.* Be willing to take (measured) risks. Preserving the status quo is not humility; it is often merely conflict avoidance, fear, or timidity. Don't be afraid to fail.
- *Get over it!* Whether you are dealing with a success or criticism, savor the moment, drawing what you can from it. Then move

on. There is no future in living in the past, so don't revisit the glory days and don't dwell on past mistakes. Move forward.

- *Help others.* Be willing to serve. Be willing to make sacrifices to honor others or for the good of the organization or accomplishing the mission of your organization or group. Be willing to protect those who need it without being condescending.
- *Stay aware of hierarchies.* They have a function. Usually those higher up in the chain have things to teach others. Learn from them. (Yes, you have things to teach them, but a good leader seeks to be teachable.) You can learn from everyone.

St. Benedict's Rule—An Original Twelve-Step Program

Benedict of Nursia (ca. 480–550) wrote to provide guidelines for monks within a contemplative community under the authority of an abbot. Benedictines live under the motto "pray and work." Fifteen centuries of monks and other adherents to the Benedictine order have abided by and refined the Rule. There are no scientific studies of its efficacy, yet millions of people have tried it over time. The twelve steps (paraphrased) are as follows. The monk

1. makes pleasing God of first concern;
2. loves God's will more than his own;
3. subjects himself obediently to a superior to do arduous works for others;
4. accepts distasteful duties to serve others with patience and perseverance;
5. confesses failures in worship and ministry to others completely;
6. is content with little;
7. believes and declares to others that he has no worth apart from God;
8. does only what is approved by the religious community for worship and ministry to others;
9. disciplines himself through silence to contemplate God and goodness;
10. is restrained and modest in demeanor;
11. engages only in sober talk—seriously, with gravity, in few words; and
12. is not only humble of heart, seeking to honor God and all people, but lets others know he is sinful and unable to keep this intent fully without God's help.

As the monk keeps the 12 steps more often, he more often arrives at the sense of God's love. That love helps him keep the Rule even more easily and more often.

Pride is the archenemy of humility, so as a person seeks humility, he or she also seeks to defeat pride. In the 11th century, Bernard of Clairvaux wrote an expanded commentary on Benedict's 12 steps upward into humility, and he complemented it by proposing 12 steps downward into pride: curiosity, frivolity, foolish mirth, boastfulness, singularity, conceit, audacity, excusing sins, hypocritical confessions, defiance, freedom to sin, and habitual sinning. As we can see, Bernard thought that pride was powered by the self, and things that moved people away from pursuing God would inevitably lead to a descent toward a habitual sinning. In Bernard's 12 steps, we can see the descent taking steps away from honesty about oneself, acting immodestly, and finally breaking from the fellowship (i.e., defiance) and giving oneself over to self-satisfying, other-denying sin.

We can learn lessons for humility (and to avoid pride) even though we are not in a community with vows of obedience. Incredible self-discipline is required, and sustaining self-discipline is a key. Yet there is provision for failure—confession within an accountability relationship with a sincere intent to try to do better. The key steps in both the ladder to humility and the steps down into the basement of pride invoke a sincere dedication to something bigger than oneself—God in the case of religious orders. But for those who are not religiously inclined, some other noble cause or revered person might give the motivation needed. We have seen this in the hero's journey. For pursuing humility, renunciation of self and pursuit of God is first, clearing the way from effort to achieve something that would make oneself better and getting a perspective to commit oneself to God, the noble cause, or the revered person.

LEARNING HUMILITY FROM SCIENCE

Van Tongeren and Myers (2017) reviewed the social psychological and cognitive reasons for self-focus. Despite the self-perception bias blind spot, they suggested that there are steps to help people counter their self-serving biases. Here are things they suggested.

- *Be as realistic in your self-assessment as you can.* Seek to know yourself and to figure out when humility is easy and hard for you. Find your challenges and set your sights on change.
- *Build restraint of self-oriented impulses and exercise other-oriented impulses.* Exercise your "humility muscle." Consult Baumeister's ego depletion studies (Baumeister & Tierney, 2011). When you restrain self-oriented impulses, you can erode self-control. That's no reason not to limit your self-focus, but be aware that it can have unanticipated effects.

- *Shift consciously and consistently to System 2 cognition.* To fight self-focused bias and act humbly, engage your System 2, conscious willpower. This is hard to do, but it's worth a try.
- *Find an accountability partner.* Seek outside help regarding your humility. Third parties can be effective at assessing humility (D. E. Davis et al., 2013). They can also hold one's feet to the fire once people have committed to change.
- *Internalize rewards.* When people internalize rewards, they integrate behaviors into their sense of self, which makes the behaviors easier to do (see Ryan & Deci, 2000). Van Tongeren and Myers (2017) advised people to shift rewards internally so that they can seek humility because it is the right thing to do.
- *Compare upward.* Van Tongeren and Myers (2017) recommended that people who want to be humble compare themselves in light of God rather than comparing downward. That will put things in a larger perspective. Even for people who are not religious, comparing their actions with noble ideals will help put things into that larger perspective.
- *Evaluation.* These are reasonable extensions from social psychological research, but recall that even when people were told of their biases, they usually failed at self-control (Pronin, Lin, & Ross, 2002). Something more stringent, more engaging than willpower is usually needed.

LEARNING HEROIC HUMILITY BY LEARNING SUCCESSIVE STATES OF HUMILITY

Ruberton, Kruse, and Lyubomirsky (2017) designed interventions to promote trait humility indirectly. They examined three experimental interventions to increase *state humility*. They assumed that trait humility is developed by experiencing states of humility more often and more deeply. They thus developed three interventions aimed at increasing the number of times one experienced states of humility. They helped people affirm the self, practice being grateful, and experience awe. In the remainder of this section, we summarize the excellent line of research created by and reviewed by Ruberton, Kruse, and Lyubomirsky (2017). We direct the reader to their chapter (and original articles) for additional details.

Self-Affirmation

Self-affirmation combats the tendency to preserve one's positive self-image by responding defensively to information that threatens the self.

Instead, Kruse, Chancellor, and Lyubomirsky (2015) had people affirm their good qualities, which is thought to strengthen the self and reduce defensiveness. In five studies, Kruse et al. (2015) examined how self-affirmation might be related to humility. Participants who self-affirmed had greater humility, whether assessed by themselves or others. However, self-affirmation only increased people's humility when it helped them deal with a challenge to their ego. Simply repeating platitudes about the self did not help.

Gratitude

Gratitude is a moral emotion. It is experienced when people reflect on the benefit they have obtained from another person (McCullough, Kilpatrick, Emmons, & Larson, 2001). Gratitude and humility are linked for several reasons. Both are other-oriented. Also, one feels gratitude because one could not do something oneself; thus, it might indirectly highlight attention to one's limitations. Layous, Nelson, Kurtz, and Lyubomirsky (2017) found that writing thank-you letters is not always a completely positive experience; expressing gratitude makes people aware that they need to improve, so they often increase goal-directed efforts (Layous et al., 2017). Kruse, Chancellor, Ruberton, and Lyubomirsky (2014) used a diary method to examine the relationship between humility and gratitude, which predicted each other during a 2-week period. When people felt grateful one day, they usually felt more humble the next day. When they felt humble one day, they felt more grateful the next. Ruberton, Kruse, and Lyubomirsky (2017) called a "mutually-reinforcing upward spiral" (p. 266).

Awe

Awe is "an emotional response to grand, powerful, overwhelming, or unexpected environmental stimuli, such as nature, beauty, or great accomplishments by other people" (Ruberton et al., 2017, p. 266). Awe pulls from us a sense of vastness and recognition that there are things physically, socially, aesthetically, or morally larger or grander than we are. It helps us expand out mental framework (Fredrickson, 2013). Awe makes our sense of self smaller and more detached, which is consistent with humility. Chancellor, Nelson, Cornick, Blascovich, and Lyubomirsky (2016) used a virtual-reality simulation (a spaceship slowly moving away from Earth) to induce feelings of awe. Their control was a boring narration about Pluto. People who experienced the awe-inspiring simulation later reported higher levels of both awe and humility than those who did the boring simulation.

States of humility are valuable in themselves, but one value of these interventions is as part of a program. These could be worked into more clinically oriented interventions.

INTERVENTIONS DESIGNED TO PROMOTE HUMILITY

In this section, we summarize some of the research reviewed by Lavelock et al. (in press). Generally, we have expanded on the research in the following sections to emphasize the nature of the interventions more than the outcome research. For additional, but typically different, information about the interventions, see Lavelock et al. (2014).

Psychoanalytic Theory (Dwiwardani et al., 2014)

Secure attachment style in early childhood predicts humility (Dwiwardani et al., 2014). Insecure attachment can produce shame. Psychoanalytically informed psychotherapeutic modalities seek to produce corrective emotional experiences for insecure attachment. Another term from psychodynamic theory is *mentalization*, "the ability to attend to the mental states of self and others" (Worthington & Sandage, 2016, p. 190). Promoting mentalization may also lead to humility because it increases empathy. Dwiwardani et al.'s research informs treatment even though it is not psychotherapeutic evidence-based treatment.

Wisdom Therapy (Robins, 2008)

Wisdom therapy is a method to promote wisdom through promoting humility, mindfulness, and well-being. Wisdom therapy is an eclectic blend of cognitive–behavioral therapy (CBT), humility-inducing methods, and mindfulness-centered methods. It is purportedly for reducing emotional disorders like depression, anxiety, and anger, but it also is recommended for personality disorders like narcissism and antisocial personality disorder. Robins (2008) focused on fearful narcissism using CBT and grandiose narcissism using humility. The humility intervention was composed of seeking to convince people that (a) our perception is limited (by using visual illusions) and (b) we-are-usually-right assumptions are not trustworthy. People were invited to contemplate the vastness of the universe with the intent of stimulating awe and undermining our certainty that what we see is real. At root, the treatment is Buddhist consistent, inducing profound doubt of temporal reality.

The research is weak in several ways. The research was made public by being presented at a conference and was never adjudicated by peer review.

Robins (2008) did not show that humility was actually promoted by the intervention or that people achieved wisdom. In fact, one dissertation (McCulloh, 2009) using substance-dependent clients found that wisdom therapy equaled rational emotive behavior therapy in producing humility. Although wisdom therapy claims to induce humility, there is no support for the claim.

Shibboleth (Romanowska, Larsson, & Theorell, 2014)

Shibboleth is an art intervention directed at leaders. It seeks to stimulate humility, self-awareness, and rejection of hubris in leaders. In this study, 20 leaders and 64 employees watched a multiple-genre, 60- to 70-minute art performance and then were in a group discussion. They completed assessments. Participants were compared with 20 leaders and 66 employees who attended a leadership-training seminar. Leaders in the art group improved on several measures. These included humility, self-awareness, and stress-and-coping measures. Their leadership style was less laissez-faire than for those who completed a traditional leadership seminar. Romanowska et al.'s (2014) intervention focused on leadership, not explicitly on humility.

PROVE HUMILITY

In her master's research beginning in fall 2011, Caroline Lavelock took my group manual to REACH Forgiveness (http://www.EvWorthington-Forgiveness.com) and adapted it into a 6- to 7-hour workbook (Lavelock et al., 2014, in press). As an innovation in psychological treatment, we saw workbooks available on the web and accessible by psychotherapy clients (free) or by anyone interested in self-improvement (free) to be the next great thing in giving psychology away (see Kazdin & Rabbitt, 2013). Lavelock created four other similarly structured 6- to 7-hour workbooks to compare with the five-step REACH Forgiveness workbook—workbooks to promote humility, patience, self-control, and positivity. She pilot tested each workbook on six participants ($n = 30$) and solicited their feedback on the experience. She then ran an intervention study comparing all four virtue workbooks to the positivity workbook and to a retested control condition. The clinical trial involved over 200 participants that had to be recruited, carefully monitored, and coaxed to complete assessments on all variables as well as their workbook.

As with any large project, we could not look at all the data in a single publication. In our first publication, we compared the humility intervention to the retested control participants on the degree to which the participants changed their virtuous traits of forgiveness, humility, patience, and self-control as well as on the degree to which they changed their positivity and negativity of stable mood. This was a randomized clinical trial to study the efficacy of an 80-page workbook intervention. The workbook revolves around five steps to PROVE Humility: Pick a time when you were not humble, Remember your abilities within the big picture, Open yourself, Value all things, and Examine limitations (for a description of exercises, see Lavelock et al., 2014). We excerpt some practical exercises from each of the steps in Exhibit 13.1.

Considering the three-part definition of humility we have used throughout this book, let's evaluate the workbook. We have identified six elements of Lavelock et al.'s (2014) workbook: (1) acknowledging accuracy of one's strengths and limitations, (2) inducing awe by considering things greater than oneself, (3) performing unimportant tasks responsibly, (4) challenging the ego by asking for forgiveness, (5) experiencing and expressing gratitude, and (6) seeking to have close relationships. Our definition involved an accurate view of oneself leading to teachability, a modest self-presentation, and an orientation to build others up. Lavelock et al.'s (2014) workbook covered accurate self-appraisal in Element 1. It covered the other-orientation in Elements 4, 5, and 6. However, little attention was given to modest self-presentation. Furthermore, we suggest that much more could be done to strengthen awareness of accurate self-assessment and especially to promote an orientation to help others. Finally, based on our approach in this book, which supplements cognition, awareness, and behavioral engagement with narratives about exemplars, we suggest that many additional examples could have been used to engage participants' imaginations. Thus, much more could be done to improve the PROVE Humility intervention.

In the first of two outcome studies, we randomly assigned the people who signed up for a workbook study to become more virtuous. We assessed them on how much their character traits changed from baseline. We were hoping to see whether we could produce changes in people's traits—not just feelings of virtue—through their work in the workbook. We made it doubly hard on ourselves to find changes in humility (or other virtues) by first giving people a treatment that they did not specifically sign up for (a treatment to help them build some unspecified character strength) and then measuring traits, not just states or feelings. We found that people who completed the humility workbooks not only became more humble in their stable character but also became more forgiving, patient, and self-controlled and less negative.

FOLLOW-UP CLINICAL TEST TO PROVE HUMILITY

A couple of years later, we followed up on that clinical experiment by using a modified version of the same humility workbook, integrating new findings but comparing it with the retested control group. In the second study,

EXHIBIT 13.1
What Is Involved in the PROVE Humility Intervention?

PROVE Humility originally was configured to follow the same structure as the already created REACH Forgiveness model, which was delivered in groups and in a workbook form (C. L. Greer, Worthington, Lin, Lavelock, & Griffin, 2014; Harper et al., 2014). Let's walk through some practical exercises to PROVE Humility. I will summarize only a few to give you a sense of the exercises. It is important to note that at the outset, people describe a situation in which they failed to act humbly, and it disappointed them. They work with that throughout.

P = Pick a time when you weren't humble

EXERCISE P-1: RECALL, IN VIVID IMAGINATION, THE SITUATION IN WHICH YOU WERE NOT HUMBLE

Take some deep breaths before beginning this section. We are about to really start working toward humility. Quiet yourself, relax. Picture the situation. Picture the experiences you had during and before and after the situation. Remember conversations and other experiences of events. Answer these questions: (1) Did you set out to intentionally not be humble? (2) Did the situation just unfold, and you realized afterwards, or in the middle of it, that you were being prideful, not humble, or downright arrogant? (3) Did you actually behave immodestly so that others could see that you were not being humble, or was your experience more of an internal self-judgment on your lack of humility? *Lesson: Sometimes we fail to be humble even when we are trying our hardest, but other times the failures just seem to come out of nowhere and blindside us. Sometimes our failures in humility can remain relatively hidden from others, though they trouble us in our spirit. But other times, we simply act immodestly or arrogantly, and then our failures in humility are apparent to all who see us.*

EXERCISE P-2: GIVING THE BURDEN OF PRIDE AWAY

You will get the most out of this exercise if you use your body. Stand. Imagine you are holding your failed humility in your hands. Hold your arms out, hands squeezed together, and imagine you are holding the pride you felt from the situation you've described. Keep it contained inside your hands and at arm's length from you. If you, in fact, stand and hold your arms out for a while, after about a minute of this, your arms will get tired and feel heavy and burdensome. Can you see how this is a metaphor for the burden of pride?

Now, if you are still doing this, imagine yourself making a decision to release the pride. To symbolize this—regardless of whether you feel like really being humble at this moment—open your hands and suddenly let your arms fall to your sides. (You may choose to do this exercise while actually holding an object that represents pride.)

You might want to make a decision to start a more humble lifestyle right now. If you do, you probably won't feel any differently toward the situation or humility in general. Your feelings will be more affected as we keep working on emotional humility. But in decisional humility, you make a decision to act differently. You agree with yourself to stop acting pridefully and start trying to treat all people as valuable. If you do not decide to make this decision now, then later, after trying some of the exercises, you can come back to this and make a definite decision to become a more humble person. *Lesson: We can decide to be more humble. If we make a conscious decision, we probably won't succeed 100% of the time. But we will succeed way more than if we just wait for humility to happen to us. Act to become more humble.*

(*continues*)

EXHIBIT 13.1
What Is Involved in the PROVE Humility Intervention? *(Continued)*

R = Remember the place of your abilities and achievements within the big picture

EXERCISE R-1: THINK ABOUT "THE BIG PICTURE"

Rank the following things in importance relative to "The Big Picture," with 1 being the most important. There are no wrong answers. This is so you can remember what you think are your most important things in life. [A list of experiences follows.] *Lesson: Humility involves an accurate self-assessment, including our limitations. Understanding our values keeps our accomplishments from looking too big or too small to us and also keeps our failures from looking too big or small to us.*

O = Open yourself and be adaptable

EXERCISE O-1: WHEN DID YOU DO SOMETHING HUMBLE FOR SOMEONE ELSE?

Write about a time when you did something in the interest of somebody else that required you to be humble, to set aside your own agenda and act in his or her best interest instead of your own. Describe what you did. Describe how you felt about doing it. How did you feel after you had done this humble act (or refrained from a prideful/selfish act)? *Lesson: Most people feel good about helping others, even doing things that are costly.*

EXERCISE O-2: WHEN WAS SOMEONE OPEN TO YOU?

Think back to a time in your past when someone put his or her opinion or agenda aside and let you choose something that would affect both of you. Write a description of the event.

Now, answer the following questions in writing by jotting a few notes. (1) What did it feel like for someone to put aside his or her agenda and let you lead the way? (2) What emotions did you experience as you realized that this person had humbled himself or herself to you? (3) Why would this person give you this gift of humility? *Lesson: Being humble makes the other person also want to be humble. Humility is other-oriented, and makes all participants more other-oriented.*

EXERCISE O-3: THE GIFT OF HUMILITY

Just as you have benefitted from someone else showing you humility, you can give the gift of humility to others by being open to them and adapting yourself to their benefit. Imagine the people involved in your target situation when you weren't humble. If given the opportunity *now* to give them the gift of humility, how would you act?

Lesson: It often feels as good (or better) to give the gift of acting humbly toward others to help them as it does to get such a gift.

EXHIBIT 13.1
What Is Involved in the PROVE Humility Intervention? *(Continued)*

V = Value others to lower self-focus

EXERCISE V-1: GETTING IN TOUCH WITH THE GRATITUDE WE FEEL BECAUSE OTHERS HAVE BLESSED US

Focus on how good it felt in the last section to talk about receiving a gift of humility. When you have been able to adopt this state of gratitude, do this exercise. If you were going to write a letter of gratitude for all of the opportunities you have been given because someone showed his or her humility by blessing you, what would you say? Write a few notes here:

Lesson: Being humble is knowing we can't do everything on our own. We need to constantly look out for others who have helped us and show sincere gratitude to them. Don't just think how grateful you are. Tell the person! Lesson: We can't do everything on our own. Be alert to how others help you constantly. (Consider helping others more often than you might now.)

EXERCISE V-2: WHAT WE'RE GRATEFUL FOR

One of the best ways to get in touch with our humility is to count our blessings. List 10 things that people have done for you that you are thankful for. Try to remind yourself of them as often as you can.

Lesson: We have been blessed through others' humility. We can pay it forward (or pay it back), and that will make our relationships work more smoothly. We often would like to believe that "I am the master of my fate/I am the captain of my soul." But that rarely is the case. Usually, we are indebted to many, many people for who we are and what we achieve. Being grateful is a way of acknowledging our strengths and limitations accurately, motivating ourselves to be modest in the way we portray ourselves to others, and being other-oriented to lift others up and not squash them down.

(*continues*)

EXHIBIT 13.1
What Is Involved in the PROVE Humility Intervention? *(Continued)*

E = Examine your limitations and commit to a humble lifestyle

EXERCISE E-1: A HUMBLE ACT YOU'VE OBSERVED

Now describe an event you have witnessed that you admire for its humility. (Maybe it's a confession or a selfless act. Maybe it happened to you or someone else.) *Lesson: If we are teachable, we are always looking to learn from others.*

EXERCISE E-2: YOU CAN CHANGE CHANNELS

You have a choice to control your emotions. You can hold onto pride, or if you have replaced it with love or empathy, sympathy, or compassion that lifts others up, you can now hold on to emotional humility—even in the face of powerful challenges to your humility. Psychologist Fred Luskin suggests that experiencing negative emotions is like watching a television channel that is depressing, angering, fear producing, or bitterness enhancing. We often think we are stuck watching the same channels. But you can change channels. Choose a more positive, humble channel. (1) What pride-stimulating channels do you often watch? (2) What humility-inspiring channels do you want to watch more of? (3) What is stopping you from changing channels? (4) Can you remove the roadblock and change channels? *Lesson: Humility doesn't just happen to us. We can actively shape our character, even though we have to deal with the realities of life. We have some control. Exercise it.*

EXERCISE E-3: THINGS THAT MIGHT MAKE YOU DOUBT WHETHER YOU'RE REALLY HUMBLE NOW

You've worked hard and experienced either complete or at least partial emotional humility when compared with when you began the workbook. But it's possible you might doubt that you actually have become more humble. Can you think of some times in your life when you might have a hard time staying humble?

Ponder this: There are hot reminders (being publicly recognized, being praised for you work, etc.) and cold reminders (when you just start thinking about your "greatness"). List the danger spots. *Lesson: Anticipate trouble spots. Plan how to deal with them now.*

---

we recruited people who specifically wanted to become more humble. We did measure the same virtues, though, as traits to see whether completing the humility workbook had the same effects on other virtues as it had in the first study. The results were even stronger in the second study than in the first. A manuscript reporting these findings is under editorial consideration as this book goes to press. We believe we have a psychological workbook intervention that worked strongly. Thus, we feel confident that we have a practical and demonstrated successful workbook intervention that is available to anyone without any fee (http://www.EvWorthington-Forgiveness.com; look under DIY workbooks).

THE NEW SCIENCE OF WISE PSYCHOLOGICAL INTERVENTIONS—WHAT COULD BE OUR NEW CANDIDATES?

We are going to go out on a limb here. (That almost certainly is not our most humble decision.) Walton (2014) suggested that some recent brief intervention studies in psychological science have shown evidence of proportionately large changes. Some things come immediately to mind, like Robert Cialdini's *Yes! 50 Scientifically Proven Ways to Be Persuasive* (which reports studies in influence; Goldstein, Martin, & Cialdini, 2008), Ellen Langer and Judith Rodin's nursing home studies (Langer & Rodin, 1976), and Jamie Pennebaker's (Pennebaker & Smyth, 2016) writing studies. Are there wise humility interventions?

What Are the Characteristics of Wise Psychological Interventions?

Walton (2014) described interventions to change civic behavior, relationships, educational performance, health behavior, and intergroup relations. He identified properties of the brief wise interventions that he thought were responsible for the changes they induced. These were psychologically precise with a targeted theory that identifies a focus of change, targeting recursive processes (rather than a fixed snapshot of behavior), and they were context dependent (not silver bullets).

I (Ev) might add other considerations that could potentially qualify a brief intervention for "wise psychological intervention" (Walton, 2014, p. 73) status, based on about 40 years of intervention research. First, the intervention needs to be *engaging*. If people do not participate, they won't change. Second, the intervention needs to be *hope inspiring*. This includes being perceived as doable, likely to produce change, positive, and nonobvious. Third, it needs to *keep people involved* long after the intervention ceases. If people do not carry the changes with them outside of the intervention, they will not experience lasting change. This involves also raising questions to keep people engaged or involving some cues to trigger repetitions. Fourth, it should involve senses other than those engaged with talking—such as writing, visualizing imagery, watching videos or listening to audio recordings, enlisting emotions, and involving interactions. Fourth, it should *engage people's questioning mind.* Fifth, it should be *consistent with one's values, beliefs, and practices* and ideally the intervention should be *easy to integrate* into current life. Sixth, it should involve *choice among a set of interventions.* Different people learn differently. Providing choices will broaden the scope of people for whom the intervention might work. Let's consider three that have not been used previously.

Three Suggested Potential Wise Humility Interventions

We have drawn from other fields to suggest three potential wise humility interventions. These look to family therapy, cognitive mind mapping, and studies of heroes to come up with other potential ways to bring about more humility.

Use Scaling to Determine Small Steps That Might Make a Big Difference

In solution-focused therapy (de Shazer, 1985, 1988), Minuchin's (1974) structural family therapy, or Worthington's (2005) hope-focused couple approach, people physically represent a numerical rating of their problem by using the room (see below) as a 0-to-10 rating scale. They then try to make a minimal positive change and rerate. The idea is to make a small change that will eventuate in a big change when it reaches fruition in the future (see Tyler, 1973). As an analogy, it is like starting from Los Angeles to drive across country to Atlanta. Change direction by 3 degrees and one ends in Raleigh instead of in Atlanta.

They might be asked to do the following sequence of behaviors. First, pick a day and time that is generally available for reflection. This may be, for example, before breakfast on Sunday morning. Second, imagine the room they are in represents a scale from 0 to 10. Zero is the least humility possible; 10 is the humility of the greatest hero of humility they can imagine. Third, rate their current humility by physically moving to a point representing the current status. Fourth, move to the place they would like to settle into in their life. Fifth, move back to the current position, then step one half a point toward their ideal (so if they were at 4, they move to 4.5). Sixth, imagine standing in the room next week at this time and rating themselves at the target (4.5, in our example). Seventh, write down three things to do this week to move from 4 to 4.5. Eighth, sign it as a good-faith contract with themselves. Ninth, place it where it will be seen daily (e.g., on top of their handwritten daily journal, beside their computer, or as a daily reminder on their phone calendar). Tenth, evaluate progress next week. (We are omitting the little *Rocky-10* victory dance that they could do when successful.) Eleventh, repeat weekly.

Draw a Mind Map or Concept Map

First, draw a mind map of humility and its associations. There are software programs available if you don't want to do this by hand (see https://en.wikipedia.org/wiki/List_of_concept-_and_mind-mapping_software); however, the "hands-on" do-it-yourself experience might be the best for lasting learning. We have created a sample (see Figure 13.1). There is clearly no one correct mind map. Each person will have different associations. Place

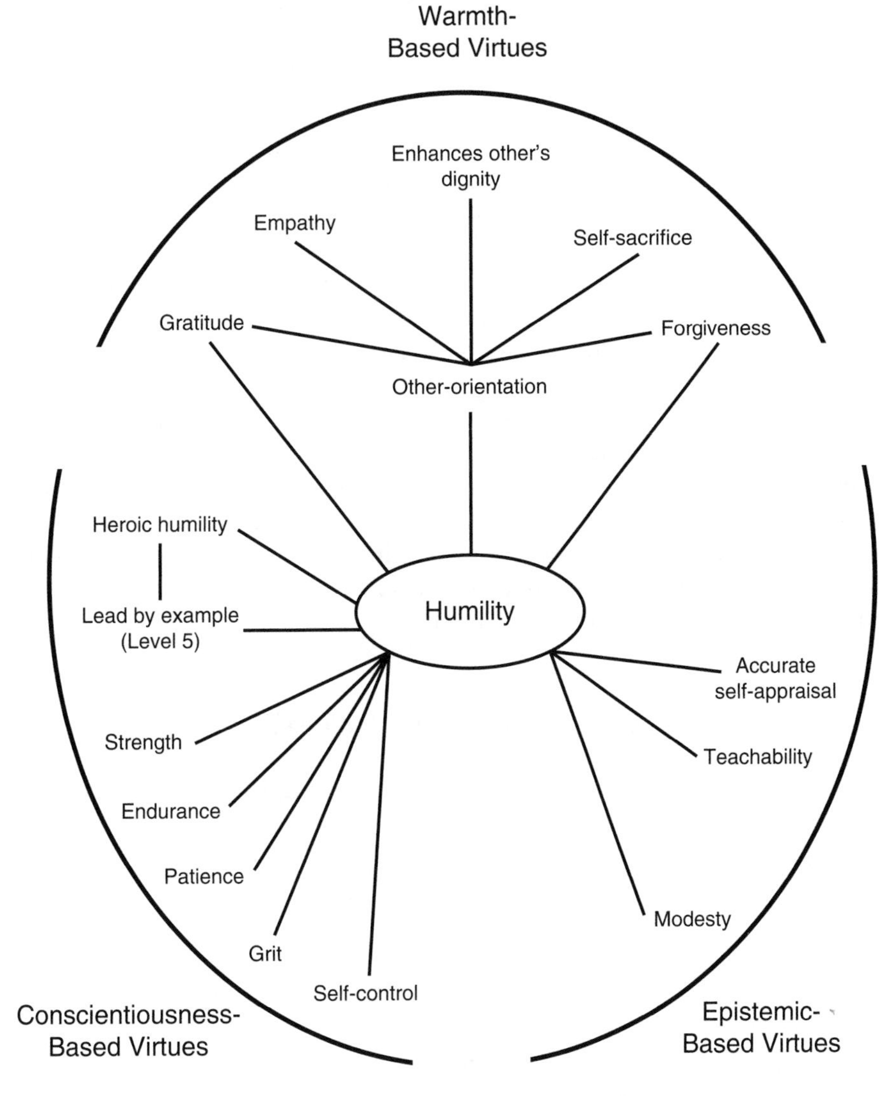

Figure 13.1. A mind map for humility. Reprinted with permission from Brandon Griffin.

the circled word *humility* near the center of a piece of paper. Associate words with it using closeness of association represented by distance from the circle. Second, at one's weekly time of reflection (Sunday morning in the previous example), look at your own mind map (not Figure 13.1), and ask whether you think it is the best representation of humility. Make changes if needed. Third, come up with specific acts during the next week to move yourself a half point higher (back to the scaling intervention). Consider the associations and make up concrete actions for each. For example, if you had drawn Figure 13.1, you might ask, how can I be more forgiving this week? More teachable? Show more gratitude?

Find Your Humility Heroes

Pick humility exemplars. Think back to films, books, or stories. Who are the humility heroes who fire up your imagination? Think about the people you've known, and identify heroes of humility. Think of what inspires you. Identify examples. Flip back through this book and find the stories that are the most inspiring for you. Reflect on why. Did that fit with your mind map? Did that move you along your humility scale?

We don't know if these three interrelated exercises will change people in lasting ways, but we think they might. They meet many of the criteria: engaging, hope-inspiring, renewing (i.e., different from week to week and inspiring thought after the Sunday morning reflection ends), using cues (i.e., Sunday morning) to keep people engaged, involving multiple modalities and senses (i.e., moving the body, drawing), raising questions (i.e., how can I improve the mind map?), being consistent with one's practices, and providing choices rather than one way. But could they make large changes in a person's humility? Only empirical testing will tell.

LOOKING, BACK, LOOKING AHEAD

With a number of approaches that people could use to build their humility, we are cautiously optimistic that they might move closer to the noble goal of heroic humility. But those who are more humble will want to help others. Can humble leaders really help others? We explore that question in Chapter 14.

WHAT DID WE LEARN IN THIS CHAPTER?

1. Historically, Benedict's Rule has been used by perhaps millions of people. So, it might be considered to be the basis of an effective intervention to promote humility.

2. Several recent, scientifically based interventions have aimed at helping people become more humble. These include suggestions based on social psychology, accumulations of states of humility, several programs that contain but did not focus on humility, and PROVE Humility. We were critical of all of these. We believe that no definitive evidence-based intervention to promote humility exists.
3. PROVE Humility is closest, with two outcome studies. However, we were also critical of many aspects of the workbook intervention.

THREE QUESTIONS FOR THOUGHT AND DISCUSSION

1. How do you evaluate the strength of evidence of high use (but no scientific support) for Benedict's Rule versus two scientific studies supporting PROVE Humility (but of little general use)?
2. Did you find any intervention in this chapter that you thought you could use?
3. How important is using exemplars within a scientific program to promote humility?

14

HEROICALLY HUMBLE LEADERS, TEAMS, AND ORGANIZATIONS

If people might indeed build their humility, as the PROVE Humility workbook studies suggest, can heroically humble leaders help others? We suggest that this is possible. We also suggest that several scientific literatures can help inform people of how to do it. In this chapter, we look at humility within organizations. Then, we examine leadership within those organizations. Finally, we look at becoming a more effective and humble leader.

VARIETIES OF HUMILITY WITHIN ORGANIZATIONS

A. S. Wallace, Chiu, and Owens (2017) reviewed the literature on humility within organizations as it stood at the end of 2015. They organized their findings under three categories—*leader humility*, *team humility*, and

http://dx.doi.org/10.1037/0000079-015
Heroic Humility: What the Science of Humility Can Say to People Raised on Self-Focus, by E. L. Worthington Jr. and S. T. Allison

organizational humility. In this section, we draw on their analysis and supplement it with more recent research.

Leader Humility

Humble leaders are not necessarily the leaders out front. Instead of seeing themselves as the most influential contributors to organizational functioning, humble leaders put their contributions in perspective (Kallasvuo, 2007). A. S. Wallace et al. (2017) suggested that leader humility is consistent with their employees perceiving them to have three core components of humility: self-awareness of strengths and weaknesses; appreciation of others' strengths, weaknesses, and contributions; and evidence of being teachable (Owens & Hekman, 2012; Owens, Johnson, & Mitchell, 2013). Other organizational scholars have suggested that two other characteristics are part of being a humble leader: self-transcendence and low self-focus (Ou et al., 2014).

Each of the components of humble leadership has been associated with different behaviors (Gunn & Gullickson, 2006). First, humble leaders exemplify self-awareness by several behaviors. First, they keep a humble perspective by admitting mistakes and having compassion for others and for themselves when they fail. In fact, they admit their fallibility and intellectual limitations and also admit it when they fail. Second, humble leaders show appreciation for others' strengths and contributions. Third, humble leaders model a willingness to be teachable by being responsive to others' feedback. They avoid the spotlight unless public attention is necessary for the good of the company. They create an organizational environment where it is safe to express thoughts that run against the "party line." A. S. Wallace et al. (2017) argued that the expression of humility by leaders builds a common bond of humanness, which is consistent with the social bonds hypothesis (see Chapter 3, this volume). Having a humble leader has many advantages. For example, humble leaders are related to teams that focus on learning goals. Humble leadership is also related to job engagement, affective attachment to the job, satisfaction, and lower job turnover rates. In addition, when others perceive the leader to be humble, they also perceive the leader to be more trustworthy and to forgive mistakes more readily. There are better leader–follower relationships.

Team Humility

A good team works well as a group, and this is enhanced when the team members all (or most) exhibit humility. As with leaders, team humility also involves the same core components: self-awareness of one's own strengths and weaknesses, appreciation of others' strengths and contributions, and willingness to be teachable (Owens & Hekman, 2016). T. W. Greer (2013) also found that team humility means that other team members feel included and cared for. Inclusion of other team members can prevent subgroups or cliques from forming. Care for other team members can help the team function better. Humble team members view their fellow team members as being as valuable to the team as they are themselves. They appreciate that individual contributions differ. Being a humble team member does not mean one is oblivious to people's weaknesses. Greer found that team humility is highest when team members feel like they can learn from and teach each other. This builds on itself in a virtuous circle, and showing humility often becomes a normative behavior on the team.

Since A. S. Wallace et al. (2017) reviewed the literature in late 2015, other studies have supported benefits of humble team leadership to team performance. For example, Chiu, Owens, and Tesluk (2016) sampled 62 Taiwanese professional work teams. They found that in work teams, leader humility facilitates shared leadership by promoting leadership-claiming and leadership-granting interactions among team members. They also found that teams with proactive characteristics had the highest effects of leader humility on shared leadership. In addition, they noted that when team members were highly task focused, shared leadership was most strongly related to team performance. Second, Rego, Cunha, and Simpson (2016) assessed the perceived impact on team effectiveness of self-reported leaders' humility and reports by workers on their leaders' humility. The relationship between humility and team effectiveness was mediated by balanced processing of information. Ninety-six leaders (plus 307 subordinates, 96 supervisors, and 656 peers of those leaders) participated. Humility in leaders (as reported by others/peers) was indirectly (i.e., through balanced processing) related to leaders' perceived impact on team effectiveness. The study also corroborated literature pointing out the benefits of using other-reports (rather than self-reports) to measure humility. Third, Walters and Diab (2016) examined the relationships among leader humility, psychological safety, and employee engagement. Workers ($N = 140$) reported their perceptions of their immediate supervisor's humility and also their own psychological safety and work engagement. Humble leadership was related to employee engagement by the employees' feelings of psychological safety. When leaders admit to their limitations and mistakes as well as acknowledge their workers' strengths and the contributions workers are making, Walters and Diab suggested that this modeled leader teachability. These three recent studies add to pre-2016 summaries of humility and leadership (e.g., Collins, 2001; A. S. Wallace, Chiu, & Owens, 2017).

Organizational Humility

A humble organization is characterized by openness to dialogue, commitment to cooperation, creativity allowing the expression of new ideas, a realistic view of itself as an organization with strengths and weaknesses, and a willingness to admit mistakes (A. S. Wallace et al., 2017). A. S. Wallace et al. (2017) suggested that the same qualities as make up leader and team humility make up organizational humility—self-awareness of strengths and weaknesses of one's own organization, appreciation of other organizations' strengths and contributions, and being (as an organization) teachable (Owens & Hekman, 2016). Organizational self-awareness of strengths and weaknesses includes both leaders' and rank-and-file members' awareness. When the organization seeks assistance from other organizations, it is exhibiting appreciation of other organizations. Being teachable is illustrated when an organization can accept and receive feedback gracefully and can learn from other organizations. These characteristics are built into the organization's mission statement, values, preferences, policies, and procedures.

LEADERSHIP WITHIN ORGANIZATIONS

Let's look a little more deeply at leadership, especially within humble organizations.

Jim Collins's Research on the Good-to-Great Companies

Let's take an example of a great leader and see how he helped other leaders develop. In his 2001 book, *Good to Great: Why Some Companies Make the Leap . . . and Others Don't*, Jim Collins profiled numerous excellent leaders. He found that all 11 companies that outperformed other companies in their own market and sustained that exalted performance over time had one thing in common: They were led by "Level 5 leaders" (Collins, 2001, p. 21).

He identified four other effective, but not exemplary, levels of leadership. Level 1 leaders were very capable workers, not necessarily in leadership positions. They had excellent talent, knowledge, skills, and good work habits. Level 2 leaders had the attributes of Level 1 leaders, but they also were great team contributors. Level 3 leaders had risen to management. They could organize people and resources and get things done. Level 4 leaders were effective not just at management but also at leadership. They could inspire commitment and superior performance.

Level 5 leaders, though, were special. Collins (2001) called them executives who could build "enduring greatness through a paradoxical blend of personal humility and professional will" (p. 20). They were not merely servant-leaders (Greenleaf, 1977) or selfless executives—though they were both of those. Rather, their uniqueness was the rare blend of will and humility. One of the people Collins discussed was Alan Wurtzel. Wurtzel had inherited the position of CEO of Circuit City from his father in 1973. Circuit City was close to bankruptcy. *Forbes* published an article on the surprising great run of success on August 27, 1984. This "overnight success" had been on the road to success for over 10 years. Let's make a comparison. Jack Welch, CEO at General Electric, has been widely regarded as one of the best leaders in business history. When he took over GE, he proclaimed that if one of the divisions of GE was not number one or two in the world, he would fix it, kill it, or sell it. He moved a hugely successful company into record growth. But as Collins pointed out, if a person had invested one dollar in GE and another dollar in Circuit City when Welch took over in 1981 and held it during Wurtzel's reign until January 1, 2000, the person would have made 6 times as much money with Circuit City.

Collins (2001) interviewed Wurtzel, asking him to list and rank the top five qualities responsible for Circuit City's success. The number one quality, according to Wurtzel, was luck. Collins asked him to elaborate, and he responded, "We were in a great industry with the wind at our back" (Collins, 2001, p. 33). But Collins observed that all companies were compared with other similar companies in the same industry with the same wind at their back. After debating the issue, Wurtzel stuck to his guns. "The first thing that comes to mind is luck. . . . I was lucky to find the right successor" (Collins, 2001, p. 33). Yet Wurtzel was not the only CEO to attribute success to luck.

What comes to mind is the farewell speech by baseball great, Yankee first-baseman Lou Gehrig. Gehrig was "The Iron Horse" who played 17 seasons with the Yankees from 1923 to 1939, and at one point, he played 2,130 consecutive games (a record that stood until Cal Ripken Jr. broke it in 1995). Gehrig developed amyotrophic lateral sclerosis (ALS), named Lou Gehrig's disease. In his emotional speech to Yankee fans on July 4, 1939, the humble Gehrig said,

> You have been reading about a bad break I got. Yet today I consider myself the luckiest man on the face of the earth. I have been in ballparks for seventeen years and have never received anything but kindness and encouragement from you fans. Look at these grand men. Which of you wouldn't consider it the highlight of his career just to associate with them for even one day? . . . Sure, I'm lucky. ("Luckiest Man," n.d.)

Level 5 Leaders

The Level 5 leaders tended to have a particular attributional style. Collins (2001) called it the window or the mirror:

> Level 5 leaders look out the window to apportion credit to factors outside themselves when things go well (and if they cannot find a specific person

> or event to give credit to, they credit good luck). At the same time, they look in the mirror to apportion responsibility, never blaming bad luck when things go poorly. (p. 35)

In this chapter on helping others become more heroically humble leaders, it is necessary to consider what Collins (2001) said. When asked directly whether people could learn to be Level 5 leaders, Collins offered this response:

> My hypothesis is that there are two categories of people: Those who do not have the seed of Level 5 and those who do. The first category consists of people who could never in a million years bring themselves to subjugate their egoistic needs to the greater ambition of building something. . . . The second category of people—and I suspect the larger group—consists of those who have the potential to evolve to Level 5, the capability resides within them, perhaps buried or ignored but there nonetheless. And under the right circumstances—self-reflection, conscious personal development, a mentor, a great teacher, loving parents, a significant life experience, a Level 5 boss, or any number of other factors—they begin to develop. (pp. 36–37)

He called out particularly significant life experiences, such as a near-death experience, a wartime experience, or a personal religious transformative experience. Yet other leaders did not have one particular important experience. There is no single path to Level 5 leadership with its twin towers of iron will and heroic humility. In the end, Collins (2001) said, "I would love to be able to give you a list of steps for becoming Level 5, but we have no solid research data that would support a credible list" (p. 37).

So, Collins (2001) recommended carrying out the remainder of the steps in the good-to-great book and trusting that it will move people toward Level 5. These include a first step of getting the right people into the leadership team—get the right people on the bus and the wrong people off the bus, and then figure out where to drive the bus. This trumped developing a vision and enlisting followers who were on board with the vision.

As a second step, confront the brutal facts without losing faith. That is, ground change in reality, no matter how harsh, and yet, if the right people are in leadership, there is hope.

Third, be a hedgehog. Following an essay by Isaiah Berlin, "The Hedgehog and the Fox," Collins (2001) suggested that Level 5 leaders keep the main thing the main thing. That is, such leaders do not get pulled off in interesting directions. They find what they can develop into being the best in the world at. They will find this at the intersection of their passion, their judgment about what they can be best in the world at, and their economic engine (or power source). They devote their energy and resources at building that.

Fourth, create a culture of disciplined leaders who will focus on the hedgehog principle. But the main thing requires continually seeking, with passion, a best-in-the-world product empowered by a power source.

Fifth, use new technology to accelerate development along the lines of the hedgehog principle. Do not think of technology as a great hope to create momentum that is not there.

Sixth, realize that transformation has no "miracle moment." That is, most transitions are the product of steady pushing—in the same general direction—not one huge push. When one pushes steadily, acceleration builds and eventually people notice.

Seventh, move the organization from good-to-great to built-to-last principles. These principles of enduring success are (a) plan for the long haul, (b) turn either–or choices into both–and possibilities, (c) stay true to core values, and (d) preserve the core but stimulate change.

We might say, then, that the following characteristics are needed to be a Level 5 leader: social and emotional intelligence to select a leadership team (first) and people a disciplined culture. Never get away from reality. Sustain an unwavering focus on one's priority—identifying it, selecting people to build it up in a disciplined way, using technology in service of the one thing, continuing to push in the same general direction, and maintaining the core values even when prompting changes in direction. We are struck by the central importance of being able to discern one's priority and focus growth on that priority.

Evaluating What Collins Learned of Level 5 Leaders

In the classic Billy Crystal movie *City Slickers*, Jack Palance (who won an Academy Award and did one-armed pushups on receiving the award) plays Curly, a crusty, churlish cowboy who tells Billy Crystal's character (Mitch) the secret of life. He holds up one finger. "Your finger?" says Mitch. Curly says, "One thing." He never explains. But in Collins's (2001) *Good to Great*, it looks like organizational success at any rate has been due to people listening to Curly: Identify, focus on, and maintain the one thing that will lead to success for your organization.

But this is probably great advice for life success as well as organizational success. Talented people often have lots of choices. But successful people focus. They organize their efforts around the object of their focus. They are realistic and disciplined, and they select friends and romantic partners with consonant values. And they never stray from their core values.

Heroic humility is one of those organizing priorities, and there is no five-step method to get there. In fact, in this book we have seen a variety of paths to personal development of your own heroic humility or paths to developing your own research program to study heroic humility.

We know that programs like PROVE Humility can help people develop a more humble character. It also can help build other virtues. We don't know what parts of that complex 7-hour workbook program might be the active ingredients. We also have advice from Collins (2001) that suggests that putting into practice the seven actions to build a good-to-great organization might help people become Level 5 leaders, just as people who might be naturally Level 5 leaders might be able to put the steps into action more easily. For Collins, prioritizing is crucial.

You might be a CEO who is seeking to turn yourself into a Level 5 leader. Perhaps you are a social psychology professor who leads a research team in which you are attempting to develop Level 5 leaders who can have successful research careers. Maybe you are even a politician who wants to become a Level 5 public servant. Or perhaps you are just a person in any career who wants to become a better, more humble, Level 5 leader in your romantic relationship, family, community organization, and workplace. Regardless, we believe that prioritizing is crucial. Assay your values. See whether you think that developing humility is in line with them and is a worthy personal goal. It will involve, as you well know by now, accurate self-assessment and an attitude of teachability, modesty, and (most of all) an other-orientation showing power under control to build others up and not put them down.

LEADERSHIP AND BEING TEACHABLE

There is a vast supply of leadership material, and as it has accumulated, much of it supports the notion of being a humble leader. Jim Collins (2001) has been vocal about leaders also being servants. Robert Greenleaf (1977) formulated the servant-leader model, and business leaders like Max De Pree (1989) have made it popular. Recently, Jit, Sharma, and Kawatra (2016) conducted a qualitative study using interpretative phenomenological analysis to determine the conflict management styles of servant-leaders. Servant-leaders were described as being more persuasive, humane, and participative than other leaders. Their principal strategies aimed at resolving subordinate–subordinate conflict were sequential. They made an initial diagnosis of the situation. They then intervened with the aim of helping bring about a mutually acceptable solution. Throughout, they sought to remain impartial, self-controlled, patient, composed, and humble. They attempted not to be provoked when employees were provocative. The qualitative study provided personal accounts of leaders' experiences analyses.

Leadership expert John P. Kotter (2012) closed his book, *Leading Change*, with a reflection on humility as an essential trait of an effective leader. He emphasized having a humble view of oneself so you could watch more closely, listen more carefully, relentlessly test new ideas, be open-minded, try new things, and reflect honestly on successes and failures. That leads to being a lifelong learner. We have incorporated that idea in our definition as being teachable. For Kotter, a lifelong learner takes risks, uses humble self-reflection, seeks opinions, listens carefully, and stays open to new ideas. He said,

> The very best lifelong learners and leaders I've known seem to have high standards, ambitious goals, and a real sense of mission in their lives. Such goals and aspirations spur them on, put their accomplishments in a humbling perspective, and help them endure the short-term pain associated with growth. (p. 192)

Being a lifelong learner is what education should lead to. Rabbi Jacob Neuser gave a convocation welcoming frosh to Elizabethtown College (Pennsylvania) on September 25, 1991. William Safire (1997) described Rabbi Neuser like this:

> [He] is the more provocative and prolific scholar in the world of Judaic studies. While a professor at Brown University, a fellow of the Institute for Advanced Studies at Princeton, and a research professor at the University of South Florida in Tampa, he has written 240 learned books. (p. 1027)

No, that is not a typo: 240 learned books. Most of us haven't written 240 learned e-mails in our life.

Neuser reflected on what the teaching–learning contract is for a college education, and he concluded that if a college is successful, it will help people be lifelong learners. Great professors ask questions rather than provide information. Education provides not just experiences but guided or directed reflection on experiences. How? By questioning. Thought is not remembering and regurgitating. It is having an experience with a book, a professor, a trip to Europe, a romantic attraction and breakup, or a self-disappointing moral failure. Then, it is mentally asking why, answering one's own question, asking the next question, and so on. The train of questions is thought. Education is about getting people to interrogate their experiences and to do so throughout their lives. "Three of the all-time greats—Socrates, Jesus, and his Jewish contemporary the sage Hillel . . . always raised more questions than they answered" (Neuser, in Safire, 1997, p. 1029). Humility involves teachability, which is being open to what others can teach. Teachability is not a one-off listening experience, no matter how valuable.

Heroic humility is building listening, empathy, and questioning into a habit pattern for one's whole life.

SITUATIONS MATTER

As social psychology has repeatedly shown, strong situations can powerfully influence people's lives. Your organization can become a more humble one. If it does, that will help you. What can you do to make that organizational change? Perhaps we can draw on some of the themes and lessons of this book for ideas.

WHAT DID WE LEARN IN THIS CHAPTER?

1. A. S. Wallace et al. (2017) suggested that leaders, teams, and organizations have the same three components of humility: self-awareness of strengths and weaknesses; appreciation of others' strengths, weaknesses, and contributions; and evidence of being teachable.
2. Collins (2001) identified Level 5 leadership as essential for great companies. That leadership involves humility and iron will. The key is focus on "one thing." Heroic humility, which focuses on others, is the one thing that can build Level 5 leaders.
3. John P. Kotter (2012) found that an attitude of lifelong learning is essential for an organization, a leader, and a person. This is the humility of always being teachable.

THREE QUESTIONS FOR THOUGHT AND DISCUSSION

1. Is humility practical in highly competitive organizational environments? If you step into a competitive organization, is it professional suicide to initiate humility if that did not already characterize the organization?
2. Are you a Level 5 leader, with a core of iron will, yet the professional and personal humility to change?
3. Are you a lifelong learner?

15

TAKEAWAY LESSONS

As you close the pages of this book, we hope you will take away important learning and commitment. We have emphasized several themes. These fall into two categories. First, humility has benefits to individuals and others. It is driven by social forces. Second, its scientific study can be a public good, and it can be a scientist's way of being more humble because science emphasizes what we don't know more than what we do. And science is always aware of the limitations of the scientific method. Public intellectual Ralph Washington Sockman (1889–1970) said, "The larger the island of knowledge, the longer the shoreline of wonder."

http://dx.doi.org/10.1037/0000079-016
Heroic Humility: What the Science of Humility Can Say to People Raised on Self-Focus, by E. L. Worthington Jr. and S. T. Allison

HUMILITY IS HELPFUL TO SELF AND OTHERS

We have treated humility as involving exclusion and embrace—exclusion of pride of self and embrace of love of others. Both intrapersonal and interpersonal are needed.

Perhaps one of the biggest takeaway lessons of this book is that humility requires a humble other-orientation that seeks to elevate others. Although mere lack of self-focus and a quiet ego are important parts of humility, we have argued that warm other-orientation is the linchpin of humility, especially heroic humility. Recently, J. C. Wright, Nadelhoffer, Perini, Langville, Echols, and Venezia (2017) added support for our case. In two studies, they showed that 191 adults included other-orientation within their lay definitions of humility and that 251 middle and high school students increased their belief that other-orientation was part of humility annually from fifth grade through graduation and on into adulthood.

We have emphasized the importance of heroic humility, not the acts, states, or even trait of humility. Rather, we have found great inspiration in commitment to humility that is so deep it is costly. Heroic humility doesn't just show up one day. It is viewed, practiced until it becomes a habit of the heart, and tested in our heroic quest against the challenges of life, and it leads to ultimate satisfaction. Like all heroic quests, we don't win. We emerge scarred from the quest. But as time passes we can meet challenges easier and fail less often.

We are not on this quest alone. We are in a company of other heroic questers who together can transform relationships, families, communities, and societies. However, the world today is set up in ways that make humility more difficult than it might have been in times past. We are not today in the "crooked timber" tradition that David Brooks (2015) described. Modernity tells us we are in Frank Sinatra's "I Did It My Way" school of life. But that is tempered by postmodern skepticism that argues that no way is better than any other way. Despite these messages, Charles Taylor (2007), prophet of secularism, saw humility as the virtue of the 21st century.

People can learn to be more humble if they want to. Different learning styles are useful for different people. Some can take scientific discoveries and translate those into practical use. Many learn more from examples than from science. We have sought to provide many examples. Others learn by working through practical exercises, and again, we have provided examples.

These themes can help shape your life as a scholar, scientist, and person. We hope that you have decided that you can be a more heroically humble person yourself, practicing humility more than when you picked up this book and benefiting others from the practice. If you moved in that direction, we hope you will have found the book to be worth its price.

Understanding and Practicing Humility Can Help Individuals

Relationships drive the study of humility. The growth of humility studies has been on an upward trajectory, increasing in activity each year. Most people are drawn to study humility because they can see how humility helps relationships. It is not a quest for better health or more pleasure that makes people want to be humble, or that makes scientists want to study humility. We are drawn by the opportunity to contribute to ultimate satisfaction and a better world.

Humility is related to mental health and perhaps physical health. But frankly, these outcomes have not been well established. They need to be. Exploring the mental and physical health connections with humility can fuel many research careers.

Spirituality might be positively affected if people practiced more spiritual humility. In addition, spiritual humility can empower relational, intellectual, and general humility.

Understanding and Practicing Humility Can Help Couples and Families

Humility can be practiced in many contexts. Many of these could greatly affect society. Humility between partners or within families could save marriages and strengthen families.

The Importance of Humility in Couple and Family Contexts

Divorce is frequent (some estimate about a 42%–45% likelihood that a couple marrying today will divorce before one of them dies). Humility can make a difference in the way partners treat each other. Most marriage experts suggest that the main cause of a good marriage is the formation, maintenance and growth of a strong emotional bond and its repair when damaged (for a review, see Worthington, 2005). The same is likely for strong families. Humility is related to stronger social bonds, as we saw in Chapter 3.

How Can Couple and Family Humility Be Improved?

If people do not live in particularly humble romantic relationships or families, there is still hope. People can become more dispositionally humble. If they do, it is possible that they might also develop other virtues, like patience, forgiveness, and reduced negativity. There is some suggestion that becoming more humble might also help one develop more empathy, compassion, sympathy, altruism, or even love for others. All of these virtues (see Chapter 4) promote better couple and family relationships. By initiating personal change, especially for one of the adult partners, the entire family system might begin to be transformed. But one might also seek to influence the family system more directly, through initiating humble conversations with other family members.

Understanding and Practicing Humility Can Help Organizations

As A. S. Wallace, Chui, and Owens (2017) showed, humility at the level of leader, team, and entire organization has positive effects (and they noted a few negative effects as well) on the entire organization. Humility could spring from any level and change organizations. We are keenly aware of how Gandhi changed the United Kingdom and India (and the world's future) through his humble character coupled with iron will—Level 5 leadership (Collins, 2001). Yet, Gandhi had no official position of recognized leadership. He just had Level 5 leadership. So, in theory, we believe that anyone could turn around an organization—up to and including an organization as large as India or as complex as the entire British commonwealth.

But the fact is, the change agent is usually seen as the CEO, or today often the senior leadership team (Wageman, Nunes, Burress, & Hackman, 2008). Wageman et al. (2008) noted how we have often attributed a company's success or failure to the "heroic CEO" (p. xii) but more often today, it is the entire leadership team who direct a company's fortunes. Wageman et al. identified six elements of an effective leadership team—three essentials and three enablers. The essentials are to decide on whether to have a leadership team, to develop a compelling purpose for the team, and to get the right people on the team. The enablers are to provide the team with structure, support, and timing. But what is needed to keep the team functioning well is to create an environment that fosters good teamwork, and that begins with encouraging humility from top to bottom.

Understanding and Practicing Humility Can Help Communities

In a revision of his 1999 Presidential address to Division 27 of the American Psychological Association, the Society for Community Research and Action, Kenneth I. Maton (2000) advanced a framework for social transformation involving four goals: capacity building, group empowerment, relational community building, and the challenge of cultural inclusion. He ended with three challenges to guide community interventionists. Besides increasing awareness of the need for social transformation to the center of attention and to work with many disciplines to transform society, the third goal was to carry out the needed changes "with heart, soul, and humility" (Maton, 2000, p. 25). He closed, "Finally, we should do so with humility. The challenges are great, our knowledge is quite limited. In every situation, we have as much to learn and receive from others as we have to share with them" (p. 50). Maton, in his call to other-oriented action, addresses the essence of humility—knowing our strengths and limitations, teachability, and a modest presentation. Those qualities can help lift communities and the people in them.

Understanding and Practicing Humility Can Help Society

Cultural Humility

Humility can help transform society. To do so, we must understand people, and a humble attitude among leaders, leadership teams, communities, and individual citizens can promote generational understanding and interconnectivity across the ages, races, socioeconomic classes, genders, religions, and lifestyle choices. Cultural humility is paramount for now and the future (Foronda, Baptiste, Reinholdt, & Ousman, 2016).

In Chapter 2, we defined two types of cultural humility. In *empathic cultural humility*, a person understands the cultural diversity of another person from the perspective of a different culture, has sought to master knowledge about the culture, and yet treats the person as a valuable individual with a story to tell within the cultural framework. The person does not presume to know another person merely by being well versed in knowledge about the person's culture. In *nonpartisan cultural humility*, a person has humility about the strengths and limitations about one's own culture, and can recognize, without judgment, the strengths and limitations of other cultures. Empathic cultural humility focuses more on the interpersonal. Nonpartisan cultural humility focuses more on the intrapersonal. Foronda, Baptiste, Reinholdt, and Ousman (2016) recently provided a concept analysis and a current definition for the term *cultural humility*. Cultural humility was used in a variety of contexts from individuals having ethnic and racial differences, to differences in sexual preference, social status, and interprofessional roles, to health care provider–patient relationships. The attributes of cultural humility generally were seen to be openness, self-awareness, egolessness, supportive interactions, self-reflection, and self-critique. Cultural humility was brought forth as a need because of the pressures of dealing with increasing diversity and power imbalance within society. If people develop and practice cultural humility, the result is likely to be mutual empowerment, partnerships, respect, optimal care, and continued lifelong learning. They developed their conceptual model, and lifelong learning was seen to be at the core of cultural humility (see Figure 15.1). Individuals, communities, and societies were encouraged to use cultural humility to modify society to be more inclusive.

M. Wright, Lin, and O'Connell (2016) sought to understand, using participatory-action research, an Aboriginal worldview and to discover ways that human interactions have been shaped by social relationships in kin-based societies. A disconnection between mental health and drug and alcohol

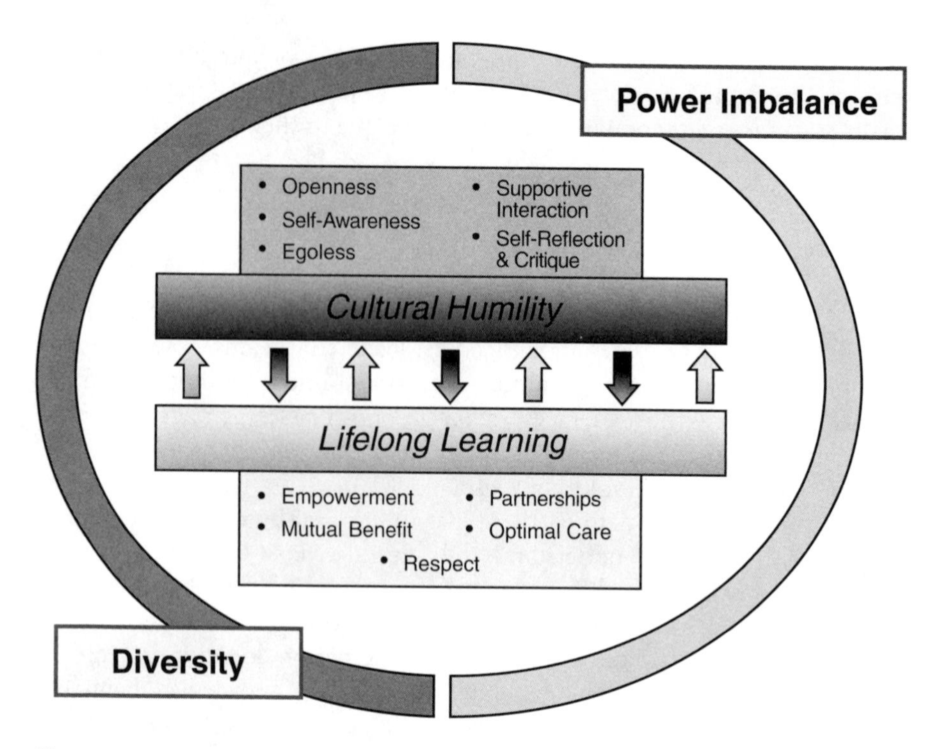

Figure 15.1. A concept analysis of cultural humility. From "Cultural Humility: A Concept Analysis," by C. Foronda, D.-L. Baptiste, M. M. Reinholdt, and K. Ousman, 2016, *Journal of Transcultural Nursing, 27,* p. 214. Copyright 2016 by Sage. Reprinted with permission.

service-providers had been uncovered in Aboriginal families in Perth, Western Australia. In 11 mental health and drug and alcohol treatment facilities, 18 Aboriginal elders and over 70 clinicians and staff shared stories. Researchers found a lack of trust between service providers and Aboriginal families that was interpreted to have arisen because most service providers did not understand the critical difference in social relationships. Clinicians who adopt a culturally humble perspective tend to be more adaptable in working with Aboriginal clients and families.

In addition, more cultural humility might improve international relations. Countries often approach each other on the basis of protecting their own interests. Empathically understanding other countries and being other-oriented can promote more international understanding.

Intellectual Humility

In Chapter 2, we also discussed types of humility needed for society to function. These included intellectual humility, especially political and religious humility, which could contribute to public discourse, improve political communication, and perhaps even lead to being able to live with religious differences. We might also include a kind of humility that invites generations to understand and empathize with each other.

SCIENTIFIC BENEFIT—JOIN IN AND DO A GREAT WORK

The scientific study of humility has just begun. If you are a social scientist entering the field, pluck the low-hanging fruit to reveal meaningful big truths. Few scientists ever become famous. Few win Nobel Prizes. As scientists, we put aside grandiose dreams of personal success. Few rewards are tangible. But we can contribute to something that can elevate people, using our talents and skills, our power under control, to build others up rather than put them down. Science at its best can be a life of heroic humility. The scientific study of heroic humility is a bold choice for the scientific scholar. We urge you to join others in that noble pursuit.

Teddy Roosevelt, the 26th president of the United States, was a sickly child who grew into a vigorous and bold adult. He advocated bold and vigorous social programs, as we might suspect would be pushed by someone who overcame adversity and rose to the presidency. In one speech, he made his philosophy succinctly apparent, and that passage inspired other presidents, like Dwight Eisenhower. Roosevelt said,

> It is not the critic who counts; not the [person] who points out . . . where the doer of deeds could have done them better. The credit belongs to the man [or woman] who is actually in the arena, . . . who strives valiantly, who errs, who comes short again and again, because there is no effort without error and shortcoming, . . . who spends himself [or herself] in a worthy cause, who at best knows in the end the triumph of high achievement, and who at the worst, if he [or she] fails, at least fails while daring greatly. (Roosevelt as cited in Safire, 1997, p. 514)

Dare greatly. Invest yourself in this humble service to humanity. You have seen many examples in this book of heroic humility. We know that we might never reach their level of humility, but we also know that we can feel ultimate satisfaction from a career that studies humility and helps others develop and practice this great virtue.

WHAT DID WE LEARN IN THIS CHAPTER?

1. Humility can help individuals—by building virtue, having better social relations, and contributing to a more noble purpose than an individual orientation might yield.

2. Humility can help friends, couples, families, organizations, communities, and nations.
3. The scientific study of humility is a noble pursuit. If you haven't joined that pursuit yet, will you consider doing so?

THREE QUESTIONS FOR THOUGHT AND DISCUSSION

1. Have we convinced you that humility requires that we are focused on others, not just a quiet ego?
2. If you assess yourself on the virtue of heroic humility, what are your conclusions? If you would like to be more humble, what concrete next steps must you take?
3. As you think back through the chapters, which do you think has made the most impact on you and why? If you are in a discussion group, what do you think of the lessons that others in your group have drawn from the book?

APPENDIX: SOME POTENTIAL ACTIVITIES FOR USE AT HOME, WITH STUDENTS, OR WITH PATIENTS

1. **Self-Reflection Paper(s)**. Do a thorough self-assessment of your own humility.
   a. Consider whether you have all three attributes of heroic humility. (1) Do you have an accurate picture of your own strengths and weaknesses? You might informally interview three people, perhaps one friend, one family member, and one schoolmate or work colleague, asking for a candid assessment of their views of your strengths and weaknesses and see if they match your own. Ask whether you show evidence of being teachable. (2) Do you behave modestly? (3) Do people perceive you as being oriented toward lifting others up, using others for your own advancement, or simply leaving others out of your life?
   b. Consider the different types of humility. Do you show humility in virtually all relationships? Do you show cultural humility by sensitivity to cultural differences? In the area of intellectual humility, are their topics that you simply cannot discuss calmly and show respect for people who differ widely from your position? Might political, religious, or social topics stimulate your intolerance? Are you spiritually humble—showing respect in the face of God, nature, humanity, transcendent reality, or whatever you hold to be Sacred?
2. **Self-Change Initiative**. Design your own self-change program to try to build the virtue of humility more prominently into your life. While you could refer to the programs mentioned in Chapter 13 to get ideas, or you could work through the *PROVE Humility* workbook and add some interventions of your own, you might also enjoy outlining your own change program from the get-go. Perhaps you would like to try a behavioral psychology spin—rewarding yourself for change, modifying the environment, and programming social reinforcers. Perhaps you would like to use a religious approach (for a summary, see Chapter 6) and draw from your religious or spiritual tradition. Design your program and put it into effect with a serious effort for at least 3 weeks. At the end of the program, do a thorough analysis about what did and didn't work for you.
3. **Learn More About Humble Heroes**. Try to identify five people who exhibit heroic humility but are not mentioned in this book.

Search them out on Wikipedia or using other biographical sources, or (if they are people you know personally) interview them about how they succeed in being humble and what challenges their humility the most.

4. **Inspire Others**. Make and post a YouTube 4-minute interview with one of the people in your life whom you believe illustrates heroic humility. Be sure they give you permission to do so.
5. **Heroic Humility Within Film**. We have suggested many films in which a protagonist shows heroic humility. Find three examples not mentioned in this book and summarize how the protagonist (or another character) illustrates heroic humility.
6. **Visualize Your Life as a Heroic Quest**. Identify the quest you have been conscripted by life to follow. What is the goal of the quest? Who is with you on the quest—a band of fellow questers or perhaps a single helper? What are the mountains, roadblocks, or challenges that stand in your way? Who will help you overcome those? Can you acknowledge that you are not able to complete your quest without help from others? Write down a brief autobiography and speculation about the future as this heroic quest.

REFERENCES

Aghababaei, N. (2013). Between you and God, where is the general factor of personality? Exploring personality–religion relationships in a Muslim context. *Personality and Individual Differences*, 55, 196–198. http://dx.doi.org/10.1016/j.paid.2013.02.021

Aghababaei, N., & Arji, A. (2014). Well-being and the HEXACO model of personality. *Personality and Individual Differences*, 56, 139–142. http://dx.doi.org/10.1016/j.paid.2013.08.037

Aghababaei, N., Błachnio, A., Arji, A., Chiniforoushan, M., Tekke, M., & Fazeli Mehrabadi, A. (2016). Honesty–humility and the HEXACO structure of religiosity and well-being. *Current Psychology*, 35, 421–426.

Aghababaei, N., Mohammadtabar, S., & Saffarinia, M. (2014). Dirty dozen vs. the H factor: Comparison of the dark triad and honesty–humility in prosociality, religiosity, and happiness. *Personality and Individual Differences*, 67, 6–10. http://dx.doi.org/10.1016/j.paid.2014.03.026

Agnew, C. R., & Dove, N. (2011). Relationship commitment and perceptions of harm to self. *Basic and Applied Social Psychology*, 33, 322–332. http://dx.doi.org/10.1080/01973533.2011.614134

Albert, T. (Producer), & Ramis, H. (Producer and Director). (1993). *Groundhog day* [Motion picture]. United States: Columbia Pictures.

Alcoholics Anonymous. (2001). *Alcoholics anonymous: The story of how many thousands of men and women have recovered from alcoholism* (4th ed.). New York, NY: Alcoholics Anonymous World Services.

Allen, W. B. (Ed.). (1988). *George Washington: A collection*. Indianapolis, IN: Liberty Fund.

Allgaier, K., Zettler, I., Wagner, W., Püttmann, S., & Trautwein, U. (2015). Honesty–humility in school: Exploring main and interaction effects on secondary school students' antisocial and prosocial behavior. *Learning and Individual Differences*, 43, 211–217. http://dx.doi.org/10.1016/j.lindif.2015.08.005

Allison, S. T. (2015). The initiation of heroism science. *Heroism Science*, 1, 1–8.

Allison, S. T., Eylon, D., Beggan, J. K., & Bachelder, J. (2009). The demise of leadership: Positivity and negativity biases in evaluations of dead leaders. *The Leadership Quarterly*, 20, 115–129. http://dx.doi.org/10.1016/j.leaqua.2009.01.003

Allison, S. T., & Goethals, G. R. (2011). *Heroes: What they do and why we need them*. New York, NY: Oxford University Press.

Allison, S. T., & Goethals, G. R. (2012). *Dakota Meyers: The hero who defied orders to save lives*. Retrieved from https://blog.richmond.edu/heroes/2012/09/26/dakota-meyer-the-hero-who-defied-orders-to-save-lives/

Allison, S. T., & Goethals, G. R. (2013). *Heroic leadership: An influence taxonomy of 100 exceptional individuals*. New York, NY: Routledge.

Allison, S. T., & Goethals, G. R. (2014). "Now he belongs to the ages": The heroic leadership dynamic and deep narratives of greatness. In G. R. Goethals, S. T. Allison, R. M. Kramer, & D. M. Messick (Eds.), *Conceptions of leadership: Enduring ideas and emerging insights* (pp. 167–183). New York, NY: Palgrave Macmillan. http://dx.doi.org/10.1057/9781137472038_10

Allison, S. T., & Goethals, G. R. (2016). Hero worship: The elevation of the human spirit. *Journal for the Theory of Social Behaviour, 46*, 187–210. http://dx.doi.org/10.1111/jtsb.12094

Allison, S. T., & Goethals, G. R. (2017). The hero's transformation. In S. T. Allison, G. R. Goethals, & R. M. Kramer (Eds.), *Handbook of heroism and heroic leadership* (pp. 379–400). New York, NY: Routledge.

Allison, S. T., Goethals, G. R., & Kramer, R. M. (Eds.). (2017a). *Handbook of heroism and heroic leadership*. New York, NY: Routledge.

Allison, S. T., Goethals, G. R., & Kramer, R. M. (2017b). Setting the scene: The rise and coalescence of heroism science. In S. T. Allison, G. R. Goethals, & R. M. Kramer (Eds.), *Handbook of heroism and heroic leadership* (pp. 1–16). New York, NY: Routledge.

Allison, S. T., & Setterberg, G. C. (2016). Suffering and sacrifice: Individual and collective benefits, and implications for leadership. In S. T. Allison, C. T. Kocher, & G. R. Goethals (Eds.), *Frontiers in spiritual leadership: Discovering the better angels of our nature* (pp. 197–214). New York, NY: Palgrave Macmillan. http://dx.doi.org/10.1007/978-1-137-58081-8_12

Allison, S. T., & Smith, G. (2015). *Reel heroes and villains*. Richmond, VA: Agile Writer Press.

Asendorpf, J. B., Banse, R., & Mücke, D. (2002). Double dissociation between implicit and explicit personality self-concept: The case of shy behavior. *Journal of Personality and Social Psychology, 83*, 380–393. http://dx.doi.org/10.1037/0022-3514.83.2.380

Ashton, M. C., & Lee, K. (2005). A defense of the lexical approach to the study of personality structure. *European Journal of Personality, 19*, 5–24. http://dx.doi.org/10.1002/per.541

Ashton, M. C., & Lee, K. (2007). Empirical, theoretical, and practical advantages of the HEXACO model of personality structure. *Personality and Social Psychology Review, 11*, 150–166. http://dx.doi.org/10.1177/1088868306294907

Ashton, M. C., & Lee, K. (2009). The HEXACO-60: A short measure of the major dimensions of personality. *Journal of Personality Assessment, 91*, 340–345. http://dx.doi.org/10.1080/00223890902935878

Ashton, M. C., & Lee, K. (2016). Age trends in HEXACO-PI-R self-reports. *Journal of Research in Personality, 64*, 102–111. http://dx.doi.org/10.1016/j.jrp.2016.08.008

Ashton, M. C., Lee, K., & de Vries, R. E. (2014). The HEXACO Honesty–Humility, Agreeableness, and Emotionality factors: A review of research and theory. *Personality and Social Psychology Review, 18*, 139–152. http://dx.doi.org/10.1177/1088868314523838

Austin, E. J., & Vahle, N. (2016). Associations of the Managing the Emotions of Others Scale (MEOS) with HEXACO personality and with trait emotional intelligence at the factor and facet level. *Personality and Individual Differences, 94*, 348–353. http://dx.doi.org/10.1016/j.paid.2016.01.047

Axelrod, R. (1984). *The evolution of cooperation*. New York, NY: Basic Books.

Ayten, A. (2012). How religion promotes forgiveness: The case of Turkish Muslims. *Archive for the Psychology of Religions, 34*, 411–425. http://dx.doi.org/10.1163/15736121-12341243

Baiocco, R., Chirumbolo, A., Bianchi, D., Ioverno, S., Morelli, M., & Nappa, M. R. (2017). How HEXACO personality traits predict different selfie-posting behaviors among adolescents and young adults. *Frontiers in Psychology, 7*, Ar 2080.

Bakic-Miric, N. (2012). *An integrated approach to interpersonal communication*. Newcastle upon Tyne, England: Cambridge Scholars.

Bandura, A. (1963). *Social learning and personality development*. New York, NY: Holt, Rinehart & Winston.

Basler, R. P. (Ed.). (1959). *Collected works of Abraham Lincoln* (Vol. 2). New Brunswick, NJ: Rutgers University Press.

Bauer, J. J., & Wayment, H. A. (2008). The psychology of the quiet ego. In H. A. Wayment & J. J. Bauer (Eds.), *Transcending self-interest: Psychological explorations of the quiet ego* (pp. 7–19). Washington, DC: American Psychological Association. http://dx.doi.org/10.1037/11771-001

Baum, L. F. (1900). *The wizard of Oz*. Chicago, IL: George M. Hill.

Baumeister, R. F., Campbell, J. D., Krueger, J. I., & Vohs, K. D. (2003). Does high self-esteem cause better performance, interpersonal success, happiness, or healthier lifestyles? *Psychological Science in the Public Interest, 4*(1), 1–44. http://dx.doi.org/10.1111/1529-1006.01431

Baumeister, R. F., & Exline, J. J. (2000). Self-control, morality, and human strength. *Journal of Social and Clinical Psychology, 19*, 29–42. http://dx.doi.org/10.1521/jscp.2000.19.1.29

Baumeister, R. F., & Exline, J. J. (2002). Mystical self loss: A challenge for psychological theory. *The International Journal for the Psychology of Religion, 12*, 15–20. http://dx.doi.org/10.1207/S15327582IJPR1201_02

Baumeister, R. F., & Tierney, J. (2011). *Willpower: Rediscovering the greatest human strength*. New York, NY: Penguin Books.

Bennett, D. (2014). *A passion for the fatherless*. Grand Rapids, MI: Kregel Ministry.

Bennett, S. H. (2003). *Radical pacifism: The war resisters league and Gandhian nonviolence in America, 1915–1963*. Syracuse, NY: Syracuse University Press.

Berger, P. L., Sacks, J., Martin, D., Weiming, T., Weigel, G., Davie, G., & An-Naim, A. A. (Eds.). (1999). *The desecularization of the world: Resurgent religion and world politics*. Washington, DC: Ethics and Public Policy Center and William B. Eerdmans.

Bergh, R., & Akrami, N. (2016). Are non-agreeable individuals prejudiced? Comparing different conceptualizations of agreeableness. *Personality and Individual Differences, 101*, 153–159. http://dx.doi.org/10.1016/j.paid.2016.05.052

Bettelheim, B. (1976). *The uses of enchantment: The meaning and importance of fairy tales*. New York, NY: Knopf. http://dx.doi.org/10.1037/e309842005-008

Bobb, D. J. (2013). *Humility: An unlikely biography of America's greatest virtue*. Nashville, TN: Nelson Books.

Bollinger, R. A., & Hill, P. C. (2012). Humility. In G. Thomas (Ed.), *Religion, spirituality, and positive psychology: Understanding the psychological fruits of faith* (pp. 31–47). Santa Barbara, CA: Praeger.

Book, A. S., Volk, A. A., & Hosker, A. (2012). Adolescent bullying and personality: An adaptive approach. *Personality and Individual Differences, 52*, 218–223. http://dx.doi.org/10.1016/j.paid.2011.10.028

Bowlby, J. (1969). *Attachment and loss: Vol. 1. Attachment*. New York, NY: Basic Books.

Brandt, R. (2014, June 25). Google divulges numbers at I/O: 20 billion texts, 93 million selfies and more. *Silicon Valley Business Journal*. Retrieved from http://www.bizjournals.com/sanjose/news/2014/06/25/google-divulges-numbers-at-i-o-20-billion-texts-93.html

Brooks, D. (2015). *The road to character*. New York, NY: Random House.

Brown, S. C., & MacDonald, R. A. R. (2014). Predictive factors of music piracy: An exploration of personality using the HEXACO PI-R. *Musicae Scientiae, 18*, 53–64. http://dx.doi.org/10.1177/1029864913510016

Bruner, J. (2002). *Making stories*. Cambridge, MA: Harvard University Press.

Burnette, J. L., McCullough, M. E., Van Tongeren, D. R., & Davis, D. E. (2012). Forgiveness results from integrating information about relationship value and exploitation risk. *Personality and Social Psychology Bulletin, 38*, 345–356. http://dx.doi.org/10.1177/0146167211424582

Bush, G. H. W. (Ed.). (1999). *All the best: My life in letters and other writings*. New York, NY: Simon and Schuster.

Cai, H., Sedikides, C., Gaertner, L., Wang, C., Carvallo, M., Xu, Y., . . . Jackson, L. E. (2011). Tactical self-enhancement in China: Is modesty at the service of self-enhancement in East Asian culture? *Social Psychological and Personality Science, 2*, 59–64. http://dx.doi.org/10.1177/1948550610376599

Calaprice, A. (1996). *The quotable Einstein*. Princeton, NJ: Princeton University Press.

Campbell, J. (1949). *The hero with a thousand faces*. New York, NY: New World Library.

Campbell, J. (1959). *Primitive mythology*. New York, NY: Penguin Books.

Campbell, J. (1972). *Myths to live by*. New York, NY: Viking Press.

Campbell, J. (1988). *The power of myth*. New York, NY: Anchor Books.

Campbell, J. (1991). *The hero's journey: Joseph Campbell on his life and work*. Novato, CA: New World Library.

Campbell, J. (1995). *Reflections on the art of living*. New York, NY: HarperCollins.

Campbell, J. (2001). *Thou art that*. Novato, CA: New World Library.

Campbell, J. (2004). *Pathways to bliss*. Novato, CA: New World Library.

Capra, F. (Producer and Director). (1946). *It's a wonderful life* [Motion picture]. United States: Liberty Films.

Carmody, P., & Gordon, K. (2011). Offender variables: Unique predictors of benevolence, avoidance, and revenge? *Personality and Individual Differences, 50*, 1012–1017. http://dx.doi.org/10.1016/j.paid.2010.12.037

Carson, C. (2001). *The autobiography of Martin Luther King, Jr*. New York, NY: Warner Books.

Carter, J. (2015). *A full life: Reflections at ninety*. New York, NY: Simon and Schuster.

Caruso, D. R., Fleming, K., & Spector, E. D. (2014). Emotional intelligence and leadership. In G. R. Goethals, S. T. Allison, R. Kramer, & D. Messick (Eds.), *Conceptions of leadership: Emerging ideas and enduring insights* (pp. 93–110). New York, NY: Palgrave Macmillan. http://dx.doi.org/10.1057/9781137472038_6

Cascio, J. (2011). A game warrior remembered. *Phi Kappa Phi Forum, 91*, 26.

Chancellor, J., & Lyubomirsky, S. (2013). Humble beginnings: Current trends, state perspectives, and hallmarks of humility. *Social and Personality Psychology Compass, 7*(11), 819–833. http://dx.doi.org/10.1111/spc3.12069

Chancellor, J., Nelson, S. K., Cornick, J., Blascovich, J., & Lyubomirsky, S. (2016). *Above the Pale Blue Dot: Awe and state humility in immersive virtual environments*. Unpublished manuscript, University of California, Riverside.

Chesterton, G. K. (1959). *Orthodoxy*. Garden City, NY: Image Books.

Chiu, C. C., Owens, B. P., & Tesluk, P. E. (2016). Initiating and utilizing shared leadership in teams: The role of leader humility, team proactive personality, and team performance capability. *Journal of Applied Psychology, 101*, 1705–1720. http://dx.doi.org/10.1037/apl0000159

Church, I. M., & Barrett, J. L. (2017). Intellectual humility. In E. L. Worthington Jr., D. E. Davis, & J. N. Hook (Eds.), *Handbook of humility: Theory, research, and applications* (pp. 62–75). New York, NY: Routledge.

Collins, J. (2001). *Good to great*. New York, NY: HarperCollins.

Comte-Sponville, A. (1996). *A small treatise on the great virtues: The uses of philosophy in everyday life*. New York, NY: Holt Paperbacks.

Contrada, R. J., & Baum, A. (2011). *The handbook of stress science: Biology, psychology, and health*. New York, NY: Springer.

Cooper, J. E. (2013). *Secular powers: Humility in modern political thought*. Chicago, IL: University of Chicago Press. http://dx.doi.org/10.7208/chicago/9780226081328.001.0001

Corazinni, J. (2011). *Advantages of group therapy*. Retrieved from https://healthandcounseling.unca.edu/advantages-group-therapy

Crocker, J., Canevello, A., & Lewis, K. A. (2017). Romantic relationships in the ecosystem: Compassionate goals, nonzero-sum beliefs, and change in relationship quality. *Journal of Personality and Social Psychology*, *112*, 58–75. http://dx.doi.org/10.1037/pspi0000076

Cuassade, J. P. (2005). *Abandonment to divine providence*. Overland Park, KS: Digireads.

Dangi, S., & Nagle, Y. K. (2015). Personality factors as determinants of psychological wellbeing among adolescents. *Indian Journal of Health and Wellbeing*, 6, 369–373.

Davis, D. E., Hook, J. N., Van Tongeren, D. R., & Worthington, E. L., Jr. (2012). Sanctification of forgiveness. *Psychology of Religion and Spirituality*, *4*, 31–39. http://dx.doi.org/10.1037/a0025803

Davis, D. E., Hook, J. N., Worthington, E. L., Jr., Van Tongeren, D. R., Gartner, A. L., & Jennings, D. J., II. (2010). Relational spirituality and forgiveness: Development of the Spiritual Humility Scale (SHS). *Journal of Psychology and Theology*, 38, 91–100.

Davis, D. E., Hook, J. N., Worthington, E. L., Jr., Van Tongeren, D. R., Gartner, A. L., Jennings, D. J., II, & Emmons, R. A. (2011). Relational humility: Conceptualizing and measuring humility as a personality judgment. *Journal of Personality Assessment*, 93, 225–234. http://dx.doi.org/10.1080/00223891.2011.558871

Davis, D. E., Hook, J. N., Worthington, E. L., Jr., Van Tongeren, D. R., Gartner, A. L., Jennings, D. J., II, & Norton, L. (2010). Relational spirituality and dealing with transgressions: Development of the Relational Engagement of the Sacred for a Transgression (REST) scale. *The International Journal for the Psychology of Religion*, 20, 288–302. http://dx.doi.org/10.1080/10508619.2010.507699

Davis, D. E., McElroy, S. E., Choe, E., Westbrook, C. J., DeBlaere, C., Van Tongeren, D. R., . . . Placeres, V. (2017). Development of the Experiences of Humility Scale. *Journal of Psychology and Theology*, 45, 3–16.

Davis, D. E., McElroy, S. E., Rice, K. G., Choe, E., Westbrook, C., Hook, J. N., . . . Worthington, E. L., Jr. (2016). Is modesty a subdomain of humility? *The Journal of Positive Psychology*, *11*, 439–446. http://dx.doi.org/10.1080/17439760.2015.1117130

Davis, D. E., Placeres, V., Choe, E., DeBlaere, C., Zeyala, D., & Hook, J. N. (2017). Relational humility. In E. L. Worthington Jr., D. E. Davis, & J. N. Hook (Eds.), *Handbook of humility: Theory, research, and applications* (pp. 119–134). New York, NY: Routledge.

Davis, D. E., Rice, K., Hook, J. N., Van Tongeren, D. R., DeBlaere, C., Choe, E., & Worthington, E. L., Jr. (2015). Development of the Sources of Spirituality Scale. *Journal of Counseling Psychology*, 62, 503–513. http://dx.doi.org/10.1037/cou0000082

Davis, D. E., Rice, K. G., McElroy, S. E., DeBlaere, C., Choe, E., Van Tongeren, D. R., & Hook, J. N. (2016). Distinguishing intellectual humility and general humility.

The Journal of Positive Psychology, 11, 215–224. http://dx.doi.org/10.1080/17439760.2015.1048818

Davis, D. E., Worthington, E. L., Jr., & Hook, J. N. (2010). Humility: Review of measurement strategies and conceptualization as a personality judgment. *The Journal of Positive Psychology*, 5, 243–252. http://dx.doi.org/10.1080/17439761003791672

Davis, D. E., Worthington, E. L., Jr., Hook, J. N., Emmons, R. A., Hill, P. C., Bollinger, R. A., & Van Tongeren, D. R. (2013). Humility and the development and repair of social bonds: Two longitudinal studies. *Self and Identity, 12*, 58–77. http://dx.doi.org/10.1080/15298868.2011.636509

Davis, D. E., Worthington, E. L., Jr., Hook, J. N., Van Tongeren, D. R., Green, J. D., & Jennings, D. J., II. (2009). Relational spirituality and the development of the Similarity of the Offender's Spirituality Scale. *Psychology of Religion and Spirituality, 1*, 249–262. http://dx.doi.org/10.1037/a0017581

Davis, J. L., Burnette, J. L., Allison, S. T., & Stone, H. (2011). Against the odds: Academic underdogs benefit from incremental theories. *Social Psychology of Education, 14*, 331–346. http://dx.doi.org/10.1007/s11218-010-9147-6

Deffler, S. A., Leary, M. R., & Hoyle, R. H. (2016). Knowing what you know: Intellectual humility and judgments of recognition memory. *Personality and Individual Differences*, 96, 255–259. http://dx.doi.org/10.1016/j.paid.2016.03.016

De Pree, M. (1989). *Leadership is an art*. New York, NY: Dell.

de Shazer, S. (1985). *Keys to solution in brief therapy*. New York, NY: W. W. Norton.

de Shazer, S. (1988). *Clues: Investigating solutions in brief therapy*. New York, NY: W. W. Norton.

De Vries, A., De Vries, R., & Born, M. P. (2011). Broad vs. narrow traits: Conscientiousness and honesty–humility as predictors of academic criteria. *European Journal of Personality*, 25, 336–348. http://dx.doi.org/10.1002/per.795

De Vries, R. E. (2012). Personality predictors of leadership styles and the self-other agreement problem. *The Leadership Quarterly*, 23, 809–821. http://dx.doi.org/10.1016/j.leaqua.2012.03.002

Dickerson, D. (2015). *It only takes a minute*. Carlsbad, CA: Motivational Press.

Dickson, J. (2011). *Humilitas: A lost key to life, love, and leadership*. Grand Rapids, MI: Zondervan.

Diehl, U. (2009). Human suffering as a challenge for the meaning of life. *International Journal of Philosophy, Religion, Politics, and the Arts*, 4(2), 36–44.

Dinger, F. C., Dickhäuser, O., Hilbig, B. E., Müller, E., Steinmayr, R., & Wirthwein, L. (2015). From basic personality to motivation: Relating the HEXACO factors to achievement goals. *Learning and Individual Differences*, 40, 1–8. http://dx.doi.org/10.1016/j.lindif.2015.03.023

Donner, L. S., Singer, B., Kinberg, S., Goodman, G. (Producers), & Vaughn, M. (Director). (2011). *X-men: First class* [Motion picture]. United States: 20th Century Fox.

Duckworth, A. (2016). *Grit: The power and passion of perseverance*. New York, NY: Scribner.

Dunlop, P. D., Bourdage, J. S., de Vries, R. E., Hilbig, B. E., Zettler, I., & Ludeke, S. G. (2016). Openness to (reporting) experiences that one never had: Overclaiming as an outcome of the knowledge accumulated through a proclivity for cognitive and aesthetic exploration. *Journal of Personality and Social Psychology*. Advance online publication. http://dx.doi.org/10.1037/pspp0000110

Dunlop, P. D., Lee, K., Ashton, M. C., Butcher, S. B., & Dykstra, A. (2015). Please accept my sincere and humble apologies: The HEXACO model of personality and the proclivity to apologize. *Personality and Individual Differences*, *79*, 140–145. http://dx.doi.org/10.1016/j.paid.2015.02.004

Dwiwardani, C., Hill, P. C., Bollinger, R. A., Marks, L. E., Steele, J. R., Doolin, H. N., . . . Davis, D. E. (2014). Virtues develop from a secure base: Attachment and resilience as predictors of humility, gratitude, and forgiveness. *Journal of Psychology and Theology*, *42*, 83–90.

Edensor, J. (2015). *Corrie ten Boom*. Retrieved from http://www.zarephath.co.uk/blog/corrie-ten-boom-happy-birthday/

Egnew, T. R. (2005). The meaning of healing: Transcending suffering. *Annals of Family Medicine*, *3*, 255–262. http://dx.doi.org/10.1370/afm.313

Eliot, T. S. (1942). *Little gidding*. London, England: Faber and Faber.

Emmons, R. A. (1984). Factor analysis and construct validity of the Narcissistic Personality Inventory. *Journal of Personality Assessment*, *48*, 291–300.

Epley, N. (2014). *Mindwise: How we understand what others think, believe, feel, and want*. New York, NY: Knopf.

Erikson, E. H. (1994). *Identity and the life cycle*. New York, NY: W. W. Norton.

Estephan, A. S. (2007). *The relationship between marital humility, marital communication, and marital satisfaction* (Doctoral dissertation). Retrieved from ProQuest Dissertations. (Order No. 3269760)

Exline, J. J. (2012). Humility and the ability to receive from others. *Journal of Psychology and Christianity*, *31*, 40–50.

Exline, J. J., & Geyer, A. L. (2004). Perceptions of humility: A preliminary study. *Self and Identity*, *3*, 95–114. http://dx.doi.org/10.1080/13576500342000077

Exline, J. J., & Hill, P. C. (2012). Humility: A consistent and robust predictor of generosity. *The Journal of Positive Psychology*, *7*, 208–218. http://dx.doi.org/10.1080/17439760.2012.671348

Farber, L. (1966). *The ways of the will*. New York, NY: Basic Books.

Farcht, J. (2007). *Building personal leadership*. Hampton, VA: Morgan James.

Farrell, J. E., Hook, J. N., Ramos, M., Davis, D. E., Van Tongeren, D. R., & Ruiz, J. M. (2015). Humility and relationship outcomes in couples: The mediating role of commitment. *Couple & Family Psychology: Research and Practice*, *4*, 14–26. http://dx.doi.org/10.1037/cfp0000033

Fell, L. (2011). *Mind and love: The human experience*. Raleigh, NC: Lulu.

Fiddick, L., Brase, G. L., Ho, A. T., Hiraishi, K., Honma, A., & Smith, A. (2016). Major personality traits and regulations of social behavior: Cheaters are not the same as the reckless, and you need to know who you're dealing with. *Journal of Research in Personality, 62*, 6–18. http://dx.doi.org/10.1016/j.jrp.2016.02.007

Finkel, E. J., & Campbell, W. K. (2001). Self-control and accommodation in close relationships: An interdependence analysis. *Journal of Personality and Social Psychology, 81*, 263–277. http://dx.doi.org/10.1037/0022-3514.81.2.263

Finkelman, P. (2009). *Encyclopedia of African-American history*. New York, NY: Oxford University Press.

Ford, C. T. (2005). *Roberto Clemente: Baseball legend*. New York, NY: Enslow.

Foronda, C., Baptiste, D.-L., Reinholdt, M. M., & Ousman, K. (2016). Cultural humility: A concept analysis. *Journal of Transcultural Nursing, 27*, 210–217. http://dx.doi.org/10.1177/1043659615592677

Franco, Z. E., Blau, K., & Zimbardo, P. G. (2011). Heroism: A conceptual analysis and differentiation between heroic action and altruism. *Review of General Psychology, 15*, 99–113. http://dx.doi.org/10.1037/a0022672

Franco, Z. E., Efthimiou, O., & Zimbardo, P. G. (2016). Heroism and eudaimonia: Sublime actualization through the embodiment of virtue. In J. Vittersø (Ed.), *Handbook of eudaimonic wellbeing* (pp. 337–348). Basel, Switzerland: Springer International.

Frankl, V. E. (1959). *Man's search for meaning: An introduction to logotherapy*. New York, NY: Pocket Books.

Frankl, V. E. (1976). *Man's search for meaning: An introduction to logotherapy*. Boston, MA: Beacon Press.

Fredrickson, B. L. (2013). Positive emotions broaden and build. *Advances in Experimental Social Psychology, 47*, 1–53.

Freud, S. (1930). *Civilization and its discontents*. London, England: Penguin Books.

Frimer, J. A., Schaefer, N. K., & Oakes, H. (2014). Moral actor, selfish agent. *Journal of Personality and Social Psychology, 106*, 790–802. http://dx.doi.org/10.1037/a0036040

Funder, D. C. (1995). On the accuracy of personality judgment: A realistic approach. *Psychological Review, 102*, 652–670. http://dx.doi.org/10.1037/0033-295X.102.4.652

Garthe, R. C., Reid, C. A., Sullivan, T. N., & Cork, B. (2017). Humility in romantic relationships. In E. L. Worthington Jr., D. E. Davis, & J. N. Hook (Eds.), *Handbook of humility: Theory, research, and applications* (pp. 221–232). New York, NY: Routledge.

Gentille, S. (2016, May 27). Bryan Rust took the glare off Sydney Crosby. *Sporting News*. Retrieved from http://www.sportingnews.com/nhl/news/bryan-rust-sidney-crosby-criticism-penguins-lightning-game-7-stanley-cup-final/bz5rng5v2lge1cotoqf9yg0re

Gergen, K. J. (2015). *An invitation to social construction* (3rd ed.). Thousand Oaks, CA: Sage.

Gerzon, R. (1998). *Finding serenity in the age of anxiety*. New York, NY: Bantam.

Gibson, E. J. (1991). *An odyssey in learning and perception*. Cambridge, MA: MIT Press.

Gilbert, D. (2007). *Stumbling on happiness*. New York, NY: Vintage.

Gill, S. (1989). *William Wordsworth: A life*. New York, NY: Oxford University Press.

Girl Scouts. (2002). *Uniquely me! Girl Scout/Unilever self-esteem program*. New York, NY: Girl Scouts of the USA.

Glover, J. (2001). *Humanity*. New Haven, CT: Yale University Press.

Goethals, G. R., & Allison, S. T. (2012). Making heroes: The construction of courage, competence, and virtue. *Advances in Experimental Social Psychology, 46*, 183–235. http://dx.doi.org/10.1016/B978-0-12-394281-4.00004-0

Goethals, G. R., & Allison, S. T. (2014). Kings and charisma, Lincoln and leadership: An evolutionary perspective. In G. R. Goethals, S. T. Allison, R. M. Kramer, & D. M. Messick (Eds.), *Conceptions of leadership: Enduring ideas and emerging insights* (pp. 111–124). New York, NY: Palgrave Macmillan. http://dx.doi.org/10.1057/9781137472038_7

Goethals, G. R., & Allison, S. T. (2016). Transforming motives and mentors: The heroic leadership of James MacGregor Burns. In G. R. Goethals & D. Bradburn (Eds.), *Politics, ethics and change: The legacy of James MacGregor Burns* (pp. 59–73). Northampton, MA: Edward Elgar. http://dx.doi.org/10.4337/9781785368936.00012

Goethals, G. R., & Allison, S. T. (2017). *Mystery and meaning: Ambiguity and the perception of leaders, heroes and villains*. Unpublished manuscript, University of Richmond, Richmond, VA.

Goethals, G. R., Messick, D. M., & Allison, S. T. (1991). The uniqueness bias: Studies of constructive social comparison. In J. Suls & B. Wills (Eds.), *Social comparison: Contemporary theory and research* (pp. 149–176). Hillsdale, NJ: Erlbaum.

Goldstein, N. J., Martin, S. J., & Cialdini, R. B. (2008). *Yes! 50 scientifically proven ways to be persuasive*. New York, NY: Simon & Schuster.

Goll, J., Goll, M. A., & King, P. (2016). *A call to compassion*. Savage, MN: Broad Street.

Green, J. D., Davis, J. L., Cairo, A. H., Griffin, B. J., Behler, A. M. C., & Garthe, R. C. (2017). Relational predictors and correlates of humility: An interdependence analysis. In E. L. Worthington Jr., D. E. Davis, & J. N. Hook (Eds.), *Handbook of humility: Theory, research, and applications* (pp. 165–177). New York, NY: Routledge.

Greenleaf, R. K. (1977). *The servant-leader within: A transformative path*. New York, NY: Paulist Press.

Greer, C. L., Worthington, E. L., Jr., Lin, Y., Lavelock, C. R., & Griffin, B. J. (2014). Efficacy of a self-directed forgiveness workbook for Christian victims of within-congregation offenders. *Spirituality in Clinical Practice, 1*, 218–230. http://dx.doi.org/10.1037/scp0000012

Greer, T. W. (2013). *Humility isn't just personal anymore: Testing group-level humility in the organization* (Doctoral dissertation). Retrieved from https://www.researchgate.net/publication/256444872_Humility_isn't_just_personal_anymore_Testing_group-level_humility_in_the_organization

Gregg, A. P., Hart, C. M., Sedikides, C., & Kumashiro, M. (2008). Everyday conceptions of modesty: A prototype analysis. *Personality and Social Psychology Bulletin, 34*, 978–992. http://dx.doi.org/10.1177/0146167208316734

Gregory, J. (2014). *The science and practice of humility: The path to ultimate freedom.* Rochester, VT: Inner Traditions.

Grewal, D. (2012, April 10). How wealth reduces compassion. *Scientific American.* Retrieved from http://www.scientificamerican.com/article/how-wealth-reduces-compassion/

Grubbs, J. B., & Exline, J. J. (2014). Humbling yourself before God: Humility as a reliable predictor of lower divine struggle. *Journal of Psychology and Theology, 42*, 41–49.

Gunn, R. W., & Gullickson, B. R. (2006). Lucky mud. *Strategic Finance*, 88, 8.

Gylfason, H. F., Halldorsson, F., & Kristinsson, K. (2016). Personality in Gneezy's cheap talk game: The interaction between Honesty–Humility and Extraversion in predicting deceptive behavior. *Personality and Individual Differences*, 96, 222–226. http://dx.doi.org/10.1016/j.paid.2016.02.075

Hagá, S., & Olson, K. R. (2017). 'If I only had a little humility, I would be perfect': Children's and adults' perceptions of intellectually arrogant, humble, and diffident people. *The Journal of Positive Psychology, 12*, 87–98. http://dx.doi.org/10.1080/17439760.2016.1167943

Haidt, J. (2012). *The righteous mind: Why good people are divided by politics and religion.* New York, NY: Pantheon Books.

Hall, E., Langer, R., & McMartin, J. (2010). The role of suffering in human flourishing: Contributions from positive psychology, theology, and philosophy. *Journal of Psychology and Theology, 38*, 111–121.

Hanh, T. N. (1999). *The heart of the Buddha's teaching.* New York, NY: Broadway Books.

Hare, R. D. (1991). *The Hare psychopathy checklist–revised.* Toronto, Ontario, CA: Multi-Health Systems.

Harper, Q., Worthington, E. L., Jr., Griffin, B. J., Lavelock, C. R., Hook, J. N., Vrana, S. R., & Greer, C. L. (2014). Efficacy of a workbook to promote forgiveness: A randomized controlled trial with university students. *Journal of Clinical Psychology, 70*, 1158–1169. http://dx.doi.org/10.1002/jclp.22079

Henrich, J., Heine, S. J., & Norenzayan, A. (2010, May). *The WEIRDest people in the world?* (RatSWD Working Paper No. 139). Retrieved from http://ssrn.com/abstract=1601785

The hero in the subway. (2007, January 25). [Letters to the editor]. *The New York Times*, A16. Retrieved from http://www.nytimes.com/2007/01/05/opinion/l05hero.html?_r=0

Hess, E. D., & Ludwig, K. (2017). *Humility is the new smart: Rethinking human excellence in the smart machine age*. Oakland, CA: Berrett-Koehler.

Hilbig, B. E., Thielmann, I., Hepp, J., Klein, S. A., & Zettler, I. (2015). From personality to altruistic behavior (and back): Evidence from a double-blind dictator game. *Journal of Research in Personality, 55*, 46–50. http://dx.doi.org/10.1016/j.jrp.2014.12.004

Hilbig, B. E., Thielmann, I., Wührl, J., & Zettler, I. (2015). From Honesty–Humility to fair behavior—benevolence or a (blind) fairness norm? *Personality and Individual Differences, 80*, 91–95. http://dx.doi.org/10.1016/j.paid.2015.02.017

Hilbig, B. E., & Zettler, I. (2009). Pillars of cooperation: Honesty–Humility, social value orientations, and economic behavior. *Journal of Research in Personality, 43*, 516–519. http://dx.doi.org/10.1016/j.jrp.2009.01.003

Hilbig, B. E., Zettler, I., Leist, F., & Heydasch, T. (2013). It takes two: Honesty–Humility and Agreeableness differentially predict active versus reactive cooperation. *Personality and Individual Differences, 54*, 598–603. http://dx.doi.org/10.1016/j.paid.2012.11.008

Hilbig, B. E., Zettler, I., Moshagen, M., & Heydasch, T. (2013). Tracing the path from personality—via cooperativeness—to conservation. *European Journal of Personality, 27*, 319–327. http://dx.doi.org/10.1002/per.1856

Hill, P. C., Laney, E. K., & Edwards, K. (2015, May). *The development and validation of self-report measures of humility and intellectual humility*. Paper presented at the annual meeting of the American Psychological Society, New York, NY.

Hill, P. C., Laney, E. K., Edwards, K. J., Wang, D. C., Orme, W. H., Chan, A. C., & Wang, F. L. (2017). A few good measures: Colonel Jessup and humility. In E. L. Worthington Jr., D. E. Davis, & J. N. Hook (Eds.), *Handbook of humility: Theory, research, and applications* (pp. 119–134). New York, NY: Routledge.

Hillenbrand, L. (2010). *Unbroken: A World War II story of survival, resilience, and redemption*. New York, NY: Random House.

Hilliard, M. J. (2011). *Stories and cultural humility: Exploring power and privilege through physical therapists' life histories*. Unpublished doctoral dissertation, DePaul University, Chicago, IL.

Hodge, B., & Patterson, R. (2015). *World religion and cults*. Green Forest, AR: Master Books.

Holiday, R. (2016, May 28). *The crucial thing commencement speakers get wrong about success*. Retrieved from https://www.fastcompany.com/3060275/the-crucial-thing-commencement-speakers-get-wrong-about-success

Hook, J. N., Davis, D. E., Owen, J., & DeBlaere, C. (2017). *Cultural humility: Engaging diverse identities in therapy*. Washington, DC: American Psychological Association. http://dx.doi.org/10.1037/0000037-000

Hook, J. N., Davis, D. E., Owen, J., Worthington, E. L., Jr., & Utsey, S. O. (2013). Cultural humility: Measuring openness to culturally diverse clients. *Journal of Counseling Psychology, 60*, 353–366. http://dx.doi.org/10.1037/a0032595

Hopkin, C. R., Hoyle, R. H., & Toner, K. (2014). Intellectual humility and reactions to opinions about religious beliefs. *Journal of Psychology and Theology*, *42*, 50–61.

Hort, L., & Brown, L. (2006). *Nelson Mandela: A photographic story of a life*. New York, NY: DK.

Houck, D. W. (2002). *FDR and fear itself*. College Station, TX: Texas A&M Press.

Hoyle, R. H., Davisson, E. K., Diebels, K. J., & Leary, M. R. (2016). Holding specific views with humility: Conceptualization and measurement of specific intellectual humility. *Personality and Individual Differences*, *97*, 165–172. http://dx.doi.org/10.1016/j.paid.2016.03.043

Hult, R. A. (2006). *Agnosticity*. Bloomington, IN: Trafford.

Idler, E. L., & Benyamini, Y. (1997). Self-rated health and mortality: A review of twenty-seven community studies. *Journal of Health and Social Behavior*, *38*, 21–37. http://dx.doi.org/10.2307/2955359

Ilibagiza, I. (2006). *Left to tell: Discovering God amidst the Rwandan holocaust*. Carlsbad, CA: Hay House.

Jacobs, W. J. (1994). *Mother Teresa: Helping the poor*. Minneapolis, MN: Econo-Clad Books.

Jankowski, P. J., & Sandage, S. J. (2014). Attachment to God and humility: Indirect effect and conditional effects models. *Journal of Psychology and Theology*, *42*, 70–82.

Jankowski, P. J., Sandage, S. J., & Hill, P. C. (2013). Differentiation-based models of forgivingness, mental health and social justice commitment: Mediator effects for differentiation of self and humility. *The Journal of Positive Psychology*, *8*, 412–424. http://dx.doi.org/10.1080/17439760.2013.820337

Jennings, D. J., II, Worthington, E. L., Jr., Van Tongeren, D. R., Hook, J. N., Davis, D. E., Gartner, A. L., . . . Mosher, D. K. (2016). The transgressor's response to denied forgiveness. *Journal of Psychology and Theology*, *44*, 16–27.

Jit, R. S., Sharma, C. S., & Kawatra, M. (2016). Servant leadership and conflict resolution: A qualitative study. *International Journal of Conflict Management*, *27*, 591–612. http://dx.doi.org/10.1108/IJCMA-12-2015-0086

Johnson, R. A. (1991). *Transformation: Understanding the three levels of masculine consciousness*. New York, NY: HarperOne.

Jonason, P. K., Hatfield, E., & Boler, V. M. (2015). Who engages in serious and casual sex relationships? An individual differences perspective. *Personality and Individual Differences*, *75*, 205–209. http://dx.doi.org/10.1016/j.paid.2014.11.042

Jung, C. (1970). *The structure and dynamics of the psyche* (Vol. 8). Princeton, NJ: Princeton University Press.

Kaczor, C. (2007, January 1). *A Pope's answer to the problem of pain*. Retrieved from https://www.catholic.com/magazine/print-edition/a-popes-answer-to-the-problem-of-pain

Kahneman, D. (2011). *Thinking, fast and slow*. New York, NY: Farrar, Straus, Giroux.

Kallasvuo, O. (2007). Humility. *Harvard Business Review, 85*(1), 16.

Kamath, M. V. (2007). *Gandhi, a spiritual journey*. Mumbai, India: Indus Source Books.

Kant, I. (1964). *The metaphysical principles of virtue* (J. W. Ellington, Trans.). Indianapolis, IN: Bobbs-Merrill. (Original work published 1797)

Kawamoto, T. (2016). Cross-sectional age differences in the HEXACO personality: Results from a Japanese sample. *Journal of Research in Personality, 62*, 1–5. http://dx.doi.org/10.1016/j.jrp.2016.03.001

Kazdin, A. E., & Rabbitt, S. M. (2013). Novel models for delivering mental health services and reducing the burdens of mental illness. *Clinical Psychological Science, 1*, 170–191. http://dx.doi.org/10.1177/2167702612463566

Kelley, H. H., & Thibaut, J. (1978). *Interpersonal relations: A theory of interdependence*. New York, NY: Wiley.

Kesebir, P. (2014). A quiet ego quiets death anxiety: Humility as an existential anxiety buffer. *Journal of Personality and Social Psychology, 106*, 610–623. http://dx.doi.org/10.1037/a0035814

King, M. L., Jr., & Armstrong, T. (2007). *The papers of Martin Luther King, Jr.* (Vol. VI). Berkeley: University of California Press.

Kinsella, E. L., Ritchie, T. D., & Igou, E. R. (2015a). Lay perspectives on the social and psychological functions of heroes. *Frontiers in Psychology*, 6, 130. http://dx.doi.org/10.3389/fpsyg.2015.00130

Kinsella, E. L., Ritchie, T. D., & Igou, E. R. (2015b). Zeroing in on heroes: A prototype analysis of hero features. *Journal of Personality and Social Psychology, 108*, 114–127. http://dx.doi.org/10.1037/a0038463

Kocher, C. T. (2016). Living a life of consequence: How not to chase a fake rabbit. In S. T. Allison, G. R. Goethals, & C. T. Kocher (Eds.), *Frontiers in spiritual leadership: Discovering the better nature of our angels* (pp. 183–196). New York, NY: Palgrave Macmillan. http://dx.doi.org/10.1007/978-1-137-58081-8_11

Kohlberg, L., & Hersh, R. H. (1977). Moral development: A review of the theory. *Theory Into Practice, 16*, 53–59. http://dx.doi.org/10.1080/00405847709542675

Kolakowski, L. (2007). *Why is there something rather than nothing?* New York, NY: Basic Books.

Kotter, J. P. (2012). *Leading change*. Boston, MA: Harvard Business Review Press.

Kraus, M. W., Piff, P., & Keltner, D. (2011). Social class as culture: The convergence of resources and rank in the social realm. *Current Directions in Psychological Science, 20*, 246–250. http://dx.doi.org/10.1177/0963721411414654

Krause, N. (2010). Religious involvement, humility, and self-rated health. *Social Indicators Research*, 98, 23–39. http://dx.doi.org/10.1007/s11205-009-9514-x

Krause, N. (2012). Religious involvement, humility, and change in self-rated health over time. *Journal of Psychology and Theology, 40*, 199–210.

Krause, N. (2014). Exploring the relationships among humility, negative interaction in the church, and depressed affect. *Aging & Mental Health, 18*, 970–979. http://dx.doi.org/10.1080/13607863.2014.896867

Krause, N. (2016). Assessing the relationships among wisdom, humility, and life satisfaction. *Journal of Adult Development, 23*, 140–149. http://dx.doi.org/10.1007/s10804-016-9230-0

Krause, N., & Hayward, R. D. (2015). Assessing whether practical wisdom and awe of God are associated with life satisfaction. *Psychology of Religion and Spirituality, 7*, 51–59. http://dx.doi.org/10.1037/a0037694

Krause, N., Pargament, K. I., Hill, P. C., & Ironson, G. (2016). Humility, stressful life events, and psychological well-being: Findings from the Landmark Spirituality and Health Survey. *The Journal of Positive Psychology, 11*, 499–510. http://dx.doi.org/10.1080/17439760.2015.1127991

Krumrei-Mancuso, E. J. (2017). Intellectual humility and prosocial values: Direct and mediated effects. *The Journal of Positive Psychology, 12*, 13–28. http://dx.doi.org/10.1080/17439760.2016.1167938

Krumrei-Mancuso, E. J., & Rouse, S. V. (2016). The development and validation of the Comprehensive Intellectual Humility Scale. *Journal of Personality Assessment, 98*, 209–221. http://dx.doi.org/10.1080/00223891.2015.1068174

Kruse, E., Chancellor, J., & Lyubomirsky, S. (2015). *Self-affirmation increases humility*. Manuscript submitted for publication.

Kruse, E., Chancellor, J., & Lyubomirsky, S. (2017). State humility: Measurement, conceptual validation, and intrapersonal processes. *Self and Identity, 16*, 399–438. http://dx.doi.org/10.1080/15298868.2016.1267662

Kruse, E., Chancellor, J., Ruberton, P. M., & Lyubomirsky, S. (2014). An upward spiral between gratitude and humility. *Social Psychological and Personality Science, 5*, 805–814. http://dx.doi.org/10.1177/1948550614534700

Kummer, D. W. (2015). *U.S. Marines in Afghanistan: 2001–2009: Anthology and annotated bibliography*. Annapolis, MD: U.S. Department of the Navy.

Kurtz, E., & Ketcham, K. (1992). *The spirituality of imperfection*. New York, NY: Bantam Books.

Kwan, V. S. Y., John, O. P., Kenny, D. A., Bond, M. H., & Robins, R. W. (2004). Reconceptualizing individual differences in self-enhancement bias: An interpersonal approach. *Psychological Review, 111*, 94–110. http://dx.doi.org/10.1037/0033-295X.111.1.94

Landaw, J. (2014). *Introduction to tantra*. Somerville, MA: Wisdom.

Langer, E. J., & Rodin, J. (1976). The effects of choice and enhanced personal responsibility for the aged: A field experiment in an institutional setting. *Journal of Personality and Social Psychology, 34*, 191–198. http://dx.doi.org/10.1037/0022-3514.34.2.191

Lasch, C. (1979). *The culture of narcissism: American life in an age of diminishing expectations*. New York, NY: W. W. Norton.

Lavelock, C. R., Worthington, E. L., Jr., Davis, D. E., Griffin, B. J., Reid, C., Hook, J. N., & Van Tongeren, D. R. (2014). The quiet virtue speaks: An intervention to promote humility. *Journal of Psychology and Theology*, *42*, 99–110.

Lavelock, C. R., Worthington, E. L., Jr., Elnasseh, A., Griffin, B. J., Garthe, R. C., Davis, D. E., & Hook, J. N. (in press). Still waters run deep: Humility as a master virtue. *Journal of Psychology and Theology*.

Layous, K., Nelson, S. K., Kurtz, J. L., & Lyubomirsky, S. (2017). What triggers prosocial effort? A positive feedback loop between positive activities, kindness, and well-being. *The Journal of Positive Psychology*, *12*, 385–398. http://dx.doi.org/10.1080/17439760.2016.1198924

Leach, M. M., & Ajibade, A. (2017). Spiritual and religious predictors, correlates, and sequelae of humility. In E. L. Worthington Jr., D. E. Davis, & J. N. Hook (Eds.), *Handbook of humility: Theory, research, and applications* (pp. 192–204). New York, NY: Routledge.

Leary, M. R., Adams, C. E., & Tate, E. B. (2006). Hypo-egoic self-regulation: Exercising self-control by diminishing the influence of the self. *Journal of Personality*, *74*, 1803–1832. http://dx.doi.org/10.1111/j.1467-6494.2006.00429.x

Leary, M. R., Diebels, K. J., Davisson, E. K., Jongman-Sereno, K., Isherwood, J. C., Raimi, K. T., . . . Hoyle, R. H. (2017). Cognitive and interpersonal features of intellectual humility. *Personality and Social Psychology Bulletin*, *43*, 793–813.

Leary, M. R., Tambor, E. S., Terdal, S. K., & Downs, D. L. (1995). Self-esteem as an interpersonal monitor. The sociometer hypothesis. *Journal of Personality and Social Psychology*, *68*, 518–530. http://dx.doi.org/10.1037/0022-3514.68.3.518

Lee, H. (1960). *To kill a mockingbird*. New York, NY: Warner Books.

Lee, K., & Ashton, M. C. (2005). Psychopathy, Machiavellianism, and Narcissism in the Five-Factor Model and the HEXACO model of personality structure. *Personality and Individual Differences*, *38*, 1571–1582. http://dx.doi.org/10.1016/j.paid.2004.09.016

Lee, K., & Ashton, M. C. (2012). Getting mad and getting even: Agreeableness and Honesty–Humility as predictors of revenge intentions. *Personality and Individual Differences*, *52*, 596–600. http://dx.doi.org/10.1016/j.paid.2011.12.004

Lee, K., Ashton, M. C., Wiltshire, J., Bourdage, J. S., Visser, B. A., & Gallucci, A. (2013). Sex, power, and money: Prediction from the dark triad and Honesty–Humility. *European Journal of Personality*, *27*, 169–184. http://dx.doi.org/10.1002/per.1860

Le Grice, K. (2013). *The rebirth of the hero: Mythology as a guide to spiritual transformation*. London, England: Muswell Hill Press.

Leman, J., Haggard, M. C., Meagher, B., & Rowatt, W. C. (2017). Personality predictors and correlates of humility. In E. L. Worthington Jr., D. E. Davis, & J. N. Hook (Eds.), *Handbook of humility: Theory, research, and applications* (pp. 137–149). New York, NY: Routledge.

Levinson, D. J. (1978). *Seasons of a man's life*. New York, NY: Random House.

Lewis, C. S. (1940). *The problem of pain*. Quebec, Canada: Samizdat University Press.

Lichtman, A. J. (2000). *Great presidents* (Great courses) [Audio recording]. Chantilly, VA: The Teaching Company.

Lindsey, K. (2010). *John Wooden, thank you for being such a great teacher*. Retrieved from http://bleacherreport.com/articles/401655-john-wooden-thank-you-for-being-such-a-great-teacher

Lombardi, V. (n.d.). *Vince Lombardi quotes*. Retrieved from http://www.brainyquote.com/quotes/quotes/v/vincelomba138158.html

Lucas, E. C., Alexander, D. R., Berry, R. J., Briggs, G. A. D., Humphreys, C. J., Jeeves, M. A., & Thistleton, A. C. (2016). The Bible, science and human origins. *Science and Christian Belief, 27*, 74–99.

Luckiest Man. (n.d.). Retrieved from http://baseballhall.org/discover/lou-gehrig-luckiest-man

Lyons, M. C., & Jackson, D. E. P. (1982). *Saladin: The politics of the Holy war*. Cambridge, England: Cambridge University Press.

Maimonides, M. (1998). *Mishneh Torah* (E. Touger, Trans.). New York, NY: Moznaim, Hikhot De'ot.

Maltby, J., Wood, A. M., Day, L., & Pinto, D. G. (2012). The position of authenticity within extant models of personality. *Personality and Individual Differences, 52*, 269–273. http://dx.doi.org/10.1016/j.paid.2011.10.014

Mandela, N. (1994). *A long walk to freedom*. Boston, MA: Back Bay Books.

Marino, G. (2010). Boxing with humility. *In Character: A Journal of Everyday Virtues, 5*(1), 40–44.

Maslow, A. (1943). A theory of human motivation. *Psychological Review, 50*, 370–396. http://dx.doi.org/10.1037/h0054346

Masters, L. (2010). *Naked: This is my story, this is my song*. Bloomington, IN: Authorhouse.

Maton, K. I. (2000). Making a difference: The social ecology of social transformation. *American Journal of Community Psychology, 28*, 25–57. http://dx.doi.org/10.1023/A:1005190312887

Mayer, J. D., Salovey, P., Caruso, D. R., & Sitarenios, G. (2001). Emotional intelligence as a standard intelligence. *Emotion, 1*, 232–242. http://dx.doi.org/10.1037/1528-3542.1.3.232

McAdams, D. P. (1997). *The stories we live by: Personal myths and the making of the self.* New York, NY: Guilford Press.

McCulloh, D. L. (2009). Effects of wisdom therapy on anger and mood as adapted for use among substance-dependent clients in a nonmedical residential setting. *Dissertation Abstracts International: Section B: The Sciences and Engineering*, 69(11-B), 7143.

McCullough, M. E., Kilpatrick, S. D., Emmons, R. A., & Larson, D. B. (2001). Is gratitude a moral affect? *Psychological Bulletin, 127*, 249–266. http://dx.doi.org/10.1037/0033-2909.127.2.249

McElroy, S., Rice, K., Davis, D. E., Hook, J. N., Hill, P. C., Worthington, E. L., Jr., & Van Tongeren, D. R. (2014). Intellectual humility: Scale development and theoretical elaborations in the context of religious leadership. *Journal of Psychology and Theology, 42*, 19–30.

Meacham, J. (2015). *Destiny and power: The American odyssey of George Herbert Walker Bush.* New York, NY: Random House.

Meagher, B. R., Leman, J. C., Bias, J. P., Latendresse, S. J., & Rowatt, W. C. (2015). Contrasting self-report and consensus ratings of intellectual humility and arrogance. *Journal of Research in Personality, 58*, 35–45. http://dx.doi.org/10.1016/j.jrp.2015.07.002

Merton, T. (1999). *The seven story mountain.* Boston, MA: Mariner Books.

Milgram, S. (1974). *Obedience to authority: An experimental view.* New York, NY: Harper and Row.

Milojev, P., & Sibley, C. G. (2017). Normative personality trait development in adulthood: A 6-year cohort-sequential growth model. *Journal of Personality and Social Psychology, 112*, 510–526. http://dx.doi.org/10.1037/pspp0000121

Minuchin, S. (1974). *Families and family therapy.* Oxford, England: Harvard University Press.

Moore, B. J. (2001, May). *The ways of the will.* Retrieved from http://www.firstthings.com/article/2001/05/the-ways-of-the-will

Moore, F. (2010). *Host Jimmy Fallon opens big at the Emmys.* Retrieved from http://my.xfinity.com/blogs/tv/2010/08/29/host-jimmy-fallon-opens-big-at-the-emmys/

Moradi, S., Nima, A. A., Rapp Ricciardi, M., Archer, T., & Garcia, D. (2014). Exercise, character strengths, well-being, and learning climate in the prediction of performance over a 6-month period at a call center. *Frontiers in Psychology, 5*, 497. http://dx.doi.org/10.3389/fpsyg.2014.00497

Mosher, D. K., Hook, J. N., Farrell, J. E., Watkins, C. E., Jr., & Davis, D. E. (2017). Cultural humility. In E. L. Worthington Jr., D. E. Davis, & J. N. Hook (Eds.), *Handbook of humility: Theory, research, and applications* (pp. 91–104). New York, NY: Routledge.

Mouw, R. J. (2010). *Uncommon decency: Christian civility in an uncivil world* (Rev. ed.). Downers Grove, IL: InterVarsity Press.

Muhammad Ali: Charity Work, Events, and Causes. (2016). Retrieved from https://www.looktothestars.org/celebrity/muhammad-ali

Muris, P., Merckelbach, H., Otgaar, H., & Meijer, E. (2017). The malevolent side of human nature: A meta-analysis and critical review of the literature on the dark triad (narcissism, Machiavellianism, and psychopathy). *Perspectives on Psychological Science, 12*, 183–204. http://dx.doi.org/10.1177/1745691616666070

Murphy, B. A., Lilienfeld, S. O., & Watts, A. L. (2017). Psychopathy and heroism: Unresolved questions and future directions. In S. T. Allison, G. R. Goethals, & R. M. Kramer (Eds.), *Handbook of heroism and heroic leadership* (pp. 525–546). New York, NY: Routledge.

Murphy, J. G. (2017). Humility as a moral virtue. In E. L. Worthington Jr., D. E. Davis, & J. N. Hook (Eds.), *Handbook of humility: Theory, research, and applications* (pp. 19–32). New York, NY: Routledge.

Murray, A. (2012). *Humility*. Alachua, FL: Bridge-Logos.

Muslim b. al-Ḥajjāj. (1995). *Ṣaḥīḥ Muslim* (5 volumes). Beirut, Lebanon: Dār Ibn Ḥazm. (Original work published 1415)

Ng, J. Y. Y., Ntoumanis, N., Thøgersen-Ntoumani, C., Deci, E. L., Ryan, R. M., Duda, J. L., & Williams, G. C. (2012). Self-determination theory applied to health contexts: A meta-analysis. *Perspectives on Psychological Science, 7*, 325–340. http://dx.doi.org/10.1177/1745691612447309

Nietzsche, F. (1992). Beyond good and evil. In *Basic writings of Nietzsche* (W. Kaufman, Trans. & Ed.). New York, NY: The Modern Library. (Original work published 1886)

Nonterah, C. W., Garthe, R. C., Reid, C. A., Worthington, E. L., Jr., Davis, D. E., Hook, J. N., . . . Griffin, B. J. (2016). The impact of stress on fluctuations in relational humility as couples transition to parenthood. *Personality and Individual Differences, 101*, 276–281. http://dx.doi.org/10.1016/j.paid.2016.06.016

Oh, I., Lee, K., Ashton, M. C., & De Vries, R. E. (2011). Are dishonest extraverts more harmful than dishonest introverts? The interaction effects of honesty–humility and extraversion in predicting workplace deviance. *Applied Psychology, 60*, 496–516. http://dx.doi.org/10.1111/j.1464-0597.2011.00445.x

Orth, U., & Luciano, E. C. (2015). Self-esteem, narcissism, and stressful life events: Testing for selection and socialization. *Journal of Personality and Social Psychology, 109*, 707–721. http://dx.doi.org/10.1037/pspp0000049

Ou, A. Y., Tsui, A. S., Kinicki, A. J., Waldman, D. A., Xiao, Z., & Song, L. J. (2014). Humble chief executive officers' connections to top management team integration and middle managers' responses. *Administrative Science Quarterly, 59*, 34–72. http://dx.doi.org/10.1177/0001839213520131

Owen, J., Jordan, T. A., II, Turner, D., Davis, D. E., Hook, J. N., & Leach, M. M. (2014). Therapists' multicultural orientation: Client perceptions of cultural humility, spiritual/religious commitment, and therapy outcomes. *Journal of Psychology and Theology, 42*, 91–98.

Owen, J., Tao, K. W., Drinane, J. M., Hook, J. N., Davis, D. E., & Kune, N. F. (2016). Client perceptions of therapists' multicultural orientation: Cultural (missed) opportunities and cultural humility. *Professional Psychology: Research and Practice, 47*, 30–37. http://dx.doi.org/10.1037/pro0000046

Owens, B. P., & Hekman, D. R. (2012). Modeling how to grow: An inductive examination of humble leader behaviors, contingencies, and outcomes. *Academy of Management Journal, 55*, 787–818. http://dx.doi.org/10.5465/amj.2010.0441

Owens, B. P., & Hekman, D. R. (2016). How does leader humility influence team performance? Exploring the mechanisms of contagion and collective promotion focus. *Academy of Management Journal, 59*, 1088–1111. http://dx.doi.org/10.5465/amj.2013.0660

Owens, B. P., Johnson, M. D., & Mitchell, T. R. (2013). Expressed humility in organizations: Implications for performance, teams, and leadership. *Organization Science, 24*, 1517–1538. http://dx.doi.org/10.1287/orsc.1120.0795

Owens, B. P., Rowatt, W. C., & Wilkins, A. L. (2011). Exploring the relevance and implications of humility in organizations. In K. Cameron & G. Spreitzer (Eds.), *The handbook of positive organizational scholarship* (pp. 260–272). New York, NY: Oxford University Press. http://dx.doi.org/10.1093/oxfordhb/9780199734610.013.0020

Owens, B. P., Wallace, A. S., & Waldman, D. A. (2015). Leader narcissism and follower outcomes: The counterbalancing effect of leader humility. *Journal of Applied Psychology, 100*, 1203–1213. http://dx.doi.org/10.1037/a0038698

Park, N., Peterson, C., & Seligman, M. E. P. (2004). Strengths of character and well-being. *Journal of Social and Clinical Psychology, 23*, 603–619. http://dx.doi.org/10.1521/jscp.23.5.603.50748

Parker, K. (2015). Freed: Bushes unleashed [Op/ed column]. *Richmond Times-Dispatch*, p. A11.

Paulhus, D. (1998). Interpersonal and intrapsychic adaptiveness of trait self-enhancement: A mixed blessing? *Journal of Personality and Social Psychology, 74*, 1197–1208.

Pennebaker, J. W., & Smyth, J. M. (2016). *Opening up by writing it down: How expressive writing improves health and eases emotional pain* (3rd ed.). New York, NY: Guilford Press.

Perkins, F. (2011). *The Roosevelt I knew*. New York, NY: The Penguin Group. (Original work published 1946)

Perry, A. (2013, December 6). *Mandela's jailer: "He was my prisoner, but he was my father."* Retrieved from http://world.time.com/2013/12/06/mandelas-jailer-he-was-my-prisoner-but-he-was-my-father/

Peters, A. S., Rowatt, W. C., & Johnson, M. K. (2011). Associations between dispositional humility and social relationship quality. *Psychology, 2*, 155–161. http://dx.doi.org/10.4236/psych.2011.23025

Peterson, C., & Seligman, M. E. P. (2003). Character strengths before and after September 11. *Psychological Science, 14*, 381–384. http://dx.doi.org/10.1111/1467-9280.24482

Peterson, C., & Seligman, M. E. P. (2004). *Character strengths and virtues: A handbook and classification*. Washington, DC: American Psychological Association and New York, NY: Oxford University Press.

Phillips, J. B. (1961). *Your God is too small*. New York, NY: Macmillan.

Piaget, J. (1972). Intellectual evolution from adolescence to adulthood. *Human Development, 15*, 1–12. http://dx.doi.org/10.1159/000271225

Piff, P. K., Dietze, P., Feinberg, M., Stancato, D. M., & Keltner, D. (2015). Awe, the small self, and prosocial behavior. *Journal of Personality and Social Psychology, 108*, 883–899. http://dx.doi.org/10.1037/pspi0000018

Piff, P. K., Stancato, D. M., Côté, S., Mendoza-Denton, R., & Keltner, D. (2012). Higher social class predicts increased unethical behavior. *Proceedings of the National Academy of Sciences, USA, 109*, 4086–4091. http://dx.doi.org/10.1073/pnas.1118373109

Pollock, N. C., Noser, A. E., Holden, C., & Zeigler-Hill, V. (2016). Do orientations to happiness mediate the associations between personality traits and subjective well-being? *Journal of Happiness Studies, 17*, 713–729. http://dx.doi.org/10.1007/s10902-015-9617-9

Porter, S. L., Rambachan, A., Vélez de Cea, A., Rabinowitz, D., Pardue, S., & Jackson, S. (2017). Religious perspectives on humility. In E. L. Worthington Jr., D. E. Davis, & J. N. Hook (Eds.), *Handbook of humility: Theory, research, and applications* (pp. 47–61). New York, NY: Routledge.

Powell, A. (2014). *Roberto Clemente*. Retrieved from https://www.tripsavvy.com/pittsburgh-pirate-roberto-clemente-2708329

Powell, C. L., & Persico, J. E. (1995). *My American journey*. New York, NY: Random House.

Price, R. (1978). *A palpable God*. New York, NY: Atheneum.

Pronin, E., Lin, D. Y., & Ross, L. (2002). The bias blind spot: Perceptions of bias in self versus others. *Personality and Social Psychology Bulletin, 28*, 369–381. http://dx.doi.org/10.1177/0146167202286008

Pyszczynski, T., Greenberg, J., Solomon, S., Arndt, J., & Schimel, J. (2004). Why do people need self-esteem? A theoretical and empirical review. *Psychological Bulletin, 130*, 435–468. http://dx.doi.org/10.1037/0033-2909.130.3.435

Qazi, M. (2014). *A journey into soulscape*. Triplicane, Chennai, India: Notion Press.

Quiros, A. E. (2008). The development, construct validity, and clinical utility of the Healthy Humility Inventory (Doctoral dissertation). *Dissertation Abstracts International: B. The Sciences and Engineering*, 68(9-B), 6331.

Rego, A., Cunha, M. P., & Simpson, A. V. (2016, January 30). The perceived impact of leaders' humility on team effectiveness: An empirical study. *Journal of Business Ethics*, 1–14. http://dx.doi.org/10.1007/s10551-015-3008-3

Reinhard, D. A., Konrath, S. H., Lopez, W. D., & Cameron, H. G. (2012). Expensive egos: Narcissistic males have higher cortisol. *PLoS One, 7*(7). http://dx.doi.org/10.1371/journal.pone.0030858

Rendon, J. (2015). *Upside: The new science of post-traumatic growth*. New York, NY: Touchstone.

Righetti, F., Finkenauer, C., & Finkel, E. J. (2013). Low self-control promotes the willingness to sacrifice in close relationships. *Psychological Science, 24*, 1533–1540.

Ripley, J. S., Garthe, R. C., Perkins, A., Worthington, E. L., Jr., Davis, D. E., Hook, J. N., . . . Eaves, D. (2016). Perceived partner humility predicts subjective stress during transition to parenthood. *Couple & Family Psychology*, *5*, 157–167.

Roberts, R. C., & Cleveland, W. S. (2017). Humility from a philosophical point of view. In E. L. Worthington Jr., D. E. Davis, & J. N. Hook (Eds.), *Handbook of humility: Theory, research, and applications* (pp. 33–46). New York, NY: Routledge.

Robins, S. (2008, August). *Wisdom therapy*. Paper presented at the annual meeting of the American Psychological Association, Boston, MA.

Rogers, C. R. (1958). Reinhold Niebuhr's *The self and the dramas of history:* A criticism. *Pastoral Psychology*, *9*, 15–17.

Rohr, R. (2011). *Falling upward: A spirituality for the two halves of life*. San Francisco, CA: Jossey-Bass.

Rohr, R. (2014). *Eager to love*. Cincinnati, OH: Franciscan Media.

Romanowska, J., Larsson, G., & Theorell, T. (2014). An art-based leadership intervention for enhancement of self-awareness, humility, and leader performance. *Journal of Personnel Psychology*, *13*, 97–106.

Rosenbaum, R. (2014). *Explaining Hitler: The search for the origins of his evil.* Boston, MA: Da Capo Press.

Rosenberg, M. (1965). *Society and the adolescent self-image*. Princeton, NJ: Princeton University Press.

Rowatt, W. C., Kang, L. L., Haggard, M. C., & LaBouff, J. P. (2014). A social-personality perspective on humility, religiousness, and spirituality. *Journal of Psychology and Theology*, *42*, 31–40.

Rowatt, W. C., Powers, C., Targhetta, V., Comer, J., Kennedy, S., & Labouff, J. (2006). Development and initial validation of an implicit measure of humility relative to arrogance. *The Journal of Positive Psychology*, *1*, 198–211. http://dx.doi.org/10.1080/17439760600885671

Ruberton, P. M., Huynh, H. P., Miller, T. A., Kruse, E., Chancellor, J., & Lyubomirsky, S. (2016). The relationship between physician humility, physician–patient communication, and patient health. *Patient Education and Counseling*, *99*, 1138–1145. http://dx.doi.org/10.1016/j.pec.2016.01.012

Ruberton, P. M., Kruse, E., & Lyubomirsky, S. (2017). Boosting state humility via gratitude, self-affirmation, and awe: Theoretical and empirical perspectives. In E. L. Worthington Jr., D. E. Davis, & J. N. Hook (Eds.), *Handbook of humility: Theory, research, and applications* (pp. 260–273). New York, NY: Routledge.

Rusbult, C. E., Bissonnette, V. L., Arriaga, X. B., & Cox, C. L. (1998). Accommodation processes during the early years of marriage. In T. N. Bradbury (Ed.), *The developmental course of marital dysfunction* (pp. 74–113). New York, NY: Cambridge University Press. http://dx.doi.org/10.1017/CBO9780511527814.005

Rusbult, C. E., Kumashiro, M., Stocker, S. L., & Wolf, S. T. (2005). The Michelangelo Phenomenon in close relationships. In A. Tesser, J. Wood, & D. Stapel (Eds.),

On building, defending and regulating the self: A psychological perspective (pp. 1–29). New York, NY: Psychology Press.

Rusbult, C. E., Olson, N., Davis, J. L., & Hannon, M. A. (2001). Commitment and relationship maintenance mechanisms. In J. H. Harvey & A. Wenzel (Eds.), *Close relationships: Maintenance and enhancement* (pp. 87–113). Mahwah, NJ: Erlbaum.

Ryan, R. M., & Deci, E. L. (2000). Intrinsic and extrinsic motivations: Classic definitions and new directions. *Contemporary Educational Psychology, 25*, 54–67. http://dx.doi.org/10.1006/ceps.1999.1020

Ryff, C. D., & Keyes, C. L. M. (1995). The structure of psychological well-being revisited. *Journal of Personality and Social Psychology, 69*, 719–727. http://dx.doi.org/10.1037/0022-3514.69.4.719

Safi, O. (2010). Can the truly humble attain greatness in public affairs: Six responses. In *Character: A Journal of the Everyday Virtues, 5*(3), 49–51.

Safire, W. (1997). *Lend me your ears: Great speeches in history*. New York, NY: W. W. Norton.

Samuelson, P. L., Jarvinen, M. J., Paulus, T. B., Church, I. M., Hardy, S. A., & Barrett, J. L. (2015). Implicit theories of intellectual virtues and vices: A focus on intellectual humility. *The Journal of Positive Psychology, 10*, 389–406. http://dx.doi.org/10.1080/17439760.2014.967802

Sanchez, K. (2016). *Malala Yousafzai: The young hero*. Retrieved from https://blog.richmond.edu/heroes/2016/03/03/malala-yousafzai-the-young-hero/

Sandage, S. J., Jankowski, P. J., Bissonette, C. D., & Paine, D. R. (2017). Vulnerable narcissism, forgiveness, humility, and depression: Mediator effects for differentiation of self. *Psychoanalytic Psychology, 34*, 300–310. http://dx.doi.org/10.1037/pap0000042

Schachter, S. (1959). *The psychology of affiliation*. Stanford, CA: Stanford University Press.

Schlesinger, R. (2008). *White House ghosts*. New York, NY: Simon & Schuster.

Schönbach, P. (1990). *Account episodes: The management or escalation of conflict*. New York, NY: Cambridge University Press.

Schwager, I. T. L., Hülsheger, U. R., & Lang, J. W. B. (2016). Be aware to be on the square: Mindfulness and counterproductive academic behavior. *Personality and Individual Differences, 93*, 74–79. http://dx.doi.org/10.1016/j.paid.2015.08.043

Schweitzer, A. (1998). *Out of my life and thought: An autobiography* (G. Allen & W. Unwin, Trans.). Baltimore, MD: Johns Hopkins Press. (Original work published 1931)

Seligman, M. E. P. (2011). *Flourish*. New York, NY: Atria.

Seligman, M. E. P., & Csikszentmihalyi, M. (2000). Positive psychology. An introduction. *American Psychologist, 55*, 5–14. http://dx.doi.org/10.1037/0003-066X.55.1.5

Sheppard, K. E., & Boon, S. D. (2012). Predicting appraisals of romantic revenge: The roles of Honesty–Humility, Agreeableness, and vengefulness. *Personality and Individual Differences, 52*, 128–132. http://dx.doi.org/10.1016/j.paid.2011.09.014

Shoshani, A., & Aviv, I. (2012). The pillars of strength for first-grade adjustment—Parental and children's character strengths and the transition to elementary school. *The Journal of Positive Psychology, 7*, 315–326. http://dx.doi.org/10.1080/17439760.2012.691981

Silvia, P. J., Nusbaum, E. C., & Beaty, R. E. (2014). Blessed are the meek? Honesty–humility, agreeableness, and the HEXACO structure of religious beliefs, motives, and values. *Personality and Individual Differences, 66*, 19–23.

Solomon, S., Greenberg, J., Schiel, J., Arndt, J., & Pyszczynski, T. (2014). *Human awareness of mortality and the evolution of culture*. Unpublished manuscript, Skidmore College, Saratoga Springs, NY.

Solzhenitsyn, A. (1973). *The Gulag archipelago: Vols. 1, 2, and 3*. New York, NY: Harper Perennial.

Steels, L. (2011). *Magic apples*. Indianapolis, IN: Dog Ear.

Sternberg, R. J. (2011). Leadership and education: Leadership stories. In M. Harvey & R. Riggio (Eds.), *Leadership studies: The dialogue of disciplines*. New York, NY: Edward Elgar. http://dx.doi.org/10.4337/9780857936486.00019

Tangney, J. P. (2000). Humility: Theoretical perspectives, empirical findings and directions for future research. *Journal of Social and Clinical Psychology, 19*, 70–82. http://dx.doi.org/10.1521/jscp.2000.19.1.70

Taylor, C. (2007). *A secular age*. Cambridge, MA: Belknap Press.

Teresa, M. (1995). *A simple path*. New York, NY: Ballantine Books.

Tesser, A. (1993). *On becoming a social psychologist*. Athens, GA: Instructional Resources Center.

Thibaut, J. W., & Kelley, H. H. (1959). *The social psychology of groups*. New York, NY: Wiley.

Thielmann, I., & Hilbig, B. E. (2015). The traits one can trust: Dissecting reciprocity and kindness as determinants of trustworthy behavior. *Personality and Social Psychology Bulletin, 41*, 1523–1536. http://dx.doi.org/10.1177/0146167215600530

Thomas, E. (Producer), Orbst, L. (Producer), & Nolan, C. (Producer and Director). (2014). *Interstellar* [Motion picture]. United States: Paramount Pictures.

Thurackal, J. T., Corveleyn, J., & Dezutter, J. (2016). Personality and self-compassion: Exploring their relationship in an Indian context. *European Journal of Mental Health, 11*(1–2), 18–35.

Tolkien, J. R. R. (1937). *The hobbit*. London, England: George Allen & Unwin.

Tong, E. M. W., Tan, K. W. T., Chor, A. A. B., Koh, E. P. S., Lee, J. S. Y., & Tan, R. W. Y. (2016). Humility facilitates higher self-control. *Journal of Experimental Social Psychology, 62*, 30–39. http://dx.doi.org/10.1016/j.jesp.2015.09.008

Toussaint, L. L., & Webb, J. R. (2017). The humble mind and body: A theoretical model and review of evidence linking humility to health and well-being. In E. L. Worthington Jr., D. E. Davis, & J. N. Hook (Eds.), *Handbook of humility: Theory, research, and applications* (pp. 178–191). New York, NY: Routledge.

Twenge, J. M. (2014). *Generation me—revised and updated: Why today's young Americans are more confident, assertive, entitled—and more miserable than ever before.* New York, NY: Simon and Schuster.

Twenge, J. M., & Campbell, W. K. (2009). *The narcissism epidemic: Living in the age of enlightenment.* New York, NY: Free Press.

Tyler, L. E. (1973). Design for a hopeful psychology. *American Psychologist, 28,* 1021–1029. http://dx.doi.org/10.1037/h0036044

Vande Kappelle, R. P. (2015). *Dark splendor: Spiritual fitness for the second half of life.* Searcy, AR: Resource.

Van Gelder, J., & De Vries, R. (2012). Traits and states: Integrating personality and affect into a model of criminal decision making. *Criminology, 50,* 627–671.

Van Tongeren, D. R., Davis, D. E., & Hook, J. N. (2014). Social benefits of humility: Initiating and maintaining romantic relationships. *The Journal of Positive Psychology, 9,* 313–321. http://dx.doi.org/10.1080/17439760.2014.898317

Van Tongeren, D. R., Davis, D. E., Hook, J. N., Rowatt, W., & Worthington, E. L., Jr. (2017). Religious differences in reporting and expressing humility. *Psychology of Religion and Spirituality.* Advance online publication. http://dx.doi.org/10.1037/rel0000118

Van Tongeren, D. R., & Myers, D. G. (2017). A social psychological perspective on humility. In E. L. Worthington Jr., D. E. Davis, & J. N. Hook (Eds.), *Handbook of humility: Theory, research, and applications* (pp. 150–164). New York, NY: Routledge.

Van Tongeren, D. R., Stafford, J., Hook, J. N., Green, J. D., Davis, D. E., & Johnson, K. A. (2016). Humility attenuates negative attitudes and behaviors toward religious out-group members. *The Journal of Positive Psychology, 11,* 199–208.

Verdorfer, A. P. (2016). Examining mindfulness and its relations to humility, motivation to lead, and actual servant leadership behaviors. *Mindfulness, 7,* 950–961. http://dx.doi.org/10.1007/s12671-016-0534-8

Visser, B. A., & Pozzebon, J. A. (2013). Who are you and what do you want? Life aspirations, personality, and well-being. *Personality and Individual Differences, 54,* 266–271. http://dx.doi.org/10.1016/j.paid.2012.09.010

Wageman, R., Nunes, D. A., Burress, J. A., & Hackman, J. R. (2008). *Senior leadership teams: What it takes to make them great.* Cambridge, MA: Harvard Business School.

Wagner, P. C. (2002). *Humility.* Bloomington, MN: Chosen Books.

Wallace, A. S., Chiu, C. Y., & Owens, B. P. (2017). Organizational humility and the better functioning business non-profit and religious organizations. In E. L. Worthington Jr., D. E. Davis, & J. N. Hook (Eds.), *Handbook of humility: Theory, research, and applications* (pp. 246–259). New York, NY: Routledge.

Wallace, H. M., & Baumeister, R. F. (2002). The performance of narcissists rises and falls with perceived opportunity for glory. *Journal of Personality and Social Psychology, 82,* 819–834. http://dx.doi.org/10.1037/0022-3514.82.5.819

Walling, M. G. (2015). *Enduring freedom, enduring voices*. Oxford, England: Osprey.

Wallis, C. L. (1983). *The treasure chest*. New York, NY: HarperCollins.

Walters, K. N., & Diab, D. L. (2016). Humble leadership: Implications for psychological safety and follower engagement. *The Journal of Leadership Studies, 10*(2), 7–18. http://dx.doi.org/10.1002/jls.21434

Walton, G. M. (2014). The new science of wise psychological interventions. *Current Directions in Psychological Science, 23*, 73–82. http://dx.doi.org/10.1177/0963721413512856

Watkins, C. E., Jr., & Hook, J. N. (2016). On a culturally humble psychoanalytic supervision perspective: Creating the cultural third. *Psychoanalytic Psychology, 33*, 487–517. http://dx.doi.org/10.1037/pap0000044

Wayment, H. A., & Bauer, J. J. (2017). The quiet ego: Motives for self-other balance and growth in relation to well-being. *Journal of Happiness Studies*. Advance online publication. http://dx.doi.org/10.1007/s10902-017-9848-z

Wayment, H. A., Bauer, J. J., & Sylaska, K. (2015). The Quiet Ego Scale: Measuring the compassionate self-identity. *Journal of Happiness Studies, 16*, 999–1033. http://dx.doi.org/10.1007/s10902-014-9546-z

Weick, K. E. (2001). Leadership as the legitimization of doubt. In W. Bennis, G. M. Spreitzer, & T. G. Cummings (Eds.), *The future of leadership: Today's top leadership thinkers speak to tomorrow's leaders* (pp. 91–102). San Francisco, CA: Jossey-Bass.

Weidman, A. C., Cheng, J. T., & Tracy, J. L. (2016). The psychological structure of humility. *Journal of Personality and Social Psychology*. Advance online publication. http://dx.doi.org/10.1037/pspp0000112

White, W. L., & Lindsey, R. J. (2017). *The Lois Wilson story, co-founder of Al-Anon*. Retrieved from http://addictioninfamily.com/family-issues/the-lois-wilson-story-co-founder-of-al-anon/

Whitfield, C. L., Whitfield, R. T., Park, R., & Prevatt, J. (2006). *The power of humility: Choosing peace over conflict in relationships*. Deerfield Beach, FL: Health Communications.

Wilson, C., Ottati, V., & Price, E. (2017). Open-minded cognition: The attitude justification effect. *The Journal of Positive Psychology, 12*, 47–58. http://dx.doi.org/10.1080/17439760.2016.1167941

Wiltshire, J., Bourdage, J. S., & Lee, K. (2014). Honesty–Humility and perceptions of organizational politics in predicting workplace outcomes. *Journal of Business and Psychology, 29*, 235–251. http://dx.doi.org/10.1007/s10869-013-9310-0

Wolfe, T. (1976, August 23). The "me" decade and the third great awakening. *New York Magazine*. Retrieved from http://nymag.com/news/features/45938/index12.html

Wood, G. (1992). *The radicalism of the American revolution*. New York, NY: Knopf.

Woodruff, E., Van Tongeren, D. R., McElroy, S., Davis, D. E., & Hook, J. N. (2014). Humility and religion: Benefits, difficulties, and a model of religious tolerance. In C. Kim-Prieto (Ed.), *Religion and spirituality across culture* (Vol. 9, pp. 271–285). New York, NY: Springer.

Worth, N. C., & Book, A. S. (2015). Dimensions of video game behavior and their relationships with personality. *Computers in Human Behavior, 50*, 132–140. http://dx.doi.org/10.1016/j.chb.2015.03.056

Worthington, E. L., Jr. (2003). *Forgiveness and reconciling: Bridges to wholeness and hope*. Downers Grove, IL: InterVarsity Press.

Worthington, E. L., Jr. (2005). *Hope-focused marriage counseling: A guide to brief therapy* (Rev. ed.). Downers Grove, IL: InterVarsity Press.

Worthington, E. L., Jr. (2007). *Humility: The quiet virtue*. Philadelphia, PA: Templeton Foundation Press.

Worthington, E. L., Jr. (2017). Political humility: A post-modern reconceptualization. In E. L. Worthington Jr., D. E. Davis, & J. N. Hook (Eds.), *Handbook of humility: Theory, research, and applications* (pp. 76–90). New York, NY: Routledge.

Worthington, E. L., Jr., Davis, D. E., & Hook, J. N. (Eds.). (2017). *Handbook of humility: Theory, research, and applications*. New York, NY: Routledge.

Worthington, E. L., Jr., Goldstein, L., Cork, B., Griffin, B. J., Garthe, R. C., Lavelock, C. R., . . . Van Tongeren, D. R. (in press). Humility: A qualitative review of definitions, theory, concept, and research support for seven hypotheses. In C. R. Snyder, S. J. Lopez, L. M. Edwards, & S. C. Marques (Eds.), *The Oxford handbook of positive psychology* (3rd ed.). New York, NY: Oxford University Press.

Worthington, E. L., Jr., Lavelock, C., Van Tongeren, D. R., Jennings, D. J., II, Gartner, A. L., Davis, D. E., & Hook, J. N. (2014). Virtue in positive psychology. In K. Timpe & C. Boyd (Eds.), *Virtues and their vices* (pp. 433–457). New York, NY: Oxford University Press.

Worthington, E. L., Jr., & Sandage, S. J. (2016). *Forgiveness and spirituality in psychotherapy: A relational approach*. Washington, DC: American Psychological Association. http://dx.doi.org/10.1037/14712-000

Wright, J. C., Nadelhoffer, T., Perini, T., Langville, A., Echols, M., & Venezia, K. (2017). The psychological significance of humility. *The Journal of Positive Psychology, 12*, 3–12. http://dx.doi.org/10.1080/17439760.2016.1167940

Wright, M., Lin, A., & O'Connell, M. (2016). Humility, inquisitiveness, and openness: Key attributes for meaningful engagement with Nyoongar people. *Advances in Mental Health, 14*, 82–95. http://dx.doi.org/10.1080/18387357.2016.1173516

Yovetich, N. A., & Rusbult, C. E. (1994). Accommodative behavior in close relationships: Exploring transformation of motivation. *Journal of Experimental Social Psychology, 30*, 138–164. http://dx.doi.org/10.1006/jesp.1994.1007

Zaslow, J. (2007, September 20). A beloved professor delivers the lecture of a lifetime. *The Wall Street Journal*. Retrieved from http://www.wsj.com/articles/SB119024238402033039

Zettler, I., Hilbig, B. E., & Heydasch, T. (2013). Two sides of one coin: Honesty–Humility and situational factors mutually shape social dilemma decision making. *Journal of Research in Personality*, *47*, 286–295. http://dx.doi.org/10.1016/j.jrp.2013.01.012

Zettler, I., Hilbig, B. E., Moshagen, M., & de Vries, R. E. (2015). Dishonest responding or true virtue? A behavioral test of impression management. *Personality and Individual Differences*, *81*, 107–111. http://dx.doi.org/10.1016/j.paid.2014.10.007

Zettler, I., Lang, J. W. B., Hülsheger, U. R., & Hilbig, B. E. (2016). Dissociating indifferent, directional, and extreme responding in personality data: Applying the three-process model to self- and observer reports. *Journal of Personality*, *84*, 461–472. http://dx.doi.org/10.1111/jopy.12172

INDEX

Note: Page numbers followed by *e*, *f*, and *t* refer to exhibits, figures, and tables, respectively.

ABOUT THE AUTHORS

Everett L. Worthington Jr., PhD, is Commonwealth Professor in the Department of Psychology at Virginia Commonwealth University and a licensed clinical psychologist in Virginia. He has published over 35 books and 400 articles and chapters, mostly on forgiveness, humility, positive psychology, marriage, family, and religion/spirituality. He provides free online resources on promoting humility, forgiveness of others and oneself, and couple relationships (http://www.EvWorthington-forgiveness.com). He attributes whatever success he has experienced to the support from his wife of 46 years, Kirby, and his family, and also to the wonderful students and colleagues he has had the privilege of working with.

Scott T. Allison, PhD, has authored numerous books, including *Heroic Leadership: An Influence Taxonomy of 100 Exceptional Individuals* and *Heroes: What They Do & Why We Need Them*. He is a professor of psychology at the University of Richmond, where he has published extensively on heroism and leadership. His other books include *Reel Heroes & Villains: Two Hero Experts Critique the Movies*, *Conceptions of Leadership: Enduring Ideas and Emerging Insights*, *Frontiers in Spiritual Leadership: Discovering the Better Angels of Our Nature*, and the *Handbook of Heroism and Heroic Leadership*. His work has been featured in *USA Today*, *The New York Times*, *The Los Angeles Times*, *Slate* online magazine, *Psychology Today*, and *The Christian Science Monitor*, as well as on *National Public Radio*, MSNBC, and CBS. He has received Richmond's Distinguished Educator Award and the Virginia Council of Higher Education's Outstanding Faculty Award.